The History of

ROBERT LOCKERBY
And
SARAH TOCK'S

Family

Marsha Pilger

Published in the USA
Amazon.com
ISBN   9798831816662
2022

Dedicated to:

Ron, Tim and Andy Pilger
Marshall and Betty Lockerby
Beulah Totten Wright,

And to Amy Plowman
for her wonderful
Inspiration!

In Appreciation:

My grateful appreciation to the following for assisting me in compiling information on the Lockerby family. My humble gratitude.

Ron, Tim and Andy Pilger for all your support.
Beulah Totten Wright for her interest, concern, family records, pictures, encouragement and faith.
Mrs. Muriel Haggman Whalen, for family records and photos.
Mrs. Susan Reynolds, Town Clerk of Catharine, N.Y.
Alice Station, Genealogist and Librarian at the W. Dale Clark Library in Omaha, Nebraska
Mrs. Bessie Lockerby Hollins, Mr. and Mrs. Ezekiel Lockerby and my parents,
Mr. and Mrs. Marshall Lockerby, for family information
And
Numerous others who contributed family data and records.

THANK YOU
Because of your interest and efforts, this history of the LOCKERBY family can be preserved for the future generations.
Marsha Lockerby Pilger

Introduction

According to *"Scots Kith and Kin"* the Lockerby family is a sept of the Douglas Clan. Most notable of this clan was Sir James, the "Black Douglas" and doughty lieutenant to King Bruce. The Douglas' originated in Douglasdale, Dumfriesshires, and Galloway, and it is in Dumfriesshires wherein we find mention of the family name Lockerbie. The country of Dumfriesshires is located in the southern upland of Scotland and touches the northwest border of England. It is in this region where we find the Town of Lockerby.

No one seems to be exact when it comes to determining how the town acquired its name. According to one local theory, the name Lockerbie stands for the "bie" (town) of locks, since locks were once a feature of the landscape there. A more plausible explanation is that the name denotes the bie (which can mean dwelling as well as town or hamlet) of Locart. It is said that Lockhart or, in some accounts, Locard, came north with Robert the Bruce who gave him a large grant of land in the area where the town now stands, Thus, arose in the 13th century the name of Lockhartby, which in later years assumed the more common form of Lockerbie.

The suffix "by" or "bie" is in fact a Norse word reflecting the major influence which the Vikings had throughout much of Britain in the 8th to 10th centuries and is found in some place names in Scandinavia and the North of England today as well as in the southwest of Scotland. The Scottish Gaelic term for Lockerbie is *"Locarbaidh"*

Lockerbie had existed since at least the days of Viking influence in this part o Scotland in the period around 900. The name (originally "Lochard's by) means *Lockard Town* in old Norse. Lockerbie first entered recorded history in the 1190's in a charter of Robert de Brus, 2nd Lord of Annandale, granting the lands of Lockerbie to Adam de Carlyle. In 1306, the name of the town is reference in early documents as *Lokardebi.*

On December 7, 1593 Clan Johnstone fought Clan Maxwell at the Battle of Dryfe Sands. These two families had been feuding between themselves for about a hundred years, The Johnstone's nearly exterminated the Maxwell's involved in the battle, leading to the expression "Lockerbie Lick." In this battle, it is known the Lockerbie's aligned with the Maxwell's thus causing great loss to the family.

As far as is known, the Lockerby families in the late 18th and early 19th centuries, were not landowners and did not occupy any positions of power or wealth, but rather were craftsmen, tradesmen and laborers. However, there is some evidence that previous generations may have belonged to the upper cases.

In an autobiographical account of one William Lockerby (known for his excursions to the Fiji Islands), he states that he was a descendant "of the Lockerby's of that ilk who were from a very early period the proprietors of considerable lands and holdings in that neighborhood. They were the master of Lockerby castle, which was a place of note during the Border wars, and in the chronicles of which many acts and deeds of valor are recorded of its Chieftains and their followers... In 1715, the Lockerby's having taken part with the exiled family of the Stewarts, their lands and holdings were forfeited."

How much credence should be attached to William Lockerby's view of the social position of his ancestors is questionable as various historical texts refer to castles or towers in and around Lockerbie as the strongholds of the Johnstone's, Maxwell's and Jardine's but, the Lockerby's are not mentioned in this context.

What I do find of interest is that the noted "William" above was the same William Lockerby who traveled to the Fiji Islands in search of Sandelwood and was associated with the ill-fated, Captain Blye. This same William did, in fact, write an autobiography leaving record of his heritage in his journal, of which the author has a copy, and since he was from this area of Scotland, as he says, then very likely he was closely related to our ancestor, Robert.

GENEALOGICAL GLEAMINGS

Our Robert was born in approximately 1738 – William was born in 1782 and was the son of John and Jannet Crighton d/o George. John's father (name unknown) would have been the same generation as the Robert here mentioned. I learned from the journal of William Lockerby that he was the ELDEST SON of John, thus it is likely, considering the early European naming standards, his father was a William Lockerby born at the approximate time (ca.1735-1740) of our Robert (1735-1738). It may be possible they share the same father, or share a near relative. I would not consider this if they were not strongly embedded in the same area of Scotland as they claim.

SPOTLIGHT ON YOUR HERITAGE:

There are numerous Heritage Societies the members of the Lockerby family qualify for, some among them being: The Daughters of the American Revolutionary War (or Sons, SDAR), Colonial Daughters, The Society of Mayflower Descendants, the Ancient and Honorable Artillery Society, and likely more. My plan is to give you some direction as to where you can begin your pursuit to join these organizations if you have an interest.

The TERRY family will lead you to all the societies listed above. Five generations from William Bradford, the Mayflower passenger in 1620 and the Governor of Plymouth Plantation for many years, you will connect to Ann Collins from Enfield, Connecticut. She married Ephraim Terry 13 Sept 1722 in Enfield. This will connect you to your Revolutionary War heritage.

Ann Collins was the daughter of Nathaniel Collins born 13 June 1677 in Enfield. His grandfather was Edward Collins born in 1603 in England. Edward served in the Ancient and Honorable Artillery Company.

To save you mountains of time and effort, before joining any of the above societies, first gain a copy of your relative's linage papers (I belong to all except Colonial Daughters) because you can reference them in your application and only prove from your connection to current day.   So much more efficient.

Descendants of Robert Lockerby and Sarah Tack

First Generation

1. John Lockerby was born from about 1700 to 1713 in (?) Scotland.

General Notes: Name of parent of Robert Lockerby and estimated birth based on the following: Birth, -- age of son Robert b. 1738 Scotland, -- if father was 25 when Rbt born, he would be born in ca. 1713; -- 1700 would leave room for other children's births in case Robert was not the first child. NAME of parent derived from European name standards that the lst child of known ancestor, Robert, would name the child after his own father --

John married someone.

His child was:

+   2   M i.   **Robert Lockerby**[1] was born in 1735 in Scotland,[2] died on 28 Jul 1819 in Catharine, Tioga Co., NY,[2] and was buried in 1819 in North Settlement Cemetery, Catharine, Tioga Co., NY.[2]

Second Generation

2. Robert Lockerby[1] was born in 1735 in Scotland,[2] died on 28 Jul 1819 in Catharine, Tioga Co., NY,[2] and was buried in 1819 in North Settlement Cemetery, Catharine, Tioga Co., NY.[2]

General Notes: FAMILY HISTORY --

The emigrant ancestor of my Lockerby family was: ROBERT LOCKERBY, born in Scotland in about 1735/8. It is believed he was born in, or near, "Lockerbie, Scotland," which is the district of Annandale. The town of Dumfries lies just 12 miles N. E. of Lockerbie and the Parish church of Lockerbie, is Dryfesdale. In 1983, microfilm at the Mormon Library in Salt Lake City, Utah, indicated numerous individuals by this surname resided in the area, however, a search of the Parish records reflected NO birth document for my ancestor. Although this discovery was disappointing to me, it is of vital importance to note the Parish records which have survived , began in September 1738, the earlier churchyard records having been washed away some centuries ago. Thus, we must conclude, if Robert was in fact born in 1738, then the event occurred preceding the month mentioned.

NOTE: Let's discuss Robert's birthdate. As is common with old sources, -- nothing agrees!!-- According to The 1901 History of the Town of Catharine, New York, by Mary L. Cleaver, "Robert at the age of 18 was pressed into the English Army and brought to America to serve under General Braddock in the War against France until 1760. He is said to have served until 1760 after which he was discharged" History reports General Braddock was killed in 1755, therefore, if Robert was 18 when he came to the new world, this would make his birthdate sometime during the year of 1737.

(NOTE: The information given by Mrs. Addie Washburn, of Odessa, for the 1901 publication of the History of the Town of Catharine, New York, says "he died in 1814 at age 76, -- but on the tombstone it reads, died 1819 age 84." --- I am inclined to believe Addie Washburn because her information holds more weight and blends with the historical data I have found during my research, besides tombstone information is often incorrect because it is given by descendants at the time of the event and they may not have known the correct data -- Marsha Pilger)

NOTE: According to Sally Delevan, Concord, NH, "two brothers came from Scotland to serve in the War with France, one was Robert and the other is thought to have been William." Since Robert named his second born son WILLIAM, I am inclined to believe there may be some truth to this family tradition. I did some minor search the Scottish Archives, and the National Archives of the United Kingdom at Rew looking for Robert but I was unable to locate a roster of soldiers who may have came to the United States with Gov. Bradford. I checked various muster and pay roster's but I still did not see Robert or William. I am certain that they must have been paid somehow for their service in the French and Indian Wars but the Military collections in England are VAST! I was hoping to confirm an absolute date of birth and place of birth from the service records, but as yet, I have been unsuccessful in locating ANY THING on him in Scotland!

Just a couple notes of interest here:
a.) In 1684, Lockerbie, Scotland, had a population of 76 adults, while, in 1791, it was about 700.
b.) From the "Surnames of Scotland, page 435" we learn: LOCKERBIE. A surname current in Dumfriesshire, derived from the small town of the name in the parish of Dryfesdale. John Lockerby in Lochmaben, 1790. The land of Lockerby of that Ilk were long possessed by Johnstons."

OK, now his tombstone reads Robert "died 1819, at the age of 84." This would indicate he was born in 1735! The noted History above, says he was born in 1738.... Maybe someday a document will be located which will fully establish Robert's actual birth year and date, but until then, researchers need to keep these things in mind when seeking his European heritage. The History of Catharine, New York, (above noted) also states "he served until 1760 after which he was discharged. He then took up his abode in New Jersey where he married in 1765 to Sarah Tock." I have not located the marriage record, although I have checked for it in Sussex County, New Jersey, and also the Dutch Reformed Church records of the area.

NOTE: Keep in mind -- There were FOUR original journals to the Walpack churches -- the one I have copied from LDS film # 0441481, Item 2, mainly deals with baptisms, however some early marriages were recorded, but the volume ends with marriages only to the year 1851. According to a history of the Walpack Church, taken from the Collections of the New York Genealogical and Biographical Society, Volume V, 1913, on page xiii, it states, -- "ONE of the journals was lost in a fire at Flatbrookville in 1902 when John S. Smith's store burned down. This book probably contained the baptisms, marriages, etc., beginning at the time the first book of records was completed."

Since the Baptism's of some of the children of Robert and Sarah are listed in these journals, there is NO DOUBT the couple was not married. I have been able to prove that Sarah's name is not Tock -- it is TACK, and she was the daughter of Isaac and Lena (Jansen) Tack. Her birth is recorded in the Dutch Reformed Church in Sussex County, Walpack Congregation on page 9. Also recorded in this same source is the birth of Sarah's sister, Gertrude Tack (p14). Sarah's family was of Dutch Heritage extending back to Aart Pietersen Tack, 1641, of Etten, Holland. The family is said to have come from Holland to the US in 1660, and settled in New York, later moving down the Minisik Valley into New Jersey. Her family was known to have operated a FISHERY on TACKS ISLAND on the Delaware River. (For further details on Sarah's line, see the records of probate in Ulster County, New York)

Robert and Sarah Lockerby resided in New Jersey for several years as the records of Probate and Wills indicate from 1778 to 1813 he frequently witnessed the settlement of various estates in Wallpack. In some of the documents he is listed as "friend, or fellow bondsman" and a couple of the records mention he was from "WAYNE COUNTY, PENN." I have not be able to investigate this area yet, however, it may be a clue to his location prior to arriving in Walpack.

Eleven children were born to Robert and Sarah; eight sons, and three daughters. (Ref: History of Catherine, NY)
John, Moses, William, Bennejah, Hannah, Catharine, Robert Jr., Samuel, Sarah, and Benjamin. It is not known the exact order of their birth, but it is thought they were all born in New Jersey.

According to the History of Catherine, New York, the family migrated to old Tioga County, New York, in 1796, and settled on a farm in the old town of Catharine near the village of Alpine. In 1807, this farm was sold to Ebenezer Mallory and he purchased another on Oak Hill. This too was sold and another bought in North Settlement, the latter comprising 150 acres. When Robert arrived in Tioga County he realized there had been no educational advantages for the children of the area. Through his untiring efforts, a school was established at Hinman, and for the next fifteen years he is said to have "wielded the scepter." From this activity, it can be assumed he himself had received some form of structured education before arriving in the New World, because at this time frame in history, most could not either read or write.

NOTE: I find it rather interesting that Robert spent so many years in this profession so late in life. When reviewing the turn of events, if the school was established within a few years of his arrival, Robert must have begun this career when he was approximately sixty-five years of age, and continued until he was eighty. Some might think this strange, but in studying the Lockerby lines, and watching the older generations, I have observed that most of them are educated, live long lives, are reasonably healthy, and remain extremely active almost to the last day. This somewhat must have held true for Roberts children because I did not find where the family had lost any of their children in early life. Those whom I have been able to trace, all grew to adulthood, married, and lived beyond.
As for Roberts children, reference is made to various members of the family becoming involved with community activities over the years, and most appear on tax lists and census records of the time.

Robert died in Catharine, New York, on July 28, 1819, at the age of 84 years, and is buried in the North Settlement Cemetery beside his wife, Sarah Tack Lockerby, who died on April 30th, 1825. In 2011, the inscription on his stone was gone, but if it originally showed 1819 as his date of death, and it was correct, then we can establish his date of birth as 1735. When his will was read his "three younger sons, Robert Jr., Samuel and Benjamin" were to receive equal shares in the farm, and as he made mention of a young horse he especially wanted Samuel to have, it is inferred that he was the favored one. To his wife, Sarah, he bequeathed "all his household furniture of every description" and appointed her executrix. To John, William, Bennejah and Moses, he willed "the sum of $2.00 over and above what he had thereto before given them," and to his daughter, Sarah, he gave" one cow and a two-year-old heifer."

In the time line of events we find the following:

> Migration: Born in Scotland ca. 1735
> Came to America abt 1753-5
> May have been in Penn (maybe Wayne Co.) until ca. 1765
> Married in New Jersey in 1765 and remained here until about 1796
> Migrated to New York about 1796 setting in old Tioga County, town of
Catharine
> Sold a farm in New York in 1807
> Was alive in 1817 as he placed an ad in the local newspaper for a "lost stray"
> Died in 1819 in Catherine, New York

I researched the New York records in SLC in October, 2007, for the Will of Robert Lockerby. I started with TIOGA County and checked the "Index to Wills, Proceedings 1800-1936 (LDS 811546)" and found NO ROBERT. Also checked "Abstracts of wills of Tioga County, NY, at the Surrogate's Court, Owego, NY, from 1799-1847 (FHL 824297, Item 3) and found NO ROBERT. I checked "Will BK A-B v. 2-3 1798-1818" (FHL 811560) and Will BK C-D v. 4-8, 1818-1840 (FHL 811561) and still found no will for Robert Lockerby. I checked the "Abstracts of wills of Tompkins county, NY, from 1817-1833 (FHL 845023) -- no Robert Lockerby. I also checked the "Abstracts of wills and administrations for Tioga Co., PA: BK 1, 1812-1833, registers A-D, 1833-1866" (FHL974.856 S2) no Robert Lockerby. Since CHEMUNG Co. NY, was originally Tioga and Schuyler formed from Chemung, I then went to Chemung to check for Robert's will but in this county the records begin in 1836! -- Schuyler Co records were later also. Therefore, I was unable to locate Robert's Will which is quoted in the 1907 History of Catherine, NY., and wonder if writing to the county might produce some positive response.

Robert married **Sarah Tack**,[4] daughter of **Isak Tack** and **Magdelena Jansen**, about 1765 in Penn ?. Sarah was born on 14 Jun 1746 in Minisink Ford, Sullivan Co., NY, died on 30 Apr 1825 in Odessa, Tioga Co., NY,[2] and was buried in 1825 in North Settlement Cemetery, Catharine, Tioga Co., NY.[2]

Children from this marriage were:

+ 3   F   i.   **Jane Lockerby**.

+ 4   M   ii.   **John Lockerby**[5] was born in 1767 in PA,[2] died on 27 Apr 1858 in Catharine, Schuyler Co., NY,[5] and was buried in 1858 in North Settlement Cemetery, Catharine, Schuyler Co., NY.[2]

+ 5   M   iii.   **William Lockerby**[4] was born on 4 Nov 1770 in PA.[6]

+ 6   M   iv.   **Bennajah Lockerby**[2] was born 1773 or (1768?) in PA. or NJ (?) and died from 1830 to 1840 in Bridgewater, Washtenaw Co., MI.

+ 7   F   v.   **Hannah Laura Lockerby**[2] died aftr 1858 (Will of Bro).

+ 8   M   vi.   **Moses Lockerby**.[2]

+ 9   M   vii.   **Robert Lockerby**[7] was born on 29 Oct 1784 in Walpack, Sussex Co., NJ[8] and died in 1880 in Cayuga, Schuyler Co., NY.[2]

+ 10   M   viii.   **Samuel Lockerby**[9] was born on 4 Apr 1787 in Walpack, Sussex Co., NJ,[10] died on 30 Oct 1855 in Catharine, Schuyler Co., NY,[5] and was buried in 1855 in North Settlement Cemetery, Catharine, Schuyler Co., NY.[2]

+ 11 M ix. **Benjamin Lockerby**[11] was born on 24 Feb 1790 in Walpack, Sussex Co., NJ[12] and died in 1841 in Menard County, IL.[13]

+ 12 F x. **Sarah Lockerby**[2] died after 1819.[2]

+ 13 F xi. **Mary Lockerby**.

+ 14 M xii. **Joseph Lockerby** died in Addison, New York.

Third Generation

3. Jane Lockerby.

General Notes: This child was added to Robert and Sarah per information found in the surname files at Thompkins County, NY, in 2011, The data says that there were eleven children born to Rbt and Sarah and names them. No official source was listed for this information.

4. John Lockerby[5] was born in 1767 in PA,[2] died on 27 Apr 1858 in Catharine, Schuyler Co., NY,[5] and was buried in 1858 in North Settlement Cemetery, Catharine, Schuyler Co., NY.[2]

General Notes: Birth: (Ref: Cem Rec. in the History of the Town of Catharine, Schuyler Co., N.Y. by Mary Louise Catlin Cleaver, p. 229) 1850 census of Chemung Co., NY indicates subject is 83 yrs -- places birth at ca. 1767 and substantiates that he was the FIRST BORN SON!! European naming system says, the First child was named after his "PATERNAL GRANDFATHER! " -- this would mean that Robert Sr.'s (b. 1738) father may be named JOHN!!) -- Special Note: the 1850 census of New York says John was born in PENNSYLVANIA and this may be true as he was not listed in the Dutch Reformed Church Records of Walpack, Sussex County, New Jersey.

In the surname files in Thompkins Co., NY, (2011) I found a list of Robert Lockerby's family and on this form it states that "John, eldest son, marries a Miss Chesney and settled in Sullivanville near Horseheads, N,Y" This is an error, he married Sarah Garrison, his brother, William married the Chestnor.

Marriage: (Ref: Town of Catharine History, by M. L. Cleaver, p. 564)

Death: (Ref: Cemetery Records of North Settlement Cem. listed in the History of the Town of Catharine, Schuyler Co., N.Y. by Cleaver, p. 229) The Cemetery records indicate that he died at the age of 91, in 1858. His wife, Sally, died in 1826 and is also buried in Catharine.

Burial: North Settlement Cemetery (Ref, N.Y. History by Cleaver, p.229)

Census Info:

1850 census of Catharine, Chemung Co, New York -- lists John, age 83 as a farmer. Born in Pennsylvania and BLIND. Mary Lockerby, age 38, is living with him. Also in the household is George Garrison, age 81, born in New York and shown as IDIOTIC. (Probably was senile..) NOTE: George Garrison was likely a brother to John's wife, Sally Garrison.

Personal data: Settled in Catharine, Schuyler Co., NY, and lived there 40 yrs as of the 1855 census (came abt 1815). The couple lived on the farm adjoining the Joseph Prince farm. If they had children born to them, none survived to adulthood as in later years, sometime between 1837 and 1855, John sold 20 acres of his land to his niece Polly Lockerby. This land was in the town of Catherine. (LDS 836053 - Schuyler co., NY, Land records transcribed from Chemung co, vol 3, p. 33)

Profession: Farmer

WILL: (Schuyler Co., NY., Probate Records 1854-1870 -- LDS #850009, Will Book 1, p. 28, dated 7 May 1858) --

NOTE: The WILL was signed on the 11th day of Sept in 1844. By the time it was probated in 1858, Robert Lockerby was the only surviving executor of John's Will, his other brother, Samuel, having proceeded him in death in 1855

I John Lockerby, considering the uncertainty of this mortal life, now being of sound mind and memory, blessed be God for the same, do make and publish this my Last Will and Testament in manner and form following, that is to say, --

FIRST, -- *I give and bequeath to my niece Polly Lockerby who now lives with and takes care of me, the use of all that ---- or tenement situate lying and being in the town of Catharine, County of Chemung and the state of New York, it being part of Lot number seventeen of Lawrence Section and the farm on which I now reside, for one year after my decease. I then give and devise all the above --- or tenement situate as above described to my two brothers, Robert Lockerby and Samuel Lockerby, on the following conditions, (to -wit) at the expiration of one year after my decease they shall cause to be sold the above described --- or tenement, the farm on which I now reside, and shall then pay to my piece Poll Lockerby one hundred dollars in money which same is to be paid to her the said Polly Lockerby at the expiration of one year after my decease, and also to my sister Laura Baker, fifty dollars, twenty five dollars to be paid to her in one year after my decease and twenty five dollars in two years after my decease if she shall be living or if she shall not be living then the said Robert Lockerby and Samuel Lockerby retain the said legacy jointly between them, and in case the said Robert Lockerby and Samuel Lockerby cannot realize the purchase money for the above farm, they the said Robert Lockerby and Samuel Lockerby shall pay to the said Polly Lockerby and Laura Baker interest on their several legacies, and I further --- that the said Robert Lockerby and Samuel Lockerby to aid and assist my brother-in-law, George Garetson in maintaining himself through life and also to place at my Grave a respectable set of Grave Stone worth around eighteen dollars to twenty dollars and I further give and bequeath to my niece Polly Lockerby one French Bedstead worth twelve dollars, together with all my other household furniture to be hers exclusively. And lastly, as to all the rest residue and remains of my personal estate goods and chattels of what kind or nature so ever, I give and bequeath to my two brothers Robert Lockerby and Samuel Lockerby whom I hereby appoint my executors to this my last will and testament, hereby revoking all former will by me made. It witness whereof I have hereunto set my hand and seal the Eleventh day of September in he year of our Lord on Thousand Eight Hundred and forty four. John Lockerby*

John married **Sarah Garrison**.[2] Sarah was born in 1764, died on 5 Sep 1826 in Catharine, Schuyler Co., NY,[2] and was buried in 1826 in North Settlement Cemetery, Catharine, Schuyler Co., NY.[2]

5. William Lockerby[4] was born on 4 Nov 1770 in PA.[6]

General Notes: FAMILY HISTORY:

William Lockerby was born November 4, 1770, and baptized in the Dutch Reformed Church (p. 36), Walpack, Sussex County, New Jersey, on September 26, 1771. He was the son of Robert and Sarah Tack Lockerby.

In approximately 1796, he married in probably, New Jersey, to Ann Chestnor, and to this union six children were born: Eleanor, Mary/Maria, Sarah, Robert, Joseph, and John.

In 1808, he was a witness to the will of Abraham Vancampen in Sussex, County, New Jersey, and in 1812, he enlisted as a corporal in Capt. William Dunn's Company of Infantry, 1nd Regiment, New Jersey Detailed Militia, in Sussex Co., N. J. (Sent to the National Archives for Military Records but they were not located)

William and Ann later settled in Sullivanville, New York, near Horseheads (formed from part of Elmira in 1854.) Probably buried in Elmira, but this researcher did not pursue at the time the Lockerby Family History was published in 1983.

William married **Ann Chestnor**, daughter of **James Chestnor** and **Susannah Custard**, about 1795 in Walpack, Sussex Co., NJ.[14] Ann was born on 4 Dec 1780 in PA.

Children from this marriage were:

+ 15   F i.   **Eleanor Lockerby**[2] was born about 1796.

+ 16	F ii.	**Mary Lockerby**[4] was born on 2 Aug 1798 in Pennsylvania,[6] died in 1874 in Odessa, Schuyler Co., New York,[2] and was buried in 1874 in North Settlement Cemetery, Catharine, Schuyler Co., NY.[2]
+ 17	F iii.	**Sarah Lockerby**.[2]
+ 18	M iv.	**Robert Lockerby**[4] was born on 20 Jan 1803 in Pennsylvania[6] and died Michigan?
+ 19	M v.	**Joseph Lockerby**.[2]
+ 20	M vi.	**John Lockerby**[6] was born on 5 Sep 1806 in Pennsylvania.[6]

6. Bennajah Lockerby[2] was born 1773 or (1768?) in PA. or NJ (?) and died from 1830 to 1840 in Bridgewater, Washtenaw Co., MI.

General Notes: FAMILY HISTORY:

I am uncertain as to Bennajah's birth but know he was among the first three children born to Robert and Sarah Tack Lockerby.   In his fathers WILL he is listed as the "third" mentioned son, John and William, being named preceding him.   Although this should bear no absolute significance, it does indicate family relationship.   He first appears in the 1810 census of Tioga County, New York, along with his brother, Robert and father, Robert Sr.   He is married by this time and has seven children: four sons under the age of 10 years, and two daughters under 10, and one daughter under 16.   I believe one of the sons is Benjamin born in 1807 who eventually spawned the Minnesota line.

The Bennajah who appears in the 1810, 1820 & 1830 census of New York, in the old county of Tioga, is our subject (son of Robert Sr.)   Since I was unable to locate a burial record for Bennajah in Catherine, and because the History of Catherine, NY, indicates "moved west, NO TRACE," I concentrated by investigation on the state of MICHIGAN for various reasons.   In checking the 1840 and 1850 census of Michigan, I did not find Bennajah listed, but I did locate some of his children in Washtenaw, County.   Likely Bennajah died shortly after emigration?

NOTE: 1985 Correspondence with Mary Balow of California listed several of the children of Bennajah.   It was only after I connected his son BENJAMIN (b. 1807) to the subject that I was able to determine that they in fact WERE the children for Bennajah.   Mary Balow said they were "siblings of Benjamin of Minnesota" --.   Later, in 1986, Linn Gustafson of Colorado gave me further data on the Benjamin line and in 2006 he visited Council Bluffs, Iowa, and in our conversation mentioned that he had a DEATH RECORD of Benjamin which showed his father as BENNAJAH.   So, strong confirmation that if we were to research further, we could complete several of the branches.

The William H. Lockerby who was born Feb 24, 1859, and "of Branch Co., Michigan" may be related to Bennajah (probably a grandson?).   William H. was a Michigan State Senator 1901-1904 and was also a candidate for the House of Representatives in 1896.   He would be worth tracing as I think we could make some clarifications here regarding the family of Bennajah.

There is much which could be done here to fill in the gaps: land records could be investigated, wills & probates, cemetery records, county history's, etc., but at the time I wrote the first issue of the Lockerby History, my research took a different path and I abandoned my search for Bennajah.

Bennajah married **Agnes** about 1798. Agnes was born about 1780 in "of Chemung Co., New York". Children from this marriage were:

+ 21	M i.	**John Lockerby** was born from about 1799 to 1800 in prob. New York.
+ 22	F ii.	**Catherine Lockerby** was born on 6 Apr 1801 in Veteran, Chemung Co., New York and died on 8 Jan 1857 in DeKalb County, Illinois.
+ 23	M iii.	**Benjamin Lockerby**[16] was born on 4 May 1807 in Tioga Co., NY,[16] died on 4 Jul 1882 in Northfield, Rice Co., MN,[16] and was buried in 1882 in Northfield, Rice Co., MN.[16]

+ 24	M iv.	**William Lockerby**.[17]
+ 25	M v.	**Bennajah Lockerby**.[17]
+ 26	F vi.	**Hannah Lockerby**.[17]
+ 27	M vii.	**Robert Lockerby**.[17]
+ 28	M viii.	**Samuel Lockerby**.[17]
+ 29	M ix.	**Moses Lockerby**.[17]

7. Hannah Laura Lockerby[2] died aftr 1858 (Will of Bro).

General Notes: FAMILY HISTORY:

Hannah's birthdate has not been established yet, and she is not referenced in her fathers Will, however, it is known from the History of Catherine, New York, that she married Daniel Baker and settled in Tioga, PA.   Nothing further is known about her as yet.

Hannah married **Daniel Baker**.[2]

8. Moses Lockerby.[2]

General Notes: FAMILY HISTORY:

I have been unable to find a lot of information on Moses.   In the History of Catherine, New York, it states there was "NO TRACE" of him.   He must have still been alive in 1819 when his father, Robert Sr., died as he is listed in his fathers will.

9. Robert Lockerby[7] was born on 29 Oct 1784 in Walpack, Sussex Co., NJ[8] and died in 1880 in Cayuga, Schuyler Co., NY.[2]

General Notes: FAMILY HISTORY:

Robert Jr. was born 29 Oct 1784, in Walpack, Sussex Co., New Jersey, and christened in the Dutch Reformed Church (page 55) on May 8, 1785.   His parents were: Robert and Sarah Tack Lockerby.

NOTE:
Birth -- (Ref: in the NYB &G 1910 Vol XL1, p.37) Mothers name, TACK.   The church register of the Walpack Congregation commenced with the Pastoral Service of John Casparus Fryenmuth. Preacher there, May 31,
1741.   Rec's of the Dutch Ref Church in Walpack, Sussex Co., N.J. reflect the date of birth and christening (p. 55)

From the Schuyler County Historical Society in Montour Falls, NY, in 2011 we learn from information found in the surname files and entitled Misc. Info: -- "Robert Lockerby settled in Cayuga in 1801/2.   His sons were William and Gabriel."

In the History of the town of Catharine, Schuyler County, New York, by Mary L. Catlin Cleaver, Robert married Sara Ann Ogden, June, 17, 1809, at Cayuga, New York.   They were married by E. S. Hinman, Esq. Sara was often referred to in the land records of the county as "Anna" and she was born April 6, 1786, in Pennsylvania.   She and Robert settled on a portion of the farm willed to him by his father in North Settlement.   The 1855 census confirms they were there and at that time had been living in Schuyler County for 20 years.   To this union nine children were born, but we know only of eight: Margaret, Polly, Jane, Catherine, William, Gabriel, Sally, and Sara.

NOTE:
Residence: North Settlement.   On a portion of the farm willed to him by his father.   (Ref: Town of Catharine, N.Y. by M.L. Cleaver, p. 564)

In the will of Robert Jr.'s father he is said to have been "one of the younger sons" of Robert and Sarah Tack Lockerby (Catharine History: p.563); the other two "younger sons" were shown as: Samuel and Benjamin. Robert and Anna are listed in the land records of the county, often in connection with his brothers.

In 1870, one of the local newspapers in Alpine, NY, (the Express) carried an article on Robert and Sarah as follows: (ref: Information provided by Carol Fagnan of Alpine NY and author of "The History of the Town of Catherine") --

"Aged Couple, Mr. Robert Lockerby of Alpine, aged 86 years is a constant reader of the Express, and is enabled to perform that labor without the aid of glasses. His wife, with whom he has lived nearly 62 years, is 84, and the happy couple, are still hale and hearty. They were married by Elijah S. Hinman, father of Dr. Hinman, of Havana, in January 1809, on the premises now occupied by Charles Swartwood, and have ever since lived in that section. They have a worthy son in the person of Mr. Gabriel Lockerby, a bachelor, who to his credit be it said, still lives with the old people and kindly and lovingly provides for all their wants, but the old lady, as has ever been her custom, still attends to all her household duties, baking, washing, and cooking for the entire family without help. They are of the old stock of New Jersey Dutch, and are most worthy representatives of that hardy, industrious and thriving race."

The History of the Town of Catharine has the listings of many of the cemeteries in the area including the one in North Settlement, but there was no record of Robert Jr.'s burial. He died in Cayuga, New York, probably about 1880, and his wife, Sara, died November 2, 1881, in Cayuga. She was listed as age 95 years.

Robert married **Sara Ann Ogden**,[18] daughter of **Capt Gabrial Ogden** and **Unknown**, on 17 Jun 1809 in Cayuga, Schuyler Co., NY.[19] Sara was born on 6 Apr 1786 in Pennsylvania,[18] died on 2 Nov 1881 in Cayuga, Schuyler Co., NY,[2] and was buried in New York.

Children from this marriage were:

+ 30   F i.   **Margaret Lockerby**.[2]
+ 31   F ii.   **Polly Lockerby**[20] was born in 1825 in Chemung Co., New York.[20]
+ 32   F iii.   **Jane Lockerby**[2] was born in 1822[2] and died on 21 Dec 1878 in Alpine, NY.[2]
+ 33   F iv.   **Catherine Lockerby**[2] was born in 1824[2] and died on 13 Dec 1854 in Alpine, NY.[2]
+ 34   M v.   **William Lockerby**[21] was born in 1815 in Alpine, Town of Catharine, Steuben Co., NY[21] and died in 1887 in Alpine, Town of Catharine, Schuyler Co., NY.
+ 35   M vi.   **Gabriel Lockerby**[22] born 1819 in Chemung Co., New York[22] and died in Nov 1887.[2]
+ 36   F vii.   **Sally Lockerby**[2] was born in 1820 in Chemung Co., New York.[2]
+ 37   F viii. **Sarah Lockerby**[22] was born on 22 May 1828 in North Settlement, Town of Catherine, New York[22] and died on 12 Nov 1903 in Alpine, New York.[2]

10. Samuel Lockerby[9] was born on 4 Apr 1787 in Walpack, Sussex Co., NJ,[10] died on 30 Oct 1855 in Catharine, Schuyler Co., NY,[5] and was buried in 1855 in North Settlement Cemetery, Catharine, Schuyler Co., NY.[2]

General Notes: FAMILY HISTORY:

Samuel Lockerby was born April 4, 1787, in Walpack, Sussex County, New Jersey, and was christened in the Dutch Reformed Church on June 3, 1787. He was the son of Robert and Sarah Tack Lockerby.

NOTES:
Birth: (Ref: NYB & G 1910 Vol. XL1, p. 40) Church Register of the Walpack Congregation Commenced with the Pastoral Service of John. Casparus Freyenmuth. Preacher there, May 31, 1741. Also have the records of the church and he appears there on page 60.

He married Eliza Hamilton on June 16, 1816, at the bride's home. She was born in 1797, and was the daughter of Dr. Walter Hamilton, a graduate of Yale. Her family lived near Newfield, New York.

NOTE:
Newfield was formed under the name of "Cayuga" Feb 22, 1811, from a part of the town of Spencer in Tioga County. On March 22, 1812, it was transferred from Tioga to Tompkins County, and on March 29th, the name was changed from Cayuga to Newfield. On June 4, 1853, a part of Newfield was annexed to the town of Catherine.

The History of the town of Catharine, NY states: "That on the same day that Samuel and Eliza were married, they returned on the back of one horse, through the dense forests to the old homestead in the town of Catharine. It is here where their children were born.." (This may explain why Samuel was devised the "horse" in his fathers Will of 1819.) To the union of Samuel and Eliza, nine children were born: Moses, Walter, Bennajah, Rosetta, Lemuel, John H., Daniel, Lucinda, and Sally.

Samuel is listed on the 1855 census of New York in the town of Cayuga. Three children are still at home, John, Daniel and Sally.

Samuel died October 30, 1855, in Catharine and Eliza died April 20, 1838. Both are buried in the North Settlement Cemetery in Catharine, Schuyler County, New York. (Ref: History of the town of Catharine, N.Y., Cleaver, p. 229)

WILL of SAMUEL LOCKERBY (Schuyler Co., NY, Probate Records 1854-1870, p. 53 of Will Book #1 (LDS 850009) -- NOTE: Will was written and signed May 4, 1854.

Be it remembered that heretofore to wit on the fifteenth day of November one thousand eight hundred and fifty five, Walter H. Lockerby, Benajah Lockerby and John Lockerby, the executors named in the Last Will and Testament of Samuel Lockerby late of the Town of Cayuga, in the county of Schuyler, deceased appeared in open court before the Surrogate of the said county of Schuyler and made application to have the said Last Will and Testament which relates to both real and personal estate proved and on such application the said Surrogate did ascertain by satisfactory proof who were heirs and next of kin of the said deceased and their places of residence so far as known and some of them appearing to be minors having no ---- guardian residing within the state of New York, a special guardian per diem was appointed in due form of law to take care of their interest in this matter in proving the said Will, by an order entered for that purpose by said Surrogate. And the said Surrogate did thereupon --- --- did require that they appear before him at his office in the Village of Watkins on the third day of December then next to attend the probate of the said Will and afterwards to wit on the said day in December, satisfactory evidence by affidavit was produced and presented to said Surrogate ----- and on that day, no one appeared to oppose the probate of said Will --- the Will is set forth to be a valid Will of real and personal estate and the proofs to be sufficient.

In the town of Cayuga in the County of Schuyler, late Chemung, and State of New York, of the age of SIXTY-SEVEN YEARS and being of sound mind and memory and considering the uncertainty of life, do make publish and declare this my last Will and Testament in the manner following. That is to say:

FIRST: It is my request and I do will and direct that my funeral expenses shall be paid out of my personal property, belonging to me at the time of my decease, by my executors, and that suitable grave stones be by them procured for me and also for my deceased daughter, Lucinda, and that the expenses there of be paid out of my personal property as above mentioned, reserving that hereinafter devised to my children, Sally and John Lockerby.

SECOND: I give devise and bequeath unto my daughter Sally one red cow I now own, one fall leaf table, one cherry stand, one looking glass, one bed and bedding for the same, a quality of feathers now on hand sufficient to make one other bed and if such feathers should be made into a bed before my death then the said Sally is to have and own such bed and one French bed stead, all of said property being now in my possession and the said articles of furniture constituting a part of my household furniture.   If the said cow should die or be disposed of at the time of my decease, then my executors are required to purchase another cow of equal quality and deliver the sane to the said Sally, the price of which shall not constitute any part of the share of my property hereinafter devised or allotted to her.

THIRD: I give and bequeath unto my son, John, the yoke of yearling steers now on my farm provided that he shall keep the said steers upon my farm until they are three years of age, and then when said steers are three years old then my said son John is to become the absolute owner thereof with the right to sell and dispose of the same as he shall see fit and not until that time.

FOURTH: I give and bequeath the proceeds of the sale of the balance of my personal property, money, notes, bonds, accounts, claims and demands, I may have at the time of my decease to my children, MOSES LOCKERBY, WALTER LOCKERBY, BENAJAH LOCKERBY, ROSETTA LOCKERBY, LEMUEL LOCKERBY, JOHN LOCKERBY, DANIEL LOCKERBY AND SALLY LOCKERBY to be divided among them equally, share and share alike, after the same shall be converted in to money whereinafter mentioned.   Third it is my wish and I so direct my executor's have full power so to do that as soon after my decease as practicable, the executors, hereinafter named and appointed by me shall sell the said practicable of personal property either at public or private sale and convert the same into money and collect what notes accounts or balances I may have outstanding and divide the said proceeds from sales equally share and share alike among my said children.

FIFTH: I also give and devise all my real estate which is situate in the town of Cayuga aforesaid being one hundred and fifty two and a half acres of land to Moses Lockerby, Benajah Lockerby and John Lockerby, my executors herein after appointed, to be held by them in trust for the use and benefit of my said children Moses, Walter, Benajah, Rosetta, Lemuel, John, Daniel and Sally Lockerby, with directions (?) - and I do order and direct that my said executors shall as soon as possible after my decease, sell, either at public or private sale all of the above mentioned lands for cash only, for the highest cash price that can be obtained therefore, and then immediately after such sale of the aforesaid lands to divide the proceeds thereof, equally share and share alike among my said children before named, and my said executors have full power to execute and deliver a good and sufficient conveyance or conveyances thereof to the purchaser or purchasers of said land.

SIXTH: In case any of my children above named shall died before my decease, then my said executors are empowered and I so direct that the share of my estate divided and bequeathed as aforesaid, to those who shall be deceased, shall by my said executors, be divided equally between the surviving children of such of my children as shall not be living at the time of my decease, and who if living, would have been entitled to receive such share as aforesaid, and in case no such grandchildren shall be living at such time then my executors are required to divide share and share alike such part or parts among my children living at the time of my death and --

LASTLY: I do hereby appoint my sons Walter Lockerby, Benajah Lockerby and John Lockerby to be my executors of this my last will and testament hereby revoking all former wills by me made.

In witness where of I have hereunto set my hand and seal this twenty fourth day of May in the year of our Lord one thousand eight hundred and fifty-four.

SAMUEL LOCKERBY

23

The WILL was probated and Phineas Catlin who resided in the Town of Catherine in the County of Schuyler declared that Samuel Lockerby died the 30th day of October 1855.

Samuel married **Eliza Hamilton**,[2] daughter of **Walter Hamilton** and **Isabel Elizabeth Lear**, on 16 Jun 1816 in Newfield, Thompkins Co., New York.[14] Eliza was born on 12 May 1797,[2] died on 20 Apr 1838 in Catharine, Schuyler Co., NY,[2] and was buried in 1838 in North Settlement Cemetery, Catharine, Schuyler Co., NY.[2]   Children from this marriage were:

+ 38   M i.   **Moses Lockerby**[23] was born from 1818 to 1819 in Catharine, Schuyler Co., NY[23] and died on 3 Apr 1887.[2]

+ 39   M ii.   **Walter H. Lockerby**[9] was born in 1820 in Catharine, Schuyler Co., NY,[24] died in Catharine, Schuyler Co., NY, and was buried in North Settlement Cemetery, Catharine, Chemung Co., NY.

+ 40   M iii. **Bennajah Lockerby**[25] was born on 1 Oct 1821 in Catharine, Tioga Co., NY,[26] died on 17 Oct 1871 in Rockford, Kent Co., MI,[27] & was buried in 1871 in Rockford, Kent Co., MI.[28]

+ 41   F iv.   **Rosetta Lockerby**[2] was born on 13 Nov 1823 in Catharine, Schuyler Co., NY,[2] died on 26 Feb 1904 in Odessa, Town of Catherine, Schuyler Co., NY,[2] and was buried in 1904.[2]

+ 42   M v.   **Lemuel H. Lockerby**[29] was born on 3 Jan 1826 in Town of Catharine, Schuyler Co., NY,[29] died on 2 Feb 1898 in Town of Catharine, Schuyler Co., NY,[2] and was buried in 1898 in Town of Catharine, Schuyler Co., NY.[2]

+ 43   M vi.   **John H. Lockerby**[30] was born in 1828 in Catharine, Schuyler Co., NY,[9] died in 1906 in Catharine, Schuyler Co., NY,[2] and was buried in 1906 in North Settlement Cemetery, Catharine, Schuyler Co., NY.[2]

+ 44   M vii. **Daniel (David) Lockerby**[9] was born in 1828 in Catharine, Schuyler Co., NY,[24] died on 19 Dec 1847,[2] and was buried in Dec 1847.

+ 45   F viii. **Lucinda Lockerby**[2] was born in 1834 in Catharine, Schuyler Co., NY,[2] died on 2 Apr 1845 in Catharine, Schuyler Co., NY,[2] and was buried in Apr 1845 in North Settlement Cemetery, Catharine, Schuyler Co., NY.[2]

+ 46   F ix.   **Sally/Sarah Lockerby**[24] was born in 1836 in Town of Cayuga, Steuben Co., NY[24] and died after 1855.

11. Benjamin Lockerby[11] was born on 24 Feb 1790 in Walpack, Sussex Co., NJ[12] and died in 1841 in Menard County, IL.[13]

General Notes: FAMILY HISTORY

Benjamin Lockerby was born 24 February 1790 in Walpack, Sussex County, New Jersey, and appears there in the christening records of the Dutch Reformed church as being baptized the 23 March 1790.   He was the son of Robert and Sarah Tack Lockerby.

NOTE: Birth: (Ref: NYB & G 1910 Vol XL1, p.42) States, Church Register of the Walpack Congregation commenced with the Pastoral Service of John Casparus Fryenmuth.   Preacher there, May 31, 1741

This child was added to Robert and Sarah per information found in the surname files at Thompkins County, NY, in 2011, the data says that there were eleven children born to Rbt and Sarah and names them, No official source was listed for this information.

Per information found in the surname files at Thompkins County, NY, in 2011, this data states that "In 1796 Benj and his family moved to Tioga Co., NY and settled in the town of Catherine on a farm now owed by Charles A. Farr." No official source was listed for this information.

Benjamin married about 1812, probably in New York in old Tioga County, in the town of Catharine, to Leah ----and from 1825 to 1830, the land records in Chemung County, New York, reflect various transactions between him and his brothers, Samuel and Robert.

NOTE:
Land rec's: (Ref: Vol 6,p. 212, #0846449 - Chemung Co. N.Y. rec's trans'd from Tioga Co 1799) Quick claim deed to Benjamin from brothers, Robert and Samuel, for 370 Acres in the town of Catharine (Tioga Co.), dated Oct 10, 1825. ON 20 OCT 1825, (VOL 6, P. 242 same film) Benjamin and LEAH his wife, sell 37 acres in Catharine, Jan 13 1826 (Vol 6, p. 494 same #) Benjamin buys 46 acres. 12 Oct 1830, Benjamin and Leah sell 46 acres (Vol 8, p 332 #0846450).

According to various sources, Benjamin is said to have moved West, and lived at one time next to Abraham Lincoln in Illinois. (Ref: History of the town of Catharine, Schuyler Co., N.Y. by Mary Louise Catlin Cleaver, p. 564) and Carl Hansen in 1994 stated, "The Benjamin of Illinois lived in MENARD COUNTY, ILL., which is next to Sangamon County where Springfield is located. Abraham Lincoln lived in Springfield." The 1850 census of Illinois does NOT list Benjamin, however there is a James and a William in Pope County, however, I did not pursue them.

There must be a lot of truth to Benjamin residing in Illinois because of all the descendants of Robert and Sarah Tack Lockerby, I can find only ONE descendant, at this time, who served in the Civil War, and this was the son of Benjamin, -- Mathew L. Lockerby.

NOTE: Diana Lockerby, 820 Hwy 128, Wilson, Wisconsin 54027-- known descendant and correspondent --1995-2007

No further investigation has been made regarding this branch however numerous doors are available for the researcher to pursue.

Benjamin married **Leah Lounsbury**,[31] daughter of **Matthew Lounsbury** and **Mary Wagon**, about 1822 in New York.[13] Leah was born in 1797 in New Jersey[13] and died in Oshkosh, WI.[13] Children from this marriage were:

> + 47   F i.   **Sarah E. Lockerby**[13] was born in 1823 in Tioga Co., NY[13] and died on 24 Nov 1891 in Greencastle, IN.[13]
>
> + 48   M ii.   **Mathew Lounsbury Lockerby**[32] was born on 24 Jan 1824 in New York,[13] died on 23 Dec 1899 in Mankato, Blue Earth Co., MN,[32] and was buried in Glenwood Cemetery, Mankato, Minnesota.[13]
>
> + 49   F iii.   **Abigail O. Lockerby**[13] was born in 1829 in New York,[13] died on 9 Jun 1884 in Cumberland, Barron Co., WI,[13] and was buried on 11 Jun 1884 in Oshkosh, WI.[13]
>
> + 50   F iv.   **Elizabeth Lockerby**[13] was born in Mar 1833 in Michigan,[13] died on 2 Jul 1903 in Janesville, WI,[13] and was buried in Riverside Cemetery, Oshkosh, WI.

12. Sarah Lockerby[2] died after 1819.[2]

General Notes: FAMILY HISTORY

Sarah was the daughter of Robert and Sarah Tack Lockerby. Her date of birth is not established. She was alive in 1819 as she is listed in her fathers WILL. He gave to his daughter, "one cow and a two-year-old heifer." (Ref: History of the town of Catharine, Schuyler County, New York)

13. Mary Lockerby.

General Notes: This child was added to Robert and Sarah per information found in the surname files at Thompkins County, NY, in 2011, the data says that there were eleven children born to Rbt and Sarah and names them. No official source was listed for this information.

14.   Joseph Lockerby died in Addison, New York.

General Notes: This child was added to Robert and Sarah per information found in the surname files at Thompkins County, NY, in 2011, the data says that there were eleven children born to Rbt and Sarah and names them. No official source was listed for this information but it also stated that Joseph married Lucretia Pratt and settled in Addison, New York when he died.

Joseph married **Lucretia Pratt**.

Fourth Generation

15. Eleanor Lockerby[2] was born about 1796.

Eleanor married **William Ray**.

16. Mary Lockerby[4] was born on 2 Aug 1798 in Pennsylvania,[6] died in 1874 in Odessa, Schuyler Co., New York,[2] and was buried in 1874 in North Settlement Cemetery, Catharine, Schuyler Co., NY.[2]

General Notes: FAMILY HISTORY:

Mary was born 2 August 1798 in Walpack, Sussex County, New Jersey, and christened in the Dutch Reformed Church on 28 April 1799. (see note).   She married as the second wife of Stephen Beardsley.   He was born 1797 in Conn and the son of James and Hannah (Beach) Beardsley. Stephen's first wife was Sally Bennett, born in 1802, and died at the age of 28 yrs in 1830.

If Mary and Stephen had family, none are known at this time, but a check of the census records for the family may shed some light on the subject.

Mary died in 1874 at the age of 74 years.   Stephen Beardsley died August 19, 1871.   All are buried in North Settlement Cemetery in Catharine, Schuyler Co., New York (Ref: History of Catherine, New York)

NOTE:
Ref: NYB &G 1910 Vol XLI p. 90;   Church Register of the Walpack Dutch Congregation. Commenced with the Pastoral Service of John Casparus Fryenmuth.   Preacher there, May 31, 1741

Mary\Maria married **Stephen Beardsley**,[2] son of **James Beardsley** and **Hannah Beach**, about 1820 in New York.[14] Stephen was born in 1797 in Conn.,[2] died on 19 Aug 1871 in Schuyler Co., New York,[2] and was buried in 1871 in North Settlement Cemetery, Catharine, Schuyler Co., NY.[2]

Children from this marriage were:

+ 51   F i.   **Ruanna Beardsley** was born on 21 Apr 1821 and died in 1892 in Elmira, New York.
+ 52   F ii.   **Alice Genet Beardsley** was born on 14 Jun 1822 in Catherine, New York, died on 15 May 1909 in Odessa, Town of Catherine, Schuyler Co., NY, and was buried in Laurel Hill Cemetery, Catherine, New York.
+ 53   M iii.   **James B. Beardsley** was born on 9 Jul 1824 in North Settlement Cemetery, Catharine, Schuyler Co., NY and died in 1893 in Battle Creek, Michigan.
+ 54   M iv.   **Aaron B. Beardsley** was born in 1826 in North Settlement Cemetery, Catharine, Schuyler Co., NY and died in Mar 1901.
+ 55   F v.   **Ruth Ann Beardsley** was born in 1827 in North Settlement Cemetery, Catharine, Schuyler Co., NY and died on 12 Jan 1913.
+ 56   F vi.   **Eunice Beardsley** was born in 1828 in North Settlement Cemetery, Catharine, Schuyler Co., NY.
+ 57   U vii.   **Beach Beardsley** died young.
+ 58   F viii.   **Maria F. Beardsley**.

17. Sarah Lockerby.[2] Sarah married **Thomas Ray**.

18. Robert Lockerby[4] was born on 20 Jan 1803 in Pennsylvania[6] and died in Michigan?

General Notes: FAMILY HISTORY:

Robert Lockerby was born Jan 20, 1803, in Walpack, Sussex County, New Jersey, and christened in the Dutch Reformed Church on May 27, 1804. (see note) He was the son of William and Ann (Chestnor) Lockerby.

The History of Catherine, Schuyler Co., New York on page 564, states "Robert married and moved to Michigan, where he died leaving a family."

Census Info: Michigan 1840 Census Index lists a Robert Lockerby in the household of Benjamin and Elizabeth Lockerby in Washington Co, MI. The 1850 Census of MI in the same county shows a Robert, Nelson and Benjamin as "heads of household" No Further Inv. --

The Robert listed in the 1850 census was William's son and nephew to the Benjamin above according to descendant: Carl Hansen, 317 Spring St, Mankato, Minnesota 56001

NOTE: (Ref: NYB & G 1910, Vol XLI p. 95 --Church Reg. of the Walpack Congregation. Dutch Ref Church Rec of Walpack p86

Robert married **Clarrisa**. She was born on 27 Sep 1812 in New York and died on 9 Jun 1884 in Northfield, Rice Co., Minnesota. Children from this marriage were:

+ 59   F i.   **Caroline Louisa Lockerby** was born on 19 Aug 1836 in Washtenaw Co., Michigan, died on 26 Apr 1914 in Northfield, Rice Co., Minnesota, and was buried in 1914.
+ 60   M ii.   **John Lockerby** was born on 2 Jan 1841 in Bridgewater, Washtenaw Co., MI and died on 21 Nov 1916 in Warsaw Twp., Rice Co., Minnesota.

19. Joseph Lockerby.[2] Joseph married **Lucretia Pratt**.[2] Joseph was the son of William and Ann (Chestnor) Lockerby. No further information.

20. John Lockerby[6] was born on 5 Sep 1806 in Pennsylvania.[6] Birth: (Ref: NYB & G 1910, Vol XLI, p. 200) Church Reg of the Walpack Congregation p. 93

21. John Lockerby was born from about 1799 to 1800 in prob. New York.

22. Catherine Lockerby was born on 6 Apr 1801 in Veteran, Chemung Co., New York and died on 8 Jan 1857 in DeKalb County, Illinois.

General Notes: FAMILY HISTORY:

The only reference I have to Catherine Lockerby was found in the book "10,000 Vital Records of Western New York 1809-1850" - by Fred Bowman. In this reference it states she married William Olmstead in Veteran, New York, on July 23, 1828. Both parties were from "Catlin, New York." If Catherine was 20-25 years of age when she married, she would have been born about 1803-1808, and probably the child of Bennajah.

Source 1 of gedcoms lists her as Bennajah's daughter

Catherine married **Mathew William Olmstead** on 23 Jul 1828 in Catlin, Veteran, New York.[33] Mathew was born on 22 Nov 1804 in Wilton, Fairfield Co., CT (see note!) and died in 1889. Children from this marriage were:

+ 61   M i.   **Robert L. Olmstead**[34] was born on 16 May 1829[34] and died on 20 Apr 1864 in Pleasant Hill, Louisiana.[34]
+ 62   F ii.   **Hannah Jennette Olmstead**[34] born on 9 May 1831[34] and died on 21 Jan 1881.[34]

+	63	F	iii.	**Araminta Agnes Olmstead**[34] was born on 29 May 1833.[35]
+	64	F	iv.	**Rebecca Margaret Olmstead**[36] born on 19 Mar 1835[37] and died on 13 May 1921.[35]
+	65	M	v.	**David Olmstead**[34] was born on 26 Apr 1840[34] and died on 4 May 1840.[35]

23.   Benjamin Lockerby[16] was born on 4 May 1807 in Tioga Co., NY,[16] died on 4 Jul 1882 in Northfield, Rice Co., MN,[16] and was buried in 1882 in Northfield, Rice Co., MN.[16]

General Notes: FAMILY HISTORY

Benjamin Lockerby, the son of Bennajah, was born May 4, 1807, in old Tioga County, New York, in the town of Catherine.   He married 5 January 1829, in Tompkins, New York (old Tioga Co), to Elizabeth Pike, the daughter of Sewell and Pamela Beardsley.   She was born September 10, 1807. To this union, seven children were born: Amanda, Oscar, Ermine, Frances, Edgar, Benjamin, and Seneca.

Benjamin and Elizabeth removed from New York to Bridgewater Township, Washtenaw County, Michigan, sometime in the 1830's and appear there on the 1840 and 1850 census records.   By 1850, the family had relocated in Northfield, Rice County, Minnesota, and appear there on the 1850 census. (ref: corresp of Carl Hansen, Jan 13, 1994)   He also appears here on the 1880 census but his wife's name is given as "Dessie" and a 5 yr old grandson, Frankie, is living with him.

Newspaper Information -- Benjamin Lockerby, FARIBAULT DAILY NEWS 'History of Rice County' 1882:   'In the summer of this year (1858 in which the territory of Minnesota was admitted as a state) the government of the county was subjected to a change by an act of the Legislature, and the management of county affairs was vested in a 'Board of Supervisors' consisting of the chairman of each board of township supervisors -- one member from each township.   On the 14th of Sept. 2858, the first meeting of this board was held in the city of Faribault and was called to order by J. A. Starks.   The roll was called and the following gentlemen, representing the towns opposite their names, answered the call ...B. Lockerby, Bridgewater..."....   "The first town meeting for Bridgewater for the purpose of organizing the township was held on the 11th of May, 1858, at the house of Fernado Thompson in the village of Dundas.   The meeting was called to order and C. C. Stetson was chosen chairman pro tem, and Benjamin Lockerby, moderator.   They next proceeded to ballot for officers, which resulted as follows: Supervisors, Benjamin Lockerby, Chairman..."

Correpondance 13 Jan 1994 -- Carl Hansen.   Mr. Hansen agrees that "Benjamin was likely the son of Benajah; son of Robert and Sarah Tack"

Benjamin died, July 4, 1882, in Northfield, Rice County, Minnesota, and is buried there in the "Old Northfield Cemetery."   Ref: Mary Balow, corresp, Aug 22, 1986, (200 So. Market St, #508, San Jose, Ca. 95113) Benjamin

Benjamin married **Elizabeth Pike**,[16] daughter of **Sewell Pike** and **Pamela Beardsley**, on 5 Jan 1829 in Tioga Co., New York. Elizabeth was born on 10 Sep 1807 in New York,[16] died on 11 Jun 1860 in Northfield, Rice Co., Minnesota,[16] and was buried in 1860 in Northfield, Rice Co., Minnesota.

Children from this marriage were:

| + | 66 | F | i. | **Amanda Melvina Lockerby**[16] was born on 13 Sep 1829 in Tompkins/Tioga County, New York,[16] died on 22 Jun 1907 in Northfield, Rice Co., Minnesota,[16] and was buried in Northfield Cemetery, Northfield, Rice Co., Minnesota.[16] |
| + | 67 | M | ii. | **Oscar Dunbooth Lockerby**[16] was born on 22 Aug 1832 in Tompkins/Tioga County, New York,[16] died on 25 Jan 1917 in Northfield, Rice Co., Minnesota,[16] and was buried in Old Northfield Cemetery, Pike Co., Minnesota.[16] |

+ 68   F iii.   **Ermine Pamela Lockerby**[16] was born on 15 Mar 1836 in Washtenaw Co., Michigan,[16] died on 11 Jun 1912 in Northfield, Rice Co., Minnesota,[16] and was buried in Northfield Cemetery, Northfield, Rice Co., Minnesota.[16]

+ 69   M iv.   **Edgar Mortimer Lockerby**[16] was born on 9 Aug 1838 in Bridgewater, Washtenaw Co., MI,[16] died on 5 Aug 1901 in Northfield, Rice Co., Minnesota,[16] and was buried in Minnesota.[16]

+ 70   F v.   **Francis Lavina Lockerby**[16] was born on 22 Jun 1840 in Washtenaw Co., Michigan,[16] died on 13 Oct 1869 in Northfield, Rice Co., Minnesota,[16] and was buried in Northfield Cemetery, Northfield, Rice Co., Minnesota.[16]

+ 71   M vi.   **Benjamin Burr Lockerby**[16] was born on 26 Dec 1842 in Washtenaw Co., Michigan,[16] died on 19 Apr 1925 in Minnesota,[16] and was buried in Northfield Cemetery, Northfield, Rice Co., Minnesota.[16]

+ 72   M vii.   **Seneca Daries Lockerby**[16] was born on 21 Apr 1845 in Washtenaw Co., Michigan,[16] died on 13 Dec 1926 in Faribault, Rice Co., MN, and was buried in Maple Lawn Cemetery in Faribault, Minnesota.

24.   William Lockerby.[17]
25.   Bennajah Lockerby.[17]
26.   Hannah Lockerby.[17]
27.   Robert Lockerby.[17]
28.   Samuel Lockerby.[17]
29.   Moses Lockerby.[17]
30.   Margaret Lockerby.[2]   Margaret married **James Beardsley**.[2]

31.   Polly Lockerby[20] was born in 1825 in Chemung Co., New York.[20]   Polly married **John Fish**.[2]

General Notes: In the 1855 State Census of New York, Polly was living with her uncle John and his wife, Sarah Garrison.   She is shown as age 44 years.   Likely she was taking care of John because on this same census, he is listed as 88 years old and blind.

32.   Jane Lockerby[2] was born in 1822[2] and died on 21 Dec 1878 in Alpine, NY.[2]
Jane married **David B. Rosebrook**.[2] David was born in 1816[2] and died on 4 Apr 1876 in Alpine, NY.[2]

33.   Catherine Lockerby[2] was born in 1824[2] and died on 13 Dec 1854 in Alpine, NY.[2]
Catherine married **Marion Lorenzo Rosebrook**.[2] Marion died in Oct 1889 in Alpine, NY.[2]

34.   William Lockerby[21] was born in 1815 in Alpine, Town of Catharine, Steuben Co., NY[21] and died in 1887 in Alpine, Town of Catharine, Schuyler Co., NY.
General Notes: I found it interesting that William was NOT LISTED on the 1855 State Census of the Town of Cayuga, Schuyler Co., NY, but all his family was, yet, -- I have his death date as 1887. Maybe this is incorrect?? -- or, he may have been away from the home serving in the CIVIL WAR? This aspect needs to be investigated.

William married **Mary L. Wakeman**,[22] daughter of **Seth Wakeman** and **Sarah**. Mary was born in 1816 in Conn.[38] and died on 17 May 1888 in New York.[2]

Children from this marriage were:

+ 73   M i.   **John B. Lockerby**[22] was born on 11 May 1844 in Alpine, Town of Catharine, Steuben Co., NY,[22] died on 5 Nov 1918,[2] and was buried in 1918 in Odessa, Town of Catherine, Schuyler Co., NY.[2]

+ 74   M ii.   **Burr Lockerby**[22] was born in 1846 in Alpine, NY,[22] died on 17 Aug 1899 in Odessa, Town of Catherine, Schuyler Co., NY,[2] and was buried in 1899 in Laurel Hill Cemetery, Odessa, Schuyler Co., NY.[2]

+ 75   M iii.   **William R. Lockerby**[22] was born in 1849 in Schuyler Co., New York,[38] died on 14 Jul 1933,[2] and was buried in 1933 in Odessa, Town of Catherine, Schuyler Co., NY.[2]

+ 76   F iv.   **Elizabeth Lockerby**[22] was born in 1852 in Schuyler Co., New York.[38]

+ 77   F v.   **Sarah Ann Lockerby**[22] was born on 14 Jun 1855 in Town of Cayuga, Schuyler Co., NY,[38] died in Feb 1923,[2] was buried in 1923 in Odessa, Town of Catherine, Schuyler Co., NY.

+ 78   M vi.   **Alfred Lockerby**[20] was born in 1856 in Town of Cayuga, Schuyler Co., NY,[20] died in 1887,[2] and was buried in 1887 in Odessa, Town of Catherine, Schuyler Co., NY.[2]

+ 79   F vii.   **Catharine Lockerby**[20] was born in 1858 in Town of Cayuga, Schuyler Co., NY,[39] died in 1920, and was buried in 1920 in Odessa, Town of Catherine, Schuyler Co., NY.

+ 80   M viii.   **Fred P. Lockerby**.[2]

+ 81   F ix.   **Mary Jane Lockerby "Jennie"**[20] was born in 1861 in Schuyler Co., New York.[39]

+ 82   F x.   **Hattie Lockerby**.[2]

35. Gabriel Lockerby[22] was born in 1819 in Chemung Co., New York[22] and died in Nov 1887.[2]

General Notes: Gabriel is residing in Catherine, Schuyler County, New York, at the time of the 1880 census. Living in his household are a sister, Sarah, age 51, and his mother, Ann, age 94.

36. Sally Lockerby[2] was born in 1820 in Chemung Co., New York.[2]

37. Sarah Lockerby[22] was born on 22 May 1828 in North Settlement, Town of Catherine, New York[22] and died on 12 Nov 1903 in Alpine, New York.[2]

General Notes: From the Schuyler County Historical Society in Montour Falls, NY, in 2011 we learn from information found in the surname files and entitled Misc. Info: -- (Death Files) -- "Miss Sarah Lockerby, d Nov 12, 1903, at the home of her niece, Mrs. Eugene Swartwood, Alpine, NY. She was the youngest and last surviving daughter of Robert and Annie Lockerby. Born May 22, 1828, in North Settlement, Town of Catherine, NY"

38. Moses Lockerby[23] was born from 1818 to 1819 in Catharine, Schuyler Co., NY[23] and died on 3 Apr 1887.[2]

General Notes: Census Info: Appears on the 1850 Census of Chemung County, New York, in VETERAN Township as age 31 born in New York and a FARMER with real estate valued at 1600. His wife is listed as Elsie age 27 and one daughter Eliza age 4.

Census Info: Appears in ALPINE township, Schuyler County, New York, on the 1880 census. At this time, his wife is still living and only the last two children are residing at home. Both Elsie and Charles are shown as being 15 yrs of age.

Moses married **Elsie Grant**[23] about 1845 in Chemung Co., New York.[40] Elsie was born in 1823 in Delaware.[41] Children from this marriage were:

+ 83   F i.   **Elizabeth Lockerby**[23] born in 1846 in Town of Catharine, Steuben Co., NY.[41]

+ 84 F ii. **Mary Lockerby**[29] born about 1851 in Town of Catharine, Steuben Co., NY.[42]

+ 85 M iii. **George Lockerby**.[2]

+ 86 M iv. **William H. Lockerby**[2] was born 24 Feb 1859 and died in Probably Michigan.

+ 87 M v. **Charles Lockerby**[2] was born about 1865 in New York,[2] died in 1883 in New York,[2] and was buried in New York.[2]

39. Walter H. Lockerby[9] was born in 1820 in Catharine, Schuyler Co., NY,[24] died in Catharine, Schuyler Co., NY, and was buried in North Settlement Cemetery, Catharine, Chemung Co., NY. Walter married **Sally M. Archibald**.[9] Sally was born in 1826 in Town of Cayuga, Steuben Co., NY,[2] died on 15 Apr 1853 in Town of Catharine, Schuyler Co., NY,[2] and was buried in North Settlement Cemetery, Catharine, Chemung Co., NY.[2] The child from this marriage was:

+ 88 F i. **Sally M. Lockerby**[9] was born in 1853 in Town of Cayuga, Steuben Co., NY.[9]

40. Bennajah Lockerby[25] was born on 1 Oct 1821 in Catharine, Tioga Co., NY,[26] died on 17 Oct 1871 in Rockford, Kent Co., MI,[27] and was buried in 1871 in Rockford, Kent Co., MI.[28]

General Notes: FAMILY HISTORY:

Bennajah Lockerby's birth is recorded in the "Lockerby Family Bible" which was on file with the DeWitt Historical Society in Tompkins, New York. It listed all the family information for generations. The bible record states he was born October 1, 1821, in "Chemung County, New York, in the Old Town of Catharine." This area today lies in Schuyler County. He very likely grew up on the old farm in Catharine.

NOTE: He says he is born in Odessa, New York, but this is all the same place. Over the years, the county lines were changing, and the names of the towns were either being changed, or new ones added.

When he was twenty-five years of age, he married Mary Ann Terry, the daughter of Ezekiel and Phebe (Canterberry) Terry. Mary Ann was born 30 Dec 1822 in Palmertown, Mass. The family bible records the marriage as follows: "By the Rev. Mr. Carr of Fairport, Chemung Co., New York, Mr. Bennajah Lockerby of Newfield, Tompkins County to Miss Maryann Terry of Veteran, Chemung County, all of New York. December 9, 1846."

The bible further records the births of their eight children born between 1848 and 1862: Marshall Samuel, Mitchell Monroe, Wallace Hiram, Jerome Bennajah, Jacob Smith, Ezekiel Terry, Ida Adelia, and Frankie Melvinia.

In 1870/71, the family migrated to Michigan and settled in Rockford, Kent County, where he is listed in the Plat book of the county as owning property in Plainfield Township. Within a year after they migrated, Bennajah died of an ulceration of the Kidneys. He was fifty years, seventeen days old. His death record in Grand Rapids, Kent Co., Michigan reads: "Benager Lockly - carpenter." Date of death was October 13, 1871. He is buried in Rockford Cemetery.

NOTE
Death: Rockford Cem. family lot 22, Block D (Cem Rec)AGE 50 -- cause of death, ulceration of the Kidneys.

Mary Ann (Terry) Lockerby was born in Mass, but left there with her parents when she was about eight years of age. The family migrated to Veteran, New York, in about 1830 and settled on property which later became known as "Terry Hill." She is a descendant of William Bradford, Mayflower passenger and first governor of Plymouth Plantation. Marsha Pilger, author of this linage, has proven her descent to William Bradford through Mary Ann Terry and is a member of the National Mayflower Society.

At the time of Mary Ann's death on June 23, 1886, she was staying at the home of her son, Ezekiel, in Keno ("Lockerby Town") in Newaygo County, Michigan, and tradition states she had a carbuncle on the back of her neck which had been draining for several days. She also had diarrhea. It is believe the poison from her body was draining through the diarrhea and when the doctor came to the home to treat the carbuncle, it is said he decided she shouldn't have to content with both discomforts and gave her medicine to stop the diarrhea. It thought by doing so, the poison backed up in her body and caused the complications which eventually lead to her death.

She is buried beside her husband, Bennajah, in the Rockford Cemetery in Rockford, Michigan.

NOTE:
Many of the "family traditions" referenced on this line were provided by Beulah (Totten) Wright, descendant of this branch. Beulah was of the generation to have known many of the individuals and lived in Michigan where she attended many family reunions, etc. She was also a genealogist and tried to collect as much family history as possible.

Bennajah married **Mary Ann Terry**,[43] daughter of **Ezekiel Terry** and **Phebe Canterburry**, on 9 Dec 1846 in Veteran, Chemung Co., NY.[44] Mary was born on 30 Dec 1822 in Palmertown, Hamden Co., Mass.,[45] died on 23 Jun 1886 in Keno, Newaygo Co., MI,[46] and was buried in 1886 in Rockford, Kent Co., MI.
Children from this marriage were:

+ 89   M i.   **Marshall Samuel Lockerby**[43] was born on 24 Feb 1848 in Town of Catherine, Chemung Co., NY,[43] died in Sep 1928 in Hokesland, WA,[47] and was buried in 1928 in Rockford, Kent Co., MI.

+ 90   M ii.   **Dr. Mitchell Monroe Lockerby**[48] was born on 14 Oct 1849 in Town of Catherine, Chemung Co., NY,[49] died on 15 Jan 1927 in Grand Rapids, Kent Co., MI,[50] and was buried in 1927 in Rockford, Kent Co., MI.[51]

+ 91   M iii.   **Wallace Hiram Lockerby**[52] was born on 7 Oct 1851 in Town of Catherine, Chemung Co., NY[47] and died on 9 Feb 1913 in Woverley, NY.[46]

+ 92   M iv.   **Jerome Bennajah Lockerby**[52] was born on 27 Jul 1852 in Town of Catherine, Chemung Co., NY,[47] died on 1 Nov 1939 in Odessa, Town of Catherine, Schuyler Co., NY,[47] and was buried in 1939 in Odessa, Town of Catherine, Schuyler Co., NY.

+ 93   M v.   **Jacob Smith Lockerby**[52] was born on 5 Mar 1855 in Town of Catherine, Schuyler Co., NY[47] and died in 1924 in Hokesland, WA.[47]

+ 94   F vi.   **Susan Lockerby**[42] was born in Jan 1855 in Catharine/Odessa, Schuyler Co., NY[42] and died before 1865 in Town of Catherine, Schuyler Co., NY.

+ 95   M vii.   **Ezekiel Terry Lockerby**[53] was born on 1 Apr 1857 in Town of Catherine, Schuyler Co., NY,[54] died from 0014 to 22 Mar 1900 in Woodville, Home Twp., Newaygo Co., MI,[55] and was buried in 1900 in Whipple Cemetery, Big Rapids, Mecosta Co., MI.[56]

+ 96   F viii.   **Ida Adelia Lockerby**[46] was born on 1 May 1859 in Town of Catherine, Schuyler Co., NY,[57] died on 10 Jul 1915 in Grand Rapids, Kent Co., MI,[50] and was buried in 1915 in Rockford, Kent Co., MI.[50]

+ 97   F ix.   **Francis Melvina Lockerby**[58] was born on 31 Aug 1862 in Town of Catherine, Schuyler Co., NY,[58] died on 2 Dec 1927 in Grand Rapids, Kent Co., MI,[47] and was buried in 1927 in Rockford, Kent Co., MI.

41. Rosetta Lockerby[2] was born on 13 Nov 1823 in Catharine, Schuyler Co., NY,[2] died on 26 Feb 1904 in Odessa, Town of Catherine, Schuyler Co., NY,[2] and was buried in 1904.[2]

General Notes: FAMILY HISTORY:

Rosetta Lockerby was born November 13, 1823, in Catharine, Schuyler Co., New York and was the daughter of Samuel and Eliza (Hamilton) Lockerby. She married Franklyn Terry. Franklyn was born July 16, 1820, in Palmerton, Mass., and was the son of Ezekiel and Phebe (Canterbury) Terry. According to the "History of Catherine, New York," he was a Civil War veteran and enlisted in Company F., 50 Reg. Engineers and discharged in 1865.

Children born to Rosetta and Franklyn: Charles, Bonaparte, Andrew, Warren, John, Caroline, Ella, and Walter Terry.

Rosetta and Franklyn spent the last years of their life in a little house that stood about where the First National Bank of Odessa was located in 1983. Their son, Andrew, owned the Odessa House just down the street from them (1945 info). Rosetta died February 26/7, 1904, in Odessa, New York. Franklyn died, at the age of 87, on May 8, 1907, in same.

Rosetta married **Franklyn Terry**,[2] son of **Ezekiel Terry** and **Phebe Canterburry**. Franklyn was born on 16 Jul 1820 in Palmertown, Mass.[2] and died on 8 May 1907 in Odessa, Town of Catherine, Schuyler Co., NY.[2] Children from this marriage were:

+ 98   M i.   **Charles F. Terry**[2] was born in 1849 in Veteran, Chemung Co., New York and died in 1924 in Veteran, Chemung Co., New York.

+ 99   M ii.   **Bonaparte Terry**[2] was born in 1852, died on 9 Feb 1862 in New York, and was buried in 1862 in North Settlement, Odessa, , New York.

+100   M iii. **Andrew Terry**[2] was born in 1853 and died in 1921.

+101   M iv.   **Warren Terry**[2] died in died young, in New York.

+102   M v.   **John Terry**[2] died in died young, in New York.

+103   F vi.   **Caroline Terry**.[2]

+104   F vii. **Ella Terry**[2] was born in 1863 and died in 1889 in Footes Hill, Odessa, New York.

+105   M viii. **Walter Terry**.[2]

42.   Lemuel H. Lockerby[29] was born on 3 Jan 1826 in Town of Catharine, Schuyler Co., NY,[29] died on 2 Feb 1898 in Town of Catharine, Schuyler Co., NY,[2] and was buried in 1898 in Town of Catharine, Schuyler Co., NY.[2]

General Notes: NOTE: The 1855 Census of the Town of Catharine, Schulyer Co., NY was taken on June 28th. It shows Lemuel at age 28, born in Schuyler County; Mary E., wife, age 24, born Schuyler Co., NY and a son, George, 10 months old, also born in Schuyler Co.

NOTE: The 1865 State Census of the Town of Catharine, Schuyler Co., NY, was taken on June 19, and shows Lemuel, Mary E., George and a daughter, Augusta, age 9 years. All born in Schuyler Co., NY.

The 1893/4 Business Directory of the Town of Cayuga (Schuyler County), New York, gave the following: Lemuel H. Lockerby, PO Alpine, Road 6, Corner 12, . 187, owns farm 50 acres and rents of Teresa Lake of N. Spencer, Tompkins Co., farm of 17 acres, has 2 horses, 1 cow, and an orchard with 75 trees. (This data from the Schuyler Co. HS in Montour Falls, NY in 2011)

Information from the Death Files of the Schuyler County Historical Society in Montour Falls, NY (2011) state the following:

"Lemuel H. Lockerby, d. Wed Feb 2, 1891. Burial North Settlement (Agard) Cemetery. Born in Town of Catharine Jan 3, 1826, married in 1848 to Miss Mary E. Hendershot. Survived by his wife; three children, George R., Waverly, NY, Mrs. Gusta A. Smith, Ithaca ad William E. at home; one brother, John Lockerby, Alpine; two sisters Mrs. George Markell, Big Flats, NY and Mrs. Frank Terry of Odessa."

In the 1914 Farm Directory for Schuyler Co., Town of Catharine, it shows the following: Mary E. Lockerby, widow of Lemuel, boards with William of Alpine. It further shows that William (b. 1866) is the son of Lemuel and a laborer (on the P. & R. Railway) owns house and lot in Alpine. ((This data from the Schuyler Co. HS in Montour Falls, NY in 2011)

Lemuel married **Mary Elizabeth Hendershot**,[29] daughter of **Isaac Hendershot** and **Unknown**, in 1848.[59] Mary was born in 1831[29] and died on 22 Sep 1915.[2] Children from this marriage were:

+ 106   M i.   **George R. Lockerby**[29] was born in 1854.[29]

+ 107   F ii.   **Augusta Lockerby**[42] was born in 1856.[42]

+ 108   M iii.   **William E. Lockerby**[60] was born on 11 Nov 1866 in Cayuga, Schuyler Co., NY,[61] died on 31 Mar 1949 in Alpine, NY, and was buried in Laurel Hill Cemetery, Catherine, Schuyler Co., New York.

43. John H. Lockerby[30] was born in 1828 in Catharine, Schuyler Co., NY,[9] died in 1906 in Catharine, Schuyler Co., NY,[2] and was buried in 1906 in North Settlement Cemetery, Catharine, Schuyler Co., NY.[2]

General Notes: The 1893/4 Business Directory of the Town of Catharine, Schuyler Co, NY shows the following: "John H. PO Alpine, off road 4, b. 1828, in Chemung County, farmer of 150 acres, has 3 horses, 4 cows, 65 sheep." (This data from the Schuyler Co. HS in Montour Falls, NY in 2011)

Burial: North Settlement Cemetery (stone - 2011)

John married **Margaret Jane Strong**,[62] daughter of **John Strong** and **Plants**. Margaret was born on 28 Sep 1851,[2] died on 13 May 1928 in Catharine, Schuyler Co., NY,[2] and was buried in 1928 in North Settlement Cemetery, Catharine, Schuyler Co., NY.[2]

+ 109   F i.   **Margaret Lockerby**.

44. Daniel (David) Lockerby[9] was born in 1828 in Catharine, Schuyler Co., NY,[24] died on 19 Dec 1847,[2] and was buried in Dec 1847.

45. Lucinda Lockerby[2] was born in 1834 in Catharine, Schuyler Co., NY,[2] died on 2 Apr 1845 in Catharine, Schuyler Co., NY,[2] and was buried in Apr 1845 in North Settlement Cemetery, Catharine, Schuyler Co., NY.[2]

46. Sally/Sarah Lockerby[24] was born in 1836 in Town of Cayuga, Steuben Co., NY[24] and died after 1855. General Notes: listed in her fathers' will

Sally/Sarah married **George Markel**[39] in Schuyler Co., New York.[24] George was born in 1835.[39] Children from this marriage were:

+ 110   F i.   **Rosella Markel**[39] was born in 1858 in Town of Cayuga, Schuyler Co., NY.[39]

+ 111   F ii.   **Mary Markel**[39] was born in 1860 in Town of Cayuga, Schuyler Co., NY.[39]

+ 112   M iii.   **Nicholas Markel**[39] was born in 1862 in Town of Cayuga, Schuyler Co., NY.[39]

+ 113   F iv.   **Siona Markel**[39] was born in 1864 in Town of Cayuga, Schuyler Co., NY.[39]

47. Sarah E. Lockerby[13] was born in 1823 in Tioga Co., NY[13] and died on 24 Nov 1891 in Greencastle, IN.[13]   Sarah married **Rev. James Leaton**.[13] James was born in 1816 in England[13] and died on 11 Sep 1891 in Carlinville, IL.[13]   Children from this marriage were:

+ 114   M i.   **James Howard Leaton**[13] was born in Sep 1847 in Illinois[13] and died on 11 May 1924 in Bloomington, McLean, IL.[13]
+ 115   F ii.   **Ann E. Leaton**[13] was born in 1849 in Illinois.[13]
+ 116   F iii.   **Martha Leaton**[13] was born in 1852 in Illinois.[13]
+ 117   F iv.   **Clara F. Leaton**[13] was born in 1854 in Illinois.[13]

48. Mathew Lounsbury Lockerby[32] was born on 24 Jan 1824 in New York,[13] died on 23 Dec 1899 in Mankato, Blue Earth Co., MN,[32] and was buried in Glenwood Cemetery, Mankato, Minnesota.[13]

General Notes: Went to Minnesota about 1863/4

Military Service: Civil War (Ref: Carl Hansen of Minn-1994) also from Diana Lockerby, descendant, correspondence of Jan 9, 1995: Civil War --37th Wisconsin Infantry.   Enlisted 30 Mar 1864 and served one year.   Was rank of Corporal and mustered out at the rank of Sargent.   Had a gunshot wound.

From a 2005 email by Diana Lockerby, descendant, she states, "the big discovery that was made for Mathew Lounsbury Lockerby, our Civil War Veteran, is that in his Military Service file at the Nat'l Archives - he had written a letter to President Lincoln. At the time, Mathew had just been shot at the Battle of Petersburg and was in a U.S. Military Hospital in York, PA. He wanted to return to a Hospital in Wisconsin and wrote to ask Lincoln for help. He describes in the letter about him knowing his Uncles - Matthew & Jonathan Lounsbury and also reminded Lincoln that when he lived in Menard Co., IL - and he was a surveyor there on the Sangamon River, that he, as a young boy, helped him with his surveying "chains" on the river."

Death Record (book G, page 174, line 3, Blue Earth County, Minnesota) Died: Dec 23, 1899; age 75 years, 4 months, 1 day; Born in NY; died of apoplexy; farmer; parents, Benjamin and Leah Lockerby.

OBITUARY: Mankato Daily Review, Saturday Evening, December 23, 1899.   "Mr. M. L. Lockerby died at his home in this city this morning at 2:40 o'clock.   His passing away was quiet and peaceful and free from pain.   About two months ago, while riding upon a load of corn, in this city, he fell to the hard ground, sustaining a severe shock to his system and suffering much pain.   He never recovered from the effect of this fall, which was very likely the cause of subsequent complications. About three weeks ago he complained of numbness of one of his limbs, which gradually developed into paralysis.   He was upon the streets the last time on about the 7th or 8th of December, resisting with his usual vigor against his ailment, which he at first interpreted as a rheumatic.   Consulting a physician, as he was then advised to do, he realized the character of his trouble, and took to his bed. Occasionally he had rallying intervals, but he gradually declined, understanding sometimes what was said to him, but unable to articulate with distinctness, he lay in this condition until death came to his relief.   He had every possible attention, and while this soothed his decline, the severity of his ailment was beyond human relief."

"Mr. Lockerby was born in New York, of Scotch-Irish parentage, seventy-five years ago last August. In early life he came west, and lived at various places in Illinois and Wisconsin.   He was a man with strong social inclinations, an ardent Republican, and in his early days numbered Lincoln, Grant and other prominent Illionian's among his acquaintances.   Afterwards moving to Walworth county, Wisconsin, he enlisted in the 37th Wisconsin Infantry, March 30, 1864, entering with the rank of corporal, served one year and was mustered out as a sergeant.   At Petersburg, VA., he suffered a gunshot wound."

"He came to Minnesota about twenty-five years ago, locating on a farm in Mapleton Township. While living there he developed a new variety of wheat, from a sample sent him from the patent office, which fro a time was very successful in its yields, sold readily and was the source of considerable income, but it finally collapsed and passed out of use." Subsequently he exchanged his farm in Mapleton township for one owned by Mr. Jenkin Williams on the Jones ford road, where he resided, gradually developing the growing of raspberries on a liberal scale. As increasing age came upon him he leased the farm and came to Mankato to reside."

"While here Mr. Lockerby took an active interest in public affairs and he was especially prominent in politics as a Republican. He was a man of large practical information, strong in his convictions, and while he had his enemies, he also made strong friends, and these appreciated his merits. He was pronounced in his sympathies with the masses, loyal to his country, and to the Grand Army of the Republic, of which he was long a member. The Review has long enjoyed his acquaintance and friendship, appreciated his many good qualities and extends its earnest sympathies to his family and afflicted friends."

"Funeral services will be held at the house at 2 o'clock Tuesday afternoon under the auspices of Wilkin Post, G. A. R."

Mathew married **Desiah T. McCurdy**,[13] daughter of **Samuel McCurdy** and **Murphy**, on 26 Jan 1851 in Oshkosh, WI.[13] Desiah was born on 11 Feb 1824 in New Brunswick, Nova Scotia,[13] died on 24 Apr 1909 in Mankato, Blue Earth Co., MN,[13] and was buried in Glenwood Cemetery, Mankato, Minnesota.[13]
Children from this marriage were:

> +118   M i.   **William Edgar Lockerby**[13] was born on 22 Aug 1853 in Winnebago Co., WI[13] and died about 1935 in Orange Co., FL.[13]

> +119   M ii.   **Charles Lounsberry Lockerby**[13] was born in 1854 in Winnebago Co., WI[13] and died in Mar 1927 in Chicago, Cook Co., IL.[13]

> +120   M iii.   **James Leaten Lockerby**[13] was born on 9 Jul 1855 in Winnebago Co., WI[13] and died on 25 Apr 1915 in Mankato, Blue Earth Co., MN.[13]

> +121   F iv.   **Mary Ellen Lockerby**[13] was born on 12 Feb 1856 in Winnebago Co., WI,[13] died on 6 Nov 1924 in Los Angeles, CA,[13] and was buried in Inglewood Cemetery, Los Angeles, California.[13]

> +122   M v.   **Elmer Ellsworth Lockerby**[32] was born on 12 Dec 1858 in Oshkosh, Winnebago Co., WI,[32] died on 23 Jul 1933 in Winthrop, Sibley Co., MN,[32] and was buried in Winthrop, Sibley Co., MN.

> +123   F vi.   **Lucy V. Lockerby**[13] was born in 1861 in Winnebago Co., WI[13] and died on 18 Nov 1883 in Mankato, Blue Earth Co., MN.[13]

> +124   M vii.   **Samuel McCarthy Lockerby**[13] was born in Aug 1864 in Winnebago Co., WI,[13] died in Oct 1923 in Seattle, WA,[13] and was buried in Seattle, WA.[13]

49.   Abigail O. Lockerby[13] was born in 1829 in New York,[13] died on 9 Jun 1884 in Cumberland, Barron Co., WI,[13] and was buried on 11 Jun 1884 in Oshkosh, WI.[13]

General Notes: Per Diane Lockerby in 2005, "Abigail died at her daughter, Maria Waterman's, home."

Abigail married **Richard Lawrence Howard**[13] on 27 May 1847 in Fond du Lac, Wisconsin.[13] Richard was born on 3 Mar 1824[13] and died about 1855.[13]   Children from this marriage were:

> +125   F i.   **Marian Eleanor Howard**[13] was born in 1848 in Oshkosh, WI.[13]

> +126   F ii.   **Maria Louisa Howard**[13] was born in Aug 1849 in Oshkosh, WI.[13]

+127   F iii.   **Sarah Howard**[13] was born in 1852 in Oshkosh, WI.[13]

50. **Elizabeth Lockerby**[13] was born in Mar 1833 in Michigan,[13] died on 2 Jul 1903 in Janesville, WI,[13] and was buried in Riverside Cemetery, Oshkosh, WI. Elizabeth married **Hiram Morley**[13] on 5 Dec 1850 in Byron, Fond du Lac Co., WI.[13] Hiram was born on 24 Oct 1826 in Oneida, NY[13] and died on 29 May 1882 in Oshkosh, WI.[13] Children from this marriage were:

+128   M i.   **Edward B. Morley**[13] was born in Jul 1853 in Wisconsin.[13]
+129   M ii.   **Eugene Morley**[13] was born in 1857 in Wisconsin[13] and died in Feb 1885 in Oshkosh, WI.[13]

Fifth Generation

51. Ruanna Beardsley was born on 21 Apr 1821 and died in 1892 in Elmira, New York. Ruanna married **Levi Lyon**.

General Notes: Died at the home of her brother, Aaron Beardsley, in Elmira, New York, Jan 1892. NO ISSUE (ref: History of Catherine New York, p. 432)

52. Alice Genet Beardsley was born on 14 Jun 1822 in Catherine, New York, died on 15 May 1909 in Odessa, Town of Catherine, Schuyler Co., NY, and was buried in Laurel Hill Cemetery, Catherine, New York.

Alice married **Aaron Ebenezer Mallory** on 27 Dec 1842 in New York. Aaron was born on 17 Oct 1817 in Alpine, NY, died on 12 May 1893 in Odessa, Town of Catherine, Schuyler Co., NY, and was buried in Laurel Hill Cemetery, Catherine, New York.

Children from this marriage were:

> + 130   M i.   **Judson D. Mallory** was born on 10 May 1844 in Alpine, NY and died on 2 Mar 1921 in Hector, NY.
> + 131   F ii.   **Anna Mallory** born on 27 Nov 1845 in Alpine, NY and died in 1875 in Alpine, NY.
> + 132   F iii.   **Charlotte Prince Mallory** was born on 12 Oct 1848 in Alpine, NY and died in 1917.
> + 133   F iv.   **Ella Ruanna Mallory** was born on 27 Mar 1857 in Alpine, NY.
> + 134   F v.   **Cora Gertrude Mallory** born 29 Jun 1864 in Alpine, NY and died on 30 Nov 1940.

53. James B. Beardsley was born on 9 Jul 1824 in North Settlement Cemetery, Catharine, Schuyler Co., NY and died in 1893 in Battle Creek, Michigan.

General Notes: James B. Beardsley married Almira Hager and took up housekeeping on a farm owned by his mother, and three years later owned it by inheritance and purchase; he sold in a few years to Thomas J. Charles, and moved to the place at Odessa and it was here his daughter, Stella, was born. He was a partner in the mercantile business with David Shelton and Merwin Bulkey for seven years, retiring to a farm on Foote's Hill, and later to Watkins. James and his daughter Sarah Wood were on their way to the Chicago World's Fair in 1893, when near Battle Creek, Michigan, they were both killed in a train wreck. (ref: History of the Town of Catherine, New York, p. 432)

James married **Almira Hager**. Almira died in Jun 1891. Children from this marriage were:

> + 135   M i.   **Stephen R. Beardsley** was born on 19 Jul 1847 in Catherine, New York and died on 16 May 1910 in Catherine, New York.
> + 136   F ii.   **Sarah D. Beardsley** was born in 1850 in Catherine, New York and died in 1893 in Battle Creek, Michigan.
> + 137   F iii.   **Stella Beardsley** was born in 1855 in Odessa, Town of Catherine, Schuyler Co., NY and died on 20 Sep 1940 in Town of Catherine, Tioga Co., NY.

54. Aaron B. Beardsley was born in 1826 in North Settlement Cemetery, Catharine, Schuyler Co., NY and died in Mar 1901. Aaron married **Lydia A. Mosher** on 27 Jan 1870 in New York. Lydia was born in Odessa, Town of Catherine, Schuyler Co., NY. They had no children

55. Ruth Ann Beardsley was born in 1827 in North Settlement Cemetery, Catharine, Schuyler Co., NY and died on 12 Jan 1913.

Ruth married **Dr. William Catlin** about Jun 1845. William was born on 16 Feb 1812 in Catherine, New York and died on 18 Jan 1876 in Catherine, New York.   Children from this marriage were:

+ 138	F	i.	**Cereles Elizabeth Catlin** was born on 10 Jul 1847 in Catherine, New York.
+ 139	M	ii.	**Abel DeLancy Catlin** was born on 11 Dec 1848 in Catherine, New York.
+ 140	M	iii.	**William Catlin (Twin)** was born on 8 Mar 1852 in Tennessee.
+ 141	M	iv.	**Willis Catlin (Twin)** was born on 8 Mar 1852 in Tennessee.

56.   Eunice Beardsley was born in 1828 in North Settlement Cemetery, Catharine, Schuyler Co., NY.

Eunice married **Levi Babcock**.

57.   Beach Beardsley died young.

58.   Maria F. Beardsley.

59.   Caroline Louisa Lockerby was born on 19 Aug 1836 in Washtenaw Co., Michigan, died on 26 Apr 1914 in Northfield, Rice Co., Minnesota, and was buried in 1914.

Caroline married **John Warren Birch**. John was born on 17 May 1830 in New York and died on 9 Jul 1908 in Minnesota.   The child from this marriage was:

+ 142	M	i.	**John Guy Birch** was born on 27 Apr 1876 in Minnesota and died on 8 Apr 1926 in Minnesota.

60.   John Lockerby was born on 2 Jan 1841 in Bridgewater, Washtenaw Co., MI and died on 21 Nov 1916 in Warsaw Twp., Rice Co., Minnesota.   NEVER MARRIED

General Notes: Migration: Went from Michigan to Minnesota with his mother, Clarrisa, in the late 1850's

61.   Robert L. Olmstead[34] was born on 16 May 1829[34] and died on 20 Apr 1864 in Pleasant Hill, Louisiana.[34]   Robert married **Louisa Clapsaddle**.[35]

62.   Hannah Jennette Olmstead[34] was born on 9 May 1831[34] and died on 21 Jan 1881.[34] Hannah married **Howell Leyson**.[35]

63.   Araminta Agnes Olmstead[34] was born on 29 May 1833.[35]   Araminta married **Lewis Larkin**.[35]

64.   Rebecca Margaret Olmstead[36] was born on 19 Mar 1835[37] and died on 13 May 1921.[35] Rebecca married **William Leonard Van Vlack**[35] on 4 Jul 1857.[35] William was born in 1836[35] and died on 6 Sep 1908.[35]   Children from this marriage were:

+ 143	M	i.	**Charles Aaron Van Vlack**[35] was born in 1861[35] and died on 5 Aug 1913.[35]
+ 144	M	ii.	**Howell E. Van Vlack (Twin)**[35] was born in 1864[35] and died on 16 Aug 1898.[35]
+ 145	M	iii.	**Eugene Wallace Van Vlack (Twin)**[35] was born in 1864[35] and died on 6 Apr 1947.[35]
+ 146	M	iv.	**Dwight L. Van Vlack**[35] was born in 1872.
+ 147	M	v.	**Oliver Judd Van Vlack**[35] was born on 6 Mar 1875[35] and died on 11 Apr 1930.[35]

65.   David Olmstead[34] was born on 26 Apr 1840[34] and died on 4 May 1840.[35]

66. Amanda Melvina Lockerby[16] was born on 13 Sep 1829 in Tompkins/Tioga County, New York,[16] died on 22 Jun 1907 in Northfield, Rice Co., Minnesota,[16] and was buried in Northfield Cemetery, Northfield, Rice Co., Minnesota.[16]

General Notes: OBITUARY: Northfield News, June 29, 1907

Mrs. Malvina Bivens, an old and respected citizen of this city and widow of the late Levi Bivens answered the call of death Saturday afternoon at two-o'clock. Miss Malvina Lockerby was born Sept 13, 1829 in Tompkins County, New York. She was the daughter of Mr. and Mrs. Benjamin Lockerby and with her parents went to Michigan in 1832. Later in 1855, the family moved to Bridgewater Township, Minnesota which township they named, the family being among the very earliest settlers. In 1857, she was married to Levi Bivens and settled in the township of Northfield, from which place they moved to the city of Northfield where she lived with her husband until the time of his death on Sept 30, 1901. One child was born to them, Eben Bivens who now resides in Dennison. Mrs. Bivens leaves besides her son, a grand-daughter, Miss Frances Bivens of Northfield, a sister, Mrs. A. F. Kingman of Northfield, and three brothers, Oscar Lockerby of Northfield, Burr B. Lockerby of Brownton and Seneca D. Lockerby of Fairbault. Funeral services were held Monday morning at 11 o'clock from the Kingman residence. Rev. S. Mills Hayes read the Episcopal service. The remains were interred in the Northfield Cemetery in the family lot. Near relatives from out of the city in attendance at the funeral were Burr Lockerby, Mr. & Mrs. Seneca Lockerby and daughter, Floy, and Burt Lockerby of Faribault, Lee Lockerby of Minneapolis and Philo Edward of Prairieville.

Amanda married **Levi Bivens**[16] on 31 May 1857 in Northfield, Rice Co., Minnesota. Levi was born in Mar 1820 in New York, died on 30 Sep 1901 in Northfield, Rice Co., Minnesota, and was buried in Northfield Cemetery, Northfield, Rice Co., Minnesota.

Children from this marriage were:

+ 148   M i.   **Elbin Bivens** was born on 27 Mar 1858 in Northfield, Rice Co., Minnesota.
+ 149   M ii.   **Guy Henry Bivens** was born on 29 Jun 1861 in Northfield, Rice Co., Minnesota and died on 14 May 1867 in Northfield, Rice Co., Minnesota.
+ 150   M iii.   **Benjamin Halsey Bivens** was born on 4 Jan 1863 in Northfield, Rice Co., Minnesota and died on 4 Mar 1863 in Northfield, Rice Co., Minnesota.

67. Oscar Dunbooth Lockerby[16] was born on 22 Aug 1832 in Tompkins/Tioga County, New York,[16] died on 25 Jan 1917 in Northfield, Rice Co., Minnesota,[16] and was buried in Old Northfield Cemetery, Pike Co., Minnesota.[16]

General Notes: According to the "History of Rice County" 1910 -- "Oscar and Genette (Tanner) Lockerby are both natives of New York. Oscar went to Michigan in 1855 and for a short time engaged in farming, and removed thence to Rice County, Minn., settling on a farm at Northfield. He afterwards engaged in the livery business and for two years served as Sheriff of Rice County. Selling his livery business, he went to Dakota and there served as deputy sheriff and later returned to Northfield, where he and his wife now reside"

Oscar Lockerby Homesteaded land in Northfield Township, Rice County, Minnesota on August 5, 1857, in the SW 1/4 of Section 19, Township 111, Range 19. For several years, He was a Deputy Sheriff in Northfield. The following are a few of the items which appeared in the Faribault Republican newspapers over the years.

Faribault Republican Nov 4, 1874 --
"Deputy Sheriffs Charley Wheeler and Lockerby went to Iowa last week with a requisition for a horse thief who was wanted in Northfield as a supposed accomplice in the recent running off of a team. They brought him as far as Austin, and while waiting yesterday morning in the depot for the train on

this road, the two Deputies fell into a doze, during which the thief walked out.   He was shackled and may therefore be retaken, unless he had friends to give him prompt assistance."

Faribault Republican 1887 --
Ara Barton, after 11 years occupation of the sheriff's office has yielded to another Democrat, O. Lockerby of Faribault.

Faribault Republican, May 28, 1890 --
Oscar Lockerby has in his possession the saddle used by Cole Younger during the famous raid of the Younger brothers in 1876.   The saddle is in a good state of preservation and is treasured highly by the present owner.

Oscar Lockerby married Genette TANNER.   She died in December 1915 and the following Obituary was published in the Northfield News Dec 31, 1915.
"Mrs. Oscar Lockerby passed away Sunday morning, Dec 26th, at her home at Eighth and Spring Streets.   Services were held at the home Tuesday afternoon at two o'clock, Rev. F. M. Garland of the All Saints Episcopal Church officiated.   Internment was made in the old cemetery.   Gennette Tanner was born Sept 19, 1832 in New York State, spending her early life there.   She came to Michigan in 1854, and in 1856 she came with her parents to Dakota County, settling just north of this city.   She was married to Oscar Lockerby, Dec 6, 1857, and together they made their home on a farm near Northfield, later moving into the city.   Five children were born to them, four of whom are living.   Mrs. Lockerby was confined to her home for many years with rheumatism, but was ever cheerful, patient, dearly beloved by all that knew her, and a loving mother.   Those left to mourn her loss are her husband, Oscar Lockerby and four children; Lee, Mrs. Elizabeth Davis, Dwight and Burt and seven grandchildren.   Those from away to attend the funeral were: Dwight Lockerby of Eau Claire, Mr. and Mrs. B. Lockerby and Mrs. Seneca Lockerby of Faribault, Lee Lockerby and daughter Luella, and Mrs. Elizabeth Davis."

OBITUARY of Oscar Lockerby:
Faribault Democrat, Feb 2, 1917
"Oscar Lockerby of Northfield, a former sheriff of Rice County died at his home in that city Tuesday, Jan 23rd, after a long illness, aged 84.   The funeral took place Saturday under Masonic auspices.   Rev. F. M. Garland rector of the Episcopal Church officiated.   Deceased was born in New York, Aug 20, 1832.   He came to Minnesota in 1855.   He is survived by three sons: Lee of Minneapolis, Dwight D. of Eau Claire and Burth of Faribault, one daughter, Mrs. Elizabeth Davis of Minneapolis, and two brothers, Burr of Northfield and S. D. Lockerby of Faribault."

OBITUARY of Oscar Lockerby
Northfield News -- Feb 2, 1917
"Oscar Lockerby, a pioneer of Minnesota, passed away Thursday morning, Jan 25th.   The funeral services were held in Northfield on Spring Street on Saturday afternoon, conducted by the Masonic Order, assisted by Rev. F. M. Garland.   Interment was made in the Northfield Cemetery.   Mr. Lockerby was born Aug 20, 1832, in New York.   He came with his parents from Michigan in Minnesota in 1855, locating on a homestead south of Northfield. On Dec. 6, 1857, he was married to Gennette Tanner who died Dec 26, 1915.   Mr. Lockerby is survived by three sons, Lee Lockerby of Minneapolis, D. D. Lockerby of Eau Claire, Wisconsin and Burt Lockerby of Faribault; one daughter, Mrs. Elizabeth Davis of Minneapolis, and two brothers Burr Lockerby of Northfield and S. D. Lockerby of Faribault.   Mr. Lockerby at one time bought alivery barn.   He became deputy sheriff for a number of years and in 1885 was elected sheriff of Rice County.   After serving one term as sheriff, he took up auctioneering in which business he continued successfully for many years."

Oscar married **Genette Tanner**[16] on 6 Dec 1857 in Northfield, Rice Co., Minnesota. Genette was born on 19 Sep 1832 in New York,[16] died on 26 Dec 1915 in Northfield, Rice Co., Minnesota,[16] and was buried in Old Northfield Cemetery, Pike Co., Minnesota.[16]

Children from this marriage were:

+ 151   M i.   **Ervin Lee Lockerby**[16] was born on 17 Apr 1860 in Northfield, Rice Co., Minnesota[16] and died in 1918 in Minneapolis, Minnesota.[16]

+ 152   F ii.   **Elizabeth Lockerby**[16] was born on 15 Aug 1862 in Northfield, Rice Co., Minnesota[16] and died in Apr 1925 in Minneapolis, Minnesota.[16]

+ 153   M iii.   **Dwight Davis Lockerby**[16] was born on 24 Jun 1867 in Northfield, Rice Co., Minnesota[16] and died on 8 Aug 1941 in Eau Claire, Wisconsin.[16]

+ 154   M iv.   **Burt Burr Lockerby**[16] was born on 1 Jul 1869 in Northfield, Rice Co., Minnesota,[16] died on 28 Feb 1938 in Rice County, Minn,[16] and was buried in St. Lawrence Cemetery, Faribault, Rice Co., Minnesota.[16]

+ 155   M v.   **Benjamin Lockerby**[16] was born on 25 Jul 1871 in Northfield, Rice Co., Minnesota,[16] died on 1 Mar 1908 in Minneapolis, Minnesota,[16] and was buried in Old Northfield Cemetery, Pike Co., Minnesota.[16]

68.   Ermine Pamela Lockerby[16] was born on 15 Mar 1836 in Washtenaw Co., Michigan,[16] died on 11 Jun 1912 in Northfield, Rice Co., Minnesota,[16] and was buried in Northfield Cemetery, Northfield, Rice Co., Minnesota.[16] Ermine married **Mathew William Olmstead**. Mathew was born on 22 Nov 1804 in Wilton, Fairfield Co., CT (see note!) and died in 1889.

General Notes: NO ISSUE

OBITUARY: Northfield News, June 15, 1912
"Mrs. Ermina Lockerby Kingman, one of Northfield's oldest residents, died at her home at 200 Linden Avenue, Tuesday morning, following an illness of several years.   Since Easter, she failed rapidly in health and although everything possible was done for her, she did not regain her health and the end came Tuesday morning.   Mrs. Kingman was 76 years of age at the time of her death and came to this state with her father in 1855 and lived here for some time.   Following her marriage to William Olmstead, they moved away for several years, but later returned to Northfield.   In 1889, she was married to Augustus F. Kingman.   Her second husband's death occurred July 10, 1910. Three brothers, Burr and Oscar Lockerby of Northfield and S. D. of Faribault are left to mourn her death.   Funeral services were held Thursday afternoon at 2 o'clock from the residence on Linden Street.   Rev. Garland officiating.   Internment was made in the old cemetery."

69.   Edgar Mortimer Lockerby[16] was born on 9 Aug 1838 in Bridgewater, Washtenaw Co., MI,[16] died on 5 Aug 1901 in Northfield, Rice Co., Minnesota,[16] and was buried in Minnesota.[16] Edgar married **Ida M. Bullock** on 9 Sep 1866 in Northfield, Rice Co., Minnesota. Children from this marriage were:

+ 156   F i.   **Ida Frances Lockerby** was born on 17 Mar 1873 in Northfield, Rice Co., Minnesota and died on 1 Jan 1883 in Northfield, Rice Co., Minnesota.

+ 157   M ii.   **Charles Edgar Lockerby** was born on 25 Nov 1876 in Northfield, Rice Co., Minnesota and died on 30 Jan 1950 in Northfield, Rice Co., Minnesota.

70.   Francis Lavina Lockerby[16] was born on 22 Jun 1840 in Washtenaw Co., Michigan,[16] died on 13 Oct 1869 in Northfield, Rice Co., Minnesota,[16] and was buried in Northfield Cemetery, Northfield, Rice Co., Minnesota.[16] Francis married **J. M. Emery**.[16] J. was born in 1842 in Jamestown, New York. General Notes: NO ISSUE

71.   Benjamin Burr Lockerby[16] was born on 26 Dec 1842 in Washtenaw Co., Michigan,[16] died on 19 Apr 1925 in Minnesota,[16] and was buried in Northfield Cemetery, Northfield, Rice Co., Minnesota.[16]

General Notes: Benjamin Burr Lockerby served in the Civil War and is listed with the Regiment of the 1st Minnesota Heavy Artillery, 1st Regiment, Minnesota.   He was inducted on 15 Feb 1865 and discharged on 2 Aug 1865.   (REF: Minnesota Civil War Soldiers)

Benjamin married **Ann L. Davis** in 1862. Ann was born in 1849, died on 13 Jul 1874 in Northfield, Rice Co., Minnesota, and was buried in Cannon City Cemetery, Minnesota.   The child from this marriage was:

+ 158   M i.   **Francis E. Lockerby** was born on 5 Jul 1874 in Northfield, Rice Co., Minnesota, died on 10 Mar 1903 in Minnesota, and was buried in Brownton, Minnesota.

72.   Seneca Daries Lockerby[16] was born on 21 Apr 1845 in Washtenaw Co., Michigan,[16] died on 13 Dec 1926 in Faribault, Rice Co., MN, and was buried in Maple Lawn Cemetery in Faribault, Minnesota.

General Notes: OBITUARY:

"Seneca Lockerby, a pioneer and for many years a resident of Rice County, died at the home of his daughter, Mrs. E. B. Kingman, on Linden Street Thursday afternoon, Dec 13th at 2:00 o'clock.   He had been ill since suffering a stroke last August.   The funeral was held at the Kingman home Saturday afternoon, Dr. Herbert P. Houghton rector of All Saints Episcopal Church, officiating.   Burial was made in the family lot, Maple Lawn Cemetery, Faribault.   Four nephews of Mr. Lockerby B. B. Lockerby of Faribault, C. E. Lockerby of Minneapolis, Richard and William Barton of St. Paul, were the pallbearers.   Seneca Lockerby was born in Michigan on April 21, 1845.   He came with his parents to Rice County in 1856 and they made their home on a farm just south of Northfield, on the Cannon City road.   He lived there until his marriage to Miss Catherine E. Barton.   They moved to Faribault and lived there until Mrs. Lockerby's death three years ago last October when Mr. Lockerby came to Northfield to make his home with his daughter Mrs. Kingman.   Mr. Lockerby is survived by three daughters, Mrs. Kingman of Northfield, Mrs. Henry Van Ruden of Faribault, and Miss Dolly Lockerby of Red Wing."

Seneca married **Katharine Barton**, daughter of **George W. Barton** and **Unknown**, on 5 Mar 1874 in Dundas, Minnesota. Katharine was born on 16 Dec 1856 in Northfield, Rice Co., Minnesota, died on 3 Mar 1925 in Faribault, Rice Co., MN, and was buried in Maple Lawn Cemetery in Faribault, Minnesota.
Children from this marriage were:

+ 159   F i.   **Ermina Bell Lockerby** was born on 7 Dec 1874 in Faribault, Rice Co., MN, died on 21 Mar 1955 in Rosemont, Minnesota, and was buried in Northfield Cemetery, Northfield, Rice Co., Minnesota.
+ 160   F ii.   **Katherine Barton Lockerby** was born on 17 Aug 1880 in Faribault, Rice Co., MN and died on 12 Mar 1968 in St. Paul, Minnesota.
+ 161   F iii.   **Dolly Lockerby** was born in 1880, died on 15 Mar 1968 in Faribault, Rice Co., MN, and was buried in Maple Lawn Cemetery in Faribault, Minnesota.
+ 162   F iv.   **Nellie Lockerby** was born on 21 Nov 1885 in Faribault, Rice Co., MN and died on 5 Jan 1887 in Faribault, Rice Co., MN.
+ 163   M v.   **Jessie E. Lockerby** was born on 9 Mar 1889 in Faribault, Rice Co., MN and died young (no mention in obit's).

73.   John B. Lockerby[22] was born on 11 May 1844 in Alpine, Town of Catharine, Steuben Co., NY,[22] died on 5 Nov 1918,[2] and was buried in 1918 in Odessa, Town of Catherine, Schuyler Co., NY.[2] John married **Cornelia Evans "Carrie"**,[2] daughter of **John J Evans** in 1866.[14] Cornelia was born in 1848 in PA,[2] died on 13 Mar 1922,[2] and was buried in 1922 in Odessa, Town of Catherine, Schuyler Co., NY.[2]

General Notes: FAMILY HISTORY:

John Lockerby was born in 1844, in Alpine, New York.   He served in the Civil War.   Company B. 141st N.Y. Vol., under Captain Andrew J Compton, 1862.   Afterwards he married (1866) Cornelia "Carrie" Evans and resided in 1914 in Alpine.   (ref: 1914 Town of Catharine Farm Directory) His profession was: Storekeeper.   He died November 5, 1918, in Alpine, and is buried in   Laurel Hill Cemetery, Odessa, New York.

(Ref: History of the Town of Catherine, New York)

The 1893/4 Business Directory of the Town of Catharine, Schuyler Co, NY, shows the following: "John Lockerby, PO Alpine, b. 1844, general store and owns house ad lot in Alpine."   (This data from the Schuyler Co. HS in Montour Falls, NY in 2011)

The 1914 Farm Directory of Schuyler Co, Town of Catharine shows the following: "John Lockerby and Carrie, Storekeeper, owns house and lot and store in Alpine."   (This data from the Schuyler Co. HS in Montour Falls, NY in 2011)

From the Schuyler County Historical Society in Montour Falls, NY, in 2011 we learn from information found in the surname files and entitled Misc. Info: --

"John Lockerby of Alpine, age 74, d. Nov 5 1918 from papralyptic stroke.   Mr. Lockerby conducted a grocery store in Alpine for many years."

NOTE: there is a photo of the grocery store in the Carol Fagnan history of the Town of Catherine.

74.   Burr Lockerby[22] was born in 1846 in Alpine, NY,[22] died on 17 Aug 1899 in Odessa, Town of Catherine, Schuyler Co., NY,[2] and was buried in 1899 in Laurel Hill Cemetery, Odessa, Schuyler Co., NY.[2]

Burr married **Caroline Swartwood "Carrie"**[2] on 27 Dec 1868.[14] Caroline was born in 1847,[2] died in 1930,[2] and was buried in 1930 in Odessa, Town of Catherine, Schuyler Co., NY.[2]

General Notes: FAMILY HISTORY:

According to the History of the Town of Catherine, Schuyler County, New York,   Burr Lockerby was married on December 27, 1868, by Rev. Mr. Cranmer to Caroline Swartwood "Carrie" of Cayuga, New York.   She married second to a --Clark-- but no children were given for either marriage.

In checking the burial listings of Laurel Hill Cemetery, Odessa, New York, I found an "Abigail Root, mother of Burr, age 82" buried next to Carrie.   Since Abigail was not Burr's mother, I wonder if this is Carrie's?   If so, could Root be her maiden name??

Information from the surname files in Schuyler Co., NY, (2011 trip) give data from the "Death Files" as follows: "Burr Lockerby of Cayuga, age 53, d. Aug 17, 1899.   Burial: Mix Cemetery.   Survived by his wife; brothers, John and William Lockerby of Cayuga; sister, Mrs. John Charles of Odessa and Mrs. Ed. Wood of Colorado."

Information from the surname files in Schuyler Co., NY, (2011 trip) give data from:
1868/9 Business Directory for Chemung and Schuyler counties: Town of Cayuga; Burr Lockerby from Alpine, farmer of 50 acres. --------
1893-94 Business Directory (Schuyler Co.) Town of Cayuga:
Burr Lockerby, PO Alpine, Road 6, born 1846, assessor and farmer, 50 acres, has 3 horses, 1 cow, 15 sheep, and orchard 200 trees.

75. William R. Lockerby[22] was born in 1849 in Schuyler Co., New York,[38] died on 14 Jul 1933,[2] and was buried in 1933 in Odessa, Town of Catherine, Schuyler Co., NY.[2] William married **Delphine Mix**.[2] Delphine was born on 1 Sep 1851, died on 22 May 1939 in Catharine, Schuyler Co., NY,[2] and was buried in 1939 in New York.

General Notes: From the Schuyler County Historical Society in Montour Falls, NY, in 2011 we learn from information found in the surname files and entitled Misc. Info: -- (Death File) -- "William R. Lockerby of Alpine, age 84, died July 14, 1933. He was a lifelong resident of Alpine. Burial in Laurel Hill Cemetery."

In his wife's obituary, there were only nieces and nephews listed, NO CHILDREN.

1893-94 Business directory (Schuyer Co.) Town of Catherine (Information from the surname files in Schuyler Co., NY, (2011 trip) give data) -- William R. Lockerby, PO Alpine, stonemason, owns house and lot in Alpine. --then the 1914 Farm Directory lists him at Alpine, N.Y. on 12 Acres

76. Elizabeth Lockerby[22] was born in 1852 in Schuyler Co., New York.[38]

General Notes: Note: Appears on the 1850 census of Schuyler Co., New York. (Ref: Town of Catharine History, p. 200)

77. Sarah Ann Lockerby[22] was born on 14 Jun 1855 in Town of Cayuga, Schuyler Co., NY,[38] died in Feb 1923,[2] and was buried in 1923 in Odessa, Town of Catherine, Schuyler Co., NY, in the Laurel Hill Cemetery. Sarah married **John Jefferson Charles**,[2] son of **Thomas J. Charles** and **Unknown**, on 23 Mar 1881 in Catherine, Schuyler Co., New York.[14] John was born in 1850 in Odessa, Town of Catherine, Schuyler Co., NY, died on 6 Oct 1909, and was buried in 1909 in Odessa, Town of Catherine, Schuyler Co., NY. Children from this marriage were:

+164	F i.	**Addie Charles**.[2]
+165	F ii.	**Grace Charles**.[2]
+166	F iii.	**Katharine Charles**[2] was born on 23 Dec 1886, died on 22 Apr 1919 in Odessa, Town of Catherine, Schuyler Co., NY, and was buried in 1919 in Laurel Hill Cemetery, Odessa, Schuyler Co., NY.
+167	M iv.	**Thomas Burr Charles**[2] was born on 11 Jan 1890.

78. Alfred Lockerby[20] was born in 1856 in Town of Cayuga, Schuyler Co., NY,[20] died in 1887,[2] and was buried in 1887 in Odessa, Town of Catherine, Schuyler Co., NY.[2] Burial: Laurel Hill Cemetery in Odessa, New York. Alfred married **Ada Harding**, daughter of **T. A. Harding** and **Unknown**, on 15 Dec 1879. Ada was born in 1857, died in 1882, and was buried in 1882 in Odessa, Town of Catherine, Schuyler Co., NY

From the Schuyler County Historical Society in Montour Falls, NY, in 2011 we learn from information found in the surname files and entitled Misc. Info: -- "Alfred Lockerby married Addie Harding of Alpine, daughter of T. A. Harding, Esq. on Dec 15, (1879?) by Elder St. John at the home of the bride's father."

79. Catharine Lockerby[20] was born in 1858 in Town of Cayuga, Schuyler Co., NY,[39] died in 1920, and was buried in 1920 in Odessa, Town of Catherine, Schuyler Co., NY. Burial: Laurel Hill Cemetery, Odessa, New York. Catharine married **Swan**.[2]

80. Fred P. Lockerby.[2]

81. Mary Jane Lockerby "Jennie"[20] was born in 1861 in Schuyler Co., New York.[39]   Mary married **E. L. Wood**.[2]   Children from this marriage were:

+168	M	i.	**Chapman Wood**.[2]
+169	M	ii.	**Robert Wood**.[2]
+170	M	iii.	**Harry Wood**.[2]
+171	F	iv.	**Alta Wood**.[2]
+172	M	v.	**Buena Wood**.[2]

82. Hattie Lockerby.[2]   Hattie married **Francis Burt**.[2] Francis was born in "of Port Alleghany, PA".[2]
Children from this marriage were:

+173	F	i.	**Prentiss Burt**.[2]
+174	M	ii.	**William Burt**.[2]
+175	M	iii.	**Frank Burt**.[2]
+176	M	iv.	**Burton Burt**.[2]

83. Elizabeth Lockerby[23] was born in 1846 in Town of Catharine, Steuben Co., NY.[41]   Elizabeth married **Frank E. Cummings**,[2] son of **Cyrus Cummings** and **Mary**, on 27 Jan 1885.[14] Frank was born in "of Meadville, PA.".

84. Mary Lockerby[29] was born about 1851 in Town of Catharine, Steuben Co., NY.[42]
85. George Lockerby.[2]
86. William H. Lockerby[2] was born on 24 Feb 1859 and died in Probably Michigan.
87. Charles Lockerby[2] was born about 1865 in New York,[2] died in 1883 in New York,[2] and was buried in New York.[2]
88. Sally M. Lockerby[9] was born in 1853 in Town of Cayuga, Steuben Co., NY.[9]
89. Marshall Samuel Lockerby[43] was born on 24 Feb 1848 in Town of Catherine, Chemung Co., NY,[43] died in Sep 1928 in Hokesland, WA,[47] and was buried in 1928 in Rockford, Kent Co., MI. Marshall married **Tressa Borden**. HAD NO ISSUE

90. Dr. Mitchell Monroe Lockerby[48] was born on 14 Oct 1849 in Town of Catherine, Chemung Co., NY,[49] died on 15 Jan 1927 in Grand Rapids, Kent Co., MI,[50] and was buried in 1927 in Rockford, Kent Co., MI.[51]

General Notes: Obituary of Mitchell Monroe Lockerby -- provided by the DeWitt Historical Society of New York - 1983   (No newspaper source given!)

"The death of Mitchell M. Lockerby, M. D., occurred at Blodgett Hospital in Grand Rapids, Michigan, on January 15, 1927.   The descendant was 79 years of age.   Dr. Lockerby was born in Odessa, N.Y., and resided there until his early twenties when he left for the Middle West where he built up a very successful practice.   For the past few years preceding his death, he resided at Pasadena, CA. The burial was made in the family plot at Rockford, Michigan, beside his parents, his brother, Ezekiel, and his sister, Ida.   The departed was survived by a son, Findley Lockerby, of the Thompson Lockerby Lumber Co., of Grand Rapids, Michigan, and a brother, Jerome B. Lockerby of Odessa, New York."

Personal data: Had two children, Arnold and Findley.   Findley was the only son to survive his father.   Arnold died at age 10 years.   In 1927, Findley was working for the Thompson Lockerby Lumber Co of Grand Rapids, Michigan.

Mitchel [63] died on 9 Jul 1940 in Rockford, Kent Co., MI,[51] and was buried in 1940 in Rockford, Kent Co., MI.[51]   Children from this marriage were:

+ 177   M i.   **Arnold Lockerby** died on 26 Jan 1949 in Rockford, Kent Co., MI[65] and was buried in 1949 in Rockford Cemetery, Kent Co., MI.[65]

+ 178   M ii.   **Findley Lockerby**.

91.   Wallace Hiram Lockerby[52] was born on 7 Oct 1851 in Town of Catherine, Chemung Co., NY[47] and died on 9 Feb 1913 in Woverley, NY.[46]   Married a Nan --- and had No desc.

92.   Jerome Bennajah Lockerby[52] was born on 27 Jul 1852 in Town of Catherine, Chemung Co., NY,[47] died on 1 Nov 1939 in Odessa, Town of Catherine, Schuyler Co., NY,[47] and was buried in 1939 in Odessa, Town of Catherine, Schuyler Co., NY.

General Notes: FAMILY HISTORY:

Jerome was born on July 27, 1852, in the Town of Catharine, Village of Odessa, New York (recorded in the family bible).   He was the son of Bennajah and Mary Ann (Terry) Lockerby.   He married on December 14, 1871, to Florence Charles the daughter of Simeon and Mary Ferguson Charles.   They were married in Odessa.   The couple had four children: Kitty, Truman and twins, Edith and Ethel. Kitty later married Jon Van and had a son by that name however, Truman died in the construction of the LeHigh Valley Railroad when he was 17 years of age.   Although Edith and Ethel both married, neither is known to have had any children.

The information in the History of the Town of Catharine states that the "farm owned by the Lockerby's was located just outside of Odessa and the Farm Directory of 1914 states that Jerome B. (occ. general repairman) and wife, Florence, did in fact reside on the farm or at least still owned the land"   Their residence was listed as Odessa.

In the same noted history, the reference is made to the fact that a toll gate once existed on the Plank Road from Havana to Mecklenburg near the residence of the late Jerome Lockerby.   It appears that the toll was abandoned on June 30, 1868, but the data confirms that the couple was residing there on the farm during that time.

By 1874, Jerome is listed as a resident of Alpine (N.Y.) and in the 1895 Directory his residence is listed as such.   Information gathered reflects that in 1879 Jerome was operating a saw mill on the Upper Pond in Odessa and in 1916 he built a new mill race in Alpine.   He owned a house in Odessa ca. 1874 and is said to have built a home for his father-in-law there.

Jerome B. Lockerby PO Odessa, b. 1853, silversmith, owns house and lot in Alpine according to the 1893/4 Business Directory of the Town of Catharine, Schuyler Co., NY   (This data from the Schuyler Co. HS in Montour Falls, NY in 2011)

His wife died in 1926 and he followed ten years later (1936).   Both are buried in Laurel Hill Cemetery.

Jerome married **Florence I. Charles**,[46] daughter of **Simeon Charles** and **Mary Ferguson**, on 14 Dec 1871 in Odessa, Town of Catherine, Schuyler Co., NY.[47] Florence was born on 3 Nov 1851,[46] died on 21 Jun 1926 in Odessa, Town of Catherine, Schuyler Co., NY,[46] and was buried in 1926 in Odessa, Town of Catherine, Schuyler Co., NY.[2]   Children from this marriage were:

+ 179   F i.   **Kitty May Lockerby**[2] was born on 4 Sep 1875 in Odessa, Town of Catherine, Schuyler Co., NY.[47]

+ 180   M ii.   **Truman B Lockerby**[2] was born on 5 May 1874 in Odessa, Town of Catherine, Schuyler Co., NY,[46] died on 29 Aug 1891 in Odessa, Town of Catherine, Schuyler Co., NY,[46] and was buried in 1891 in Odessa, Town of Catherine, Schuyler Co., NY.

+ 181   F iii.   **Edith M. Lockerby (twin)**[2] was born on 26 Jun 1879 in Odessa, Town of Catherine, Schuyler Co., NY.[47]

+ 182   F iv.   **Ethel M. Lockerby (twin)**[46] was born on 26 Jun 1879 in Odessa, Town of Catherine, Schuyler Co., NY.[47]

93.   Jacob Smith Lockerby[52] was born on 5 Mar 1855 in Town of Catherine, Schuyler Co., NY[47] and died in 1924 in Hokesland, WA.[47] Jacob married **Ann Lovett** and had three children.   No further info.

94.   Susan Lockerby[42] was born in Jan 1855 in Catharine/Odessa, Schuyler Co., NY[42] and died before 1865 in Town of Catherine, Schuyler Co., NY.   (Note: This child appeared on the 1855 Census of Catharine, Schuyler Co., New York.   She must have died young as she is never listed again.   The census taker listed her as 5 months old.)   She is likely buried in Laurel Hill or North Settlement Cemetery in New York -- ??

Ezekiel Terry Lockerby b. 1857

95.   Ezekiel Terry Lockerby[53] was born on 1 Apr 1857 in Town of Catherine, Schuyler Co., NY,[54] died from 0014 to 22 Mar 1900 in Woodville, Home Twp., Newaygo Co., MI,[55] and was buried in 1900 in Whipple Cemetery, Big Rapids, Mecosta Co., MI.[56]

General Notes: FAMILY HISTORY:

Ezekiel Terry Lockerby was the third born son of Bennajah and Mary Ann (Terry) Lockerby.   He was born April 1, 1857, (Bible Record) and named after Mary Ann's father who was a descendant of the Rev. Ezekiel Terry born in 1775 in Enfield, Conn.

Tradition states, "in the mid-1870's, Ezekiel was engaged to be married and his future bride unexpectedly died. He was very distressed so his mother, Mary Ann, decided to take him home to New York for a brief visit with her family. While there, he re met, and later married, his first cousin, Delphine Depew." It is said, "the marriage was not by complete accident, but rather planned by the parents." Tradition relates, "the young couple, Ezekiel and Delphine, were left alone in the parlor for several evenings unchaperoned, and after approximately three evenings, Mary Ann questioned Ezekiel as to his intentions because he had been given strict instructions to propose to Delphine. When it was discovered he had not done so, Mary Ann, was quite disappointed and again instructed her son to take care of this matter. He did and a few days later, the proposal was made, the engagement announced and on March 25, 1878, in Schuyler County, New York, the couple married." (PHOTO)

"MA'S WEDDING"

(Note: I have been unable to identify all the persons in the Wedding photo taken in 1876. Ezekiel Lockerby and Delphine Depew were married 20 March 1876. They are sitting in the front row, the last two people on the right. Delphine Depew's aunt, Mary Ann Terry Lockerby is in the checkered dress right behind Delphine and a little to the left. In the top row third from the left is Elizabeth Reynolds Terry and next to her is Marshall Terry with little Marshall Terry Jr. in his arms. Margaret Depew is next (she third from the right) she is the wife of Isiah G. Depew in the middle row. (note her hand on his head). Margaret and Isiah are the grandparents to the bride, Delphine Depew. Delphine's father, William Depew, is second from the right and standing next to his mother Margaret. Delphine Depew's mother and Ezekiel Lockerby's father are not pictured because they are deceased. I think the two girls in the front next to Delphine, are sisters. Your turn! I did what I could.

Delphine Wilvinia Depew "Della" as she was commonly referred to was born July 20, 1859, in Odessa, Schuyler County, New York. She was the daughter of William and Maria Melvinia (Terry) Depew.

Not long after Ezekiel and Delphine were married, they returned to Sand Lake, Kent County, Michigan, to begin their new life together. Della brought with her a riding buggy and her Reed Organ. (In 1983, the Organ was still in the family and in the possession of Mark Lockerby in Bitely, Michigan.)

The first child born to them was, Bennajah. He died on August 25, 1880, having been born on October 22, 1879. Tradition relates, "he may have died of malnutrition as Della continued to nurse him even after discovering she was pregnant with her second born, Marshall. Evidently the body could not produce enough food for both Bennajah and the new fetus." Bennajah was laid to rest in the Old Settlers portion of Rockford Cemetery. (note: there is a little lamb on the top of his stone)

The 1884 Census of Kent County, Michigan, Nelson Twp, page 69, shows the following: Family No. 57 -- Lockerby, Ezekiel, Male, age 27, Husband, Mill Owner, place of Birth NY, Father's birth, NY and mother's birth, Mass, years in state, 13; Delphine Lockerby, Female, age 25, wife, born in Canada, Father born PA and mother born NY, years in state 5; Marshall Lockerby, male, age 3, son, born Michigan; Mabel Lockerby, female, daughter, one year old, born in Michigan.

The next years passed with more children being born to the couple and in about 1885, Ezekiel purchased three-hundred-twenty acres of land from the Railroad in Home Township, Newaygo County, just north of Big Rapids. (In the year, 2000, this area is called "Bitely") The property is listed in the 1900 Plat book in sections 34 and 35 (see Plat books in White Cloud, Michigan) This is the site where "Lockerby Town" once stood. The town consisted of the Lockerby Sawmill, a dry goods store, boarding house, home site, and several small buildings. The mill itself was located on the Marquette River, which by modern standards would be considered no more than a small stream. A log dam was constructed by Ezekiel across the river enabling the logs to be transported from the mill to the loading site, etc. The home site laid in a shallow valley surrounded by a vastly wooded area. A railroad tram ran through the valley, down to the creek, and up the slip in the valley to the road where the lumber was then unloaded and transported to its destination. Ezekiel kept very good records of the company's business and his journal for the dry goods store and the desk he used were still in the family in 1983.

In his spare time, Zeke liked to play the piano. It is said " he purchased his piano 'on time' and that the payments were $20.00 a month. Whenever he would have extra money, he was known to have pushed it into the cracks in the pantry walls. At the time of his death, the family took a hat pin and checked all the cracks for bills and found $20 rolled up and pushed into place. This was used to make the last payment on the piano." Sometime during his years at the sawmill, Ezekiel had an accident and cut off three of his fingers. It said he was quite concerned because he thought he'd never be able to play the piano again, but in time, he was able to "plunk out" a few numbers without too much difficulty.

Family members retold how "after the accident, his fingers were buried in the side of the 'slip' and for several months, Ezekiel complained he still felt pain in them. It was decided to dig them up and see if they had been buried properly. No, they were crossed, so they're laid them and after this was done, Ezekiel seldom complained about feeling pain."

In about 1887, Delphine decided to return to New York to see her family. She took the children with her, traveling by train. She did not let the family know she was coming. When she arrived in New York, she took a dray wagon out to the home of her brother, Bella, and when he opened the door, instead of saying, 'hello Della, we're so glad to see you, -- or something similar,' he opened the door and said, "Oh Della, we're all so sick!" Della asked if it was diphtheria and Bela replied, "no, Anna, (his wife) has a carbuncle and the doctor will come today to lance it." Finding the illness was nothing to concern their safety, the family remained. It is known, Margaret Depew, the grandmother of Della and Bela, was in the home caring for the family.

Della and the children stayed in New York about three months. They arrived in October and were planning to return to Michigan in January, but because of extenuating circumstances, they left New York a week earlier than planned. Ezekiel had gone to New York in December to spend the holidays with the family and just after the new year, received word his housekeeper who was attending the boarders in Michigan had fallen and could not continue her duties. Ezekiel and Della rearranged their schedule and took the earlier train home. Fate must have been leading them as the train they were originally scheduled to travel on crashed killing almost all of its occupants.

The next years passed with more children being born -- two, Herbert and Erwin, both born at Lockerby Town. The family business was proceeding in its usual manner, when, on March 22, 1900, disaster struck. Ezekiel Terry Lockerby, age 43 years, was claimed by death at Woodville, Newaygo County, Michigan. The Cause of death was listed as, Heart Failure. He was laid to rest in Whipple Cemetery.

Delphine was left to raise the family and continue the business of the Mill. Although she was a strong and determined woman, not long after Ezekiel's death the business was bankrupt and eighty acres of the original property had to be sold to satisfy the creditors. Della was awarded the rights to the buildings and the remaining portion of the property which consisted of two-hundred-forty acres. Lockerby Town was dismantled and lumber from the buildings was used to construct a new residence not far from the original site of the town. Delphine and the children were relocated.

Della worked very hard through the next years to provide for her growing family. She bought a cow and sold the cream and butter, and raised chickens and sold the eggs. Family recalls one occasion "when she was cooking for the mill workers, she kept a pair of Bantam chickens in a small bird cage in the corner of the kitchen. It was during the winter and she needed them for breeding in the spring. Anyway, to keep the boarders from complaining of 'having to east with the chickens', she would keep them covered with a towel until after breakfast. This would keep the rooster quiet. In the spring, when it was warm enough, she would put them outside to breed. She would then have extra eggs to sell during the summer, and in the fall she would kill the chickens, dress them and freeze for winter meals, saving one pair for the winter, and thus the cycle would begin again."

Della married twice after Ezekiel's death. First to Elbert F. Jewell of LeRoy, Michigan, on April 7, 1908; they divorced in the summer of 1918. And second to William Bush, a stout German man, on December 16, 1928, in Big Rapids, Michigan. No children were born of either union.

Delphine met William Bush while keeping house for him and when they decided to get married, it is said she "dropped seventeen years from her actual age so she wouldn't appear so old." She was quite vain and often did this, thus the reason for such variety in the vital records! Anyway, William did not want Della's children to call him "father, dad, or grandpa." He was known to have made the following statement regarding his title, -- "I have no children or grandchildren, -- you may call me 'Father Bush,' -- if you must!"

It is reported by descendants that his "farm was quite modern and up-to-date, and in all of Michigan, they could boast of one of the first modern methods for removing waste material from the barns. He had a large home which was well furnished, and owned a CAR which was quite a novelty for the time. After his death on March 24, 1932, Della had the car put up on blocks in the garage and it was never driven again in her life."

Two years before our subject married Father Bush, Della had sold the homestead property where she spent so many years of her life. She sold this to her youngest son, Erwin A. Lockerby, and his wife, Josie. (Deed, White Cloud, Michigan, Libr 142, pg 71) At the time of this transaction, only one-hundred-sixty acres of the original three-hundred-twenty acres was still in Delphine's name. Through the years, parcels of property had been sold to various other family members, etc. The homestead, itself, was eventually passed to Dan Lockerby, the son of Erwin and Josie, and then to his children; Mark, Vance, and MaryJo.

In 1983, Dan's children were still operating the Lockerby Sawmill in Bitely, Michigan. Though it no longer rested on the initial site of the mill, it was still on original Lockerby land. Land which was purchased by Ezekiel Lockerby when he first came to Michigan in 1871. On December 31, 1976, the Michigan Genealogical Council in Lansing, Michigan, presented a special tribute to the descendants of the Lockerby family which recognized that their ancestors had settled and lived in the State of Michigan over one-hundred-years.

Delphine Wilvinia (Depew) Lockerby, Jewell, Bush, passed away April 8, 1947, in Big Rapids, Michigan, The services were conducted by Martinson-Rogers Funeral Home in Big Rapids, Michigan, at l:00 p.m., April 11, 1947, with Rev. Bruce Brown giving the eulogy. Paul Bearers for the occasion were: Marshall Lockerby, Ezekiel Lockerby, Erwin Lockerby, Herbert Lockerby, Dan Lockerby and William E. Totten. Delphine was buried next to her first husband, Ezekiel Lockerby, in Whipple Cemetery, Newaygo County, Michigan. She was of the Free Methodist faith.

NOTE: Family stories, history, and information provided by Beulah Totten Wright, Dan Lockerby, Linda Kizer, and numerous descendants of Ezekiel Terry Lockerby of Bitely, Michigan. (1982)

Ezekiel married **Delphine Wilvinia Depew**,[66] daughter of **William Depew** and **Maria Melvinia Terry**, on 20 Mar 1876 in Odessa, Town of Catherine, Schuyler Co., NY.[67] Delphine was born on 20 Jul 1859 in Belville, Ontario, Canada,[68] died on 8 Apr 1947 in Big Rapids, Mecosta Co., MI,[69] and was buried on 11 Apr 1947 in Whipple Cemetery, Big Rapids, Mecosta Co., MI.[70] Children from this marriage were:

+ 183   M i.   **Bennajah William Lockerby**[71] was born on 22 Oct 1879 in Rockford, Kent Co., MI,[71] died on 18 Aug 1880 in Sand Lake, Kent Co., MI,[71] and was buried in 1880 in Rockford, Kent Co., MI.[72]

+ 184   M ii.   **Marshall Samuel Lockerby**[73] was born on 27 Dec 1880 in Sand Lake, Kent Co., MI,[74] died on 15 Feb 1949 in St. Ignace, Mackinac Co., MI,[56] and was buried in 1949 in St. Ignace, Mackinac Co., MI.

+ 185   F iii.   **Mabel Melvinia Lockerby**[75] was born on 26 Sep 1882 in Sand Lake, Kent Co., MI,[76] died on 21 Jan 1978 in Big Rapids, Mecosta Co., MI,[77] and was buried in 1978 in Pine Plains Cemetery, Big Rapids, Mecosta Co., MI.[78]

+ 186   M iv.   **Ezekiel Terry Lockerby**[79] was born on 30 Jul 1884 in Sand Lake, Kent Co., MI,[80] died on 24 Sep 1964 in Evart, Osceola Co., MI,[81] and was buried in 1964 in Whipple Cemetery, Big Rapids, Mecosta Co., MI.[82]

+ 187   F v.   **Olive Adell Lockerby**[83] was born on 7 Aug 1888 in White Cloud, Newaygo Co., MI,[83] died on 5 Jan 1985 in Big Rapids, Mecosta Co., MI, and was buried in 1985 in Big Rapids, Mecosta Co., MI.

+ 188   F vi.   **Lena May Lockerby**[56] was born on 18 Dec 1889 in White Cloud, Newaygo Co., MI,[56] died on 13 Sep 1977 in Greenville, MI,[84] and was buried in 1977 in Pierson, Montcolm Co, MI.

+ 189   M vii.   **Herbert Bela Lockerby**[83] was born on 20 Jul 1891 in Keno, Newaygo Co., MI,[83] died on 6 May 1967 in Grand Rapids, Kent Co., MI,[84] and was buried on 8 May 1967 in Big Rapids, Mecosta Co., MI.

+ 190   M viii. **Erwin Agustus Lockerby**[83] was born on 12 Jul 1898 in Keno, Newaygo Co., MI,[83] died on 21 Nov 1977 in Bitely, Newaygo Co., MI,[84] and was buried in 1977 in Big Rapids, Mecosta Co., MI.

96. Ida Adelia Lockerby[46] was born on 1 May 1859 in Town of Catherine, Schuyler Co., NY,[57] died on 10 Jul 1915 in Grand Rapids, Kent Co., MI,[50] and was buried in 1915 in Rockford, Kent Co., MI.[50] in Rockford Cemetery. She married L. "Pud" Finley and had twin children who died young. No further issue.

97. Francis Melvina Lockerby[58] was born on 31 Aug 1862 in Town of Catherine, Schuyler Co., NY,[58] died on 2 Dec 1927 in Grand Rapids, Kent Co., MI,[47] and was buried in 1927 in Rockford, Kent Co., MI.
in Rockford Cemetery. Francis married **Horris H Childs**[2] on 14 Sep 1881 in Rockford, Michigan at the Congregational Church.[14] Children from this marriage were:

+191	M i.	**Basher Childs**. Died young
+192	F ii.	**Ida Childs**.
+193	F iii.	**Eva Childs**.

98. Charles F. Terry[2] was born in 1849 in Veteran, Chemung Co., New York and died in 1924 in Veteran, Chemung Co., New York. (NOTE --Charles F. Terry was likely born in the Town of Catherine, Schuyler County, New York, and died in 1924, probably on Terry Hill in Veteran, New York, as this was given as his residence.) He married June 8, 1877, in Veteran, Chemung Co., New York. **Lavina C. Weeks.** She was born in 1855 and died in 1935. They had four daughters:

+194	F i.	**Adda Terry** was born in Veteran, Chemung Co., New York.
+195	F ii.	**Ella Terry** was born on 19 Jul 1879 in Veteran, Chemung Co., New York.
+196	F iii.	**Lottie Terry** was born in Veteran, Chemung Co., New York.
+197	F iv.	**Mary Terry** was born in Veteran, Chemung Co., New York.

99. Bonaparte Terry[2] was born in 1852, died on 9 Feb 1862 in New York, and was buried in 1862 in North Settlement, Odessa, , New York.

100. Andrew Terry[2] was born in 1853 and died in 1921. Andrew married **Ivah Charles** on 3 Nov 1907 in Odessa, Town of Catherine, Schuyler Co., NY. NO Descendants.

Letter from Town of Catharine dated Nov 16, 1982, indicates he married Jane Sherwood on Nov 3, 1907 --??

101. Warren Terry[2] died young, in New York.

102. John Terry[2] died young, in New York.

103. Caroline Terry.[2] Caroline married **James Crowe**. They had children:

| +198 | F i. | **Ida Ann Crowe**. |
| +199 | M ii. | **William Crowe**. |

104. Ella Terry[2] was born in 1863 and died in 1889 in Foote's Hill, Odessa, New York.
Ella married **Henry A. Shelton**, son of **Lewis Shelton** and **Ruby Beardsley**. Henry was born in 1862, died in 1940 in Foote's Hill, Odessa, New York, and was buried in 1940 in New York. Children:

| +200 | M i. | **Harry Shelton**. |
| +201 | M ii. | **Lee Shelton**. |

105. Walter Terry.[2] Never married

106. George R. Lockerby[29] was born in 1854.[29]

107. Augusta Lockerby[42] was born in 1856.[42] Augusta married **Smith**.

108. William E. Lockerby[60] was born on 11 Nov 1866 in Cayuga, Schuyler Co., NY,[61] died on 31 Mar 1949 in Alpine, NY, and was buried in Laurel Hill Cemetery, Catherine, Schuyler Co., New York. William married Inez Conkright,[85] daughter of James Conkright and Unknown. Inez was born on 9 Jan 1875 in Cayuga, Schuyler Co., NY,[85] died on 17 Jan 1971 in Alpine, NY,[85] and was buried in Laurel Hill Cemetery, Catherine, Schuyler Co., New York.[85] They had NO ISSUE.

General Notes: In 1891, William E. was still living at home with his parents.   He is listed in his father's obituary.

OBITUARY: (Information provided by Carol Fagnan of Alpine NY and author of "The History of the Town of Catherine" from various newspaper articles included with her papers) --

"WILLIAM E. LOCKERBY age, 82, died Thursday, Mar 31, 1949, at his home in Alpine, following a long illness.   He was born Nov 11, 1866, the son of Elizabeth and Lemuel Lockerby.   A lifelong resident of Alpine, he was well known in public life.   He is survived by his wife, Inez; four nieces, Mrs. Flossie M. Root of Binghamton, Mrs. Harry O. Moreley of Waverly, Mrs. Bertha Moot of Ithaca, Mrs. Francis Hulslander of Endicott.   Funeral services were held at 2:30 p.m. Sunday at the Horton Funeral Chapel at Odessa, the Rev. Harrison DeWalt officiating.   Burial was in Laurel Hill Cemetery."

109. Margaret Lockerby.

General Notes: The 1914 Farm Directory for Schuyler Co., Town of Catharine shows the following: "Margaret, daughter f John H., owns house and lot and 155 acres, Alpine Side Street."   (This data from the Schuyler Co. HS in Montour Falls, NY in 2011)

110. Rosella Markel[39] was born in 1858 in Town of Cayuga, Schuyler Co., NY.[39]
111. Mary Markel[39] was born in 1860 in Town of Cayuga, Schuyler Co., NY.[39]
112. Nicholas Markel[39] was born in 1862 in Town of Cayuga, Schuyler Co., NY.[39]
113. Siona Markel[39] was born in 1864 in Town of Cayuga, Schuyler Co., NY.[39]

114. James Howard Leaton[13] was born in Sep 1847 in Illinois[13] and died on 11 May 1924 in Bloomington, McLean, IL.[13] James married **Alice Hall**.[13] Alice was born in 1850 in Ohio.[13] Children:

+202	F	i.	**May Leaton**[13] was born in 1875 in Illinois.[13]
+203	F	ii.	**Alice Grace Leaton**[13] was born in Sep 1878 in Illinois.[13]
+204	F	iii.	**Louise Leaton**[13] was born in Sep 1890 in Illinois.[13]

115. Ann E. Leaton[13] was born in 1849 in Illinois.[13] Ann married **Lucius B. Corbin**[13] on 26 May 1874 in Macoupin, Illinois.[13] Lucius was born in 1842 in Illinois.[13]   Children from this marriage were:

+205	M	i.	**Paul L. Corbin**[13] was born in Sep 1875 in Illinois.[13]
+206	M	ii.	**James R. Corbin**[13] was born in Jul 1877 in Illinois.[13]
+207	F	iii.	**Clara R. Corbin**[13] was born in Nov 1879 in Illinois.[13]
+208	F	iv.	**Laurie Corbin**[13] was born in Mar 1885 in Illinois.[13]
+209	M	v.	**Edward L. Corbin**[13] was born in Mar 1888 in Illinois.[13]
+210	F	vi.	**Annie L. Corbin**[13] was born in Jun 1890 in Illinois.[13]
+211	F	vii.	**Alice H. Corbin**[13] was born in Mar 1892 in Illinois.[13]

116. Martha Leaton[13] was born in 1852 in Illinois.[13]   Martha married **Robert E. Guthrie**.[13] Robert was born in 1850 in Illinois.[13]   Children from this marriage were:

+212	F	i.	**Blanche Guthrie**[13] was born in 1873 in Illinois.[13]
+213	F	ii.	**Lucy L. Guthrie**[13] was born in 1876 in Illinois.[13]

117. Clara F. Leaton[13] was born in 1854 in Illinois.[13] Clara married **Harry L. Beals**[13] on 16 Nov 1887 in Pike Co., IL.[13]

118. William Edgar Lockerby[13] was born on 22 Aug 1853 in Winnebago Co., WI[13] and died about 1935 in Orange Co., FL.[13] William married **Elma E LeGro**[13] on 7 Sep 1881 in Waupaca, Wisconsin.[13] Elma was born in 1862 in Wisconsin[13] and died in 1949 in Orange Co., FL.[13] The child from this marriage was:

+214   F i.   **Avis Lockerby**[13] was born on 28 Aug 1882 in Racine, Wisconsin[13] and died on 10 Apr 1967 in Orlando, Florida.[13]

General Notes: William graduated from the Normal School in Mankato, Minnesota, in 1871 and taught in a private school in Medford, Wisconsin. He was the Clerk of the Circuit Court in Medford, Taylor County, Wisconsin. He was the Assistant Train Dispatcher in So. Minnesota. He was a member of the Methodist Episcopal Church. His wife, Elma Le Gro, received her education at Northwestern University in Chicago, Cook County, Illinois.

119. Charles Lounsberry Lockerby[13] was born in 1854 in Winnebago Co., WI[13] and died in Mar 1927 in Chicago, Cook Co., IL.[13] Charles married **Ellen Traver**.[13] Ellen was born in Nov 1857 in Wisconsin.[13]
Children from this marriage were:

+215   M i.   **William Lockerby**[13] was born in Sep 1875 in Minnesota.[13]
+216   M ii. **Charles Lockerby**[13] was born in Feb 1880 in South Dakota[13] and died in Apr 1939 in Chicago, Cook Co., IL.[13]
+217   M iii. **Samuel Lockerby**[13] was born in 1882 in South Dakota[13] and died on 20 Apr 1899 in Mapleton, Minnesota.[13]
+218   F iv. **Maude Lockerby**[13] was born in 1887 in Medford, Wisconsin[13] and died on 20 Nov 1896 in Mapleton, Minnesota.[13]

120. James Leaten Lockerby[13] was born on 9 Jul 1855 in Winnebago Co., WI[13] and died on 25 Apr 1915 in Mankato, Blue Earth Co., MN.[13] James married **Alice Gibson**[13] in 1882.[13] Alice was born on 9 May 1864 in Belfast, Ireland[13] and died on 11 Jun 1945 in Kasota, Le Sueur Co., Minnesota.[13]
Children from this marriage were:

+219   F i.   **Ethel A. Lockerby**[13] was born in May 1884 in North Dakota[13] and died on 18 Mar 1956 in Kasota, Le Sueur Co., Minnesota.[13]
+220   F ii. **Bessie Alice Lockerby**[13] was born on 18 Apr 1886 in North Dakota[13] and died on 7 Jun 1977 in Kanabec, Minnesota.[13]

121. Mary Ellen Lockerby[13] was born on 12 Feb 1856 in Winnebago Co., WI,[13] died on 6 Nov 1924 in Los Angeles, CA,[13] and was buried in Inglewood Cemetery, Los Angeles, California.[13] Mary married **George Washington Conklin**[13] about 1876. George was born on 22 Feb 1855 in Brandon, Wisconsin[13] and died on 25 Dec 1924 in Milwaukee, Wisconsin.[13] Children from this marriage were:

+221   M i.   **Rosco M. Conklin**[13] was born in Jun 1879.[13]
+222   M ii. **Elmer Conklin**[13] was born in May 1883.[13]
+223   F iii. **Hazel E. Conklin**[13] was born in Oct 1888.[13]

+224 M iv. **Carl McCurdy Conklin**[13] was born on 12 Feb 1892 in Southbend, Minnesota[13] and died on 3 Apr 1979 in Minneapolis, Minnesota.[13]

122. Elmer Ellsworth Lockerby[32] was born on 12 Dec 1858 in Oshkosh, Winnebago Co., WI,[32] died on 23 Jul 1933 in Winthrop, Sibley Co., MN,[32] and was buried in Winthrop, Sibley Co., MN. Elmer married **Julia Hyler Brown**,[13] daughter of **James Brown** and **Frances Hawkins**, on 23 Jun 1886 in Wells, Minnesota.[13] Julia was born on 26 Dec 1867 in Wisconsin,[13] died on 16 Feb 1926 in Minneapolis, Minnesota,[13] and was buried in Winthrop, Sibley Co., MN.[1] Children from this marriage were:

+225 M i. **Jay Douglas Lockerby**[13] was born on 29 Apr 1887 in Sleepy Eye, MN[13] and died on 11 Jun 1957 in Lewiston, ID.[13]

+226 M ii. **Ellsworth Elmer Lockerby**[13] was born in Apr 1890 in Sleepy Eye, MN[13] and died in 1938 in Cypress Lawn, Colma Co., CA.[13]

+227 M iii. **Frances Leonard Lockerby**[13] was born on 31 Jan 1893 in Preston, MN[13] and died on 10 Oct 1963 in Delano, Minnesota.[13]

+228 F iv. **Margaret Louise Lockerby**[13] was born on 6 Jan 1896 in Preston, MN[13] and died on 15 Feb 1958 in Winthrop, Sibley Co., MN.[13]

General Notes: Elmer Ellsworth Lockerby graduated from Mankato Normal School in Mankato, Minnesota, and was the principal at the schools there. He was the Superintendent at Wells, Minnesota; Sleepy Eye, Lansboro, Preston, and lastly at Paynesville, Minnesota where he lived for thirteen years. He was a Superintendent of schools for 33 years. He later worked for Midland Lumber Company as the Manager at Montrose, Winthrop, Hamel and Darwin, Minnesota.

123. Lucy V. Lockerby[13] was born in 1861 in Winnebago Co., WI[13] and died on 18 Nov 1883 in Mankato, Blue Earth Co., MN.[13] She was a Teacher in Mankato, MN

124. Samuel McCarthy Lockerby[13] was born in Aug 1864 in Winnebago Co., WI,[13] died in Oct 1923 in Seattle, WA,[13] and was buried in Seattle, WA.[13] in Evergreen-Washell Memorial Park in Seattle, WA. Samuel married **Clara W. Presley**[13] in 1896 in Minnesota.[13] Clara was born in Jul 1864 in Canada.[13]
Children from this marriage were:

+229 M i. **Frank McCarthy Lockerby**[13] was born on 28 Dec 1899 in Illinois[13] and died on 24 Feb 1969 in Tacoma, WA.[13]

+230 F ii. **Desiah Lockerby**[13] was born in 1901 in North Dakota[13] and died on 3 Jun 1991 in Seattle, WA.[13]

General Notes: Samuel graduated from the Mankato Normal School in Minnesota. He was a lawyer and a Banker and was associated with the firm of White & Lockerby Law Firm in Bismarck, North Dakota. His partner was Frank White who became the Governor of North Dakota and Treasurer of the United States. In 1905, Samuel moved to Kennewick, Washington, and served as the town's Mayor in 1912/1913.

125. Marian Eleanor Howard[13] was born in 1848 in Oshkosh, WI.[13] Marian married **William J. Dean**[13] on 18 Oct 1865 in Winnebago Co., WI.[13] William was born in 1843 in New York.[13] Children from this marriage were:

+231 M i. **Jessie A. Dean**[13] was born in 1868 in Wisconsin.[13]

+232 M ii. **Robert H. Dean**[13] was born in 1870 in Wisconsin.[13]

126.   Maria Louisa Howard[13] was born in Aug 1849 in Oshkosh, WI.[13] Maria married **Sidney Waterman**.[13] Sidney was born in Dec 1844 in Vermont.[13]   Children from this marriage were:

+233	M	i.	**Albert Waterman**[13] was born in Mar 1867 in Wisconsin.[13]
+234	F	ii.	**Alice M. Waterman**[13] was born in 1870 in Wisconsin.[13]
+235	F	iii.	**Grace E. Waterman**[13] was born in 1877 in Wisconsin.[13]
+236	M	iv.	**Marian L. Waterman**[13] was born in Aug 1885 in Wisconsin.[13]

127.   Sarah Howard[13] was born in 1852 in Oshkosh, WI.[13] Sarah married **Rev. H. P. Haylett**[13] on 28 Aug 1879 in Oshkosh, WI.[13]

128.   Edward B. Morley[13] was born in Jul 1853 in Wisconsin.[13] Edward married **Jennie**.[13] Jennie was born in Aug 1855 in Michigan.[13]   The child from this marriage was:

+237	F	i.	**Blanche Morley**[13] was born in Aug in Michigan.[13]

129.   Eugene Morley[13] was born in 1857 in Wisconsin[13] and died in Feb 1885 in Oshkosh, WI.[13]

Sixth Generation

130. Judson D. Mallory was born on 10 May 1844 in Alpine, NY and died on 2 Mar 1921 in Hector, NY. Judson married **Flora Ely** on 26 Jan 1876.   The child from this marriage was:

+238   M i.   **William Mallory** about 1878 in Hector, NY and died in 1899 in Hector, NY.

131. Anna Mallory was born on 27 Nov 1845 in Alpine, NY and died in 1875 in Alpine, NY. Anna married **Dr. G. O. Smith** on 9 Apr 1863 in New York. G. was born on 17 Jan 1837 in Enfield, New York and died on 4 Mar 1925 in Odessa, Town of Catherine, Schuyler Co., NY.   The child from this marriage was:

+239   F i.   **Alice Smith**.

132. Charlotte Prince Mallory was born on 12 Oct 1848 in Alpine, NY and died in 1917. Charlotte married **Dr. G. O. Smith** on 7 Oct 1875. G. was born on 17 Jan 1837 in Enfield, New York and died on 4 Mar 1925 in Odessa, Town of Catherine, Schuyler Co., NY.   The child from this marriage was:

+240   F i.   **Helen M. Smith**.

133. Ella Ruanna Mallory was born on 27 Mar 1857 in Alpine, NY.   Ella married **Dr. Sidney Llewellyn Hunter** in 1883. Sidney was born on 13 Mar 1858 in Hector, NY and died on 27 Feb 1909.Children from this marriage were:

+241   F i.   **Mildred E. Hunter** was born on 18 Jul 1887 and died on 29 Apr 1942.
+242   F ii.   **Mary Alice Hunter** was born on 28 Jul 1891.

134. Cora Gertrude Mallory b. 29 Jun 1864 in Alpine, NY and died on 30 Nov 1940. NEVER MARRIED

135. Stephen R. Beardsley was born on 19 Jul 1847 in Catherine, New York and died on 16 May 1910 in Catherine, New York.   Stephen married **Mary Creith** in Glen Mt. House, Watkins, New York. Mary was born in 1839 in Ireland and died on 7 Feb 1918 in Town of Catherine, Tioga Co., NY. The child from this marriage was:

+243   M i.   **Hubert Beardsley**.

136. Sarah D. Beardsley was born in 1850 in Catherine, New York and died in 1893 in Battle Creek, Michigan. Sarah married **Wood**.   Had children and lived in Central New York.

137. Stella Beardsley was born in 1855 in Odessa, Town of Catherine, Schuyler Co., NY and died on 20 Sep 1940 in Town of Catherine, Tioga Co., NY.   Stella married **Charles Brown** on 24 Dec 1874 in Hector, NY. Charles was born in 1852 and died in Jun 1922 in Town of Catherine, Tioga Co., NY.   Stella lived in the Town of Hector until 1885 and then moved to Foote's Hill.   Children from this marriage were:

+244   F i.   **Ada Brown**.
+245   M ii.   **Walter Brown**.

138. Cereles Elizabeth Catlin b. 10 Jul 1847 in Catherine, New York.   Married **Ward Hodkiss**.
139. Abel DeLancy Catlin was born on 11 Dec 1848 in Catherine, New York.
140. William Catlin (Twin) was born on 8 Mar 1852 in Tennessee.

141. Willis Catlin (Twin) was born on 8 Mar 1852 in Tennessee. Willis married **Minnie Vaughn** on 19 Nov 1874.   The child from this marriage was:

+ 246   M i.   **Harry Catlin**.

142. John Guy Birch was born on 27 Apr 1876 in Minnesota and died on 8 Apr 1926 in Minnesota.
John married **Bertha Ann Saylor**. Bertha was born on 12 Mar 1878 in Minnesota and died on 23 Feb 1903 in Minnesota.   The child from this marriage was:

+ 247   F i.   **Myrtle Louisa Birch** was born on 7 Jan 1903 in Minnesota.

143. Charles Aaron Van Vlack[35] was born in 1861[35] and died on 5 Aug 1913.[35]   Charles married **Florence Reilly**. Florence died in 1892.

144. Howell E. Van Vlack (Twin)[35] was born in 1864[35] and died on 16 Aug 1898.[35] Howell married **Euseba Bowen**. Euseba died on 6 Feb 1917.   NO ISSUE

145. Eugene Wallace Van Vlack (Twin)[35] was born in 1864[35] and died on 6 Apr 1947.[35] Eugene married **Carrie Willey** on 1 Jun 1887. Carrie was born on 23 Mar 1864.   Children from this marriage were:

+ 248   M i.   **Earl Van Vlack** was born on 21 May 1888.
+ 249   M ii.   **Floyd Howell Van Vlack** was born on 27 Aug 1891.

146. Dwight L. Van Vlack[35] was born in 1872. Dwight married **Cora Eckhart** on 6 Feb 1900. Cora was born on 6 Feb 1875 and died on 13 Feb 1920.   The child from this marriage was:

+ 250   F i.   **Eva Marie Van Vlack**.

147. Oliver Judd Van Vlack[35] was born on 6 Mar 1875[35] and died on 11 Apr 1930.[35]   Oliver married **Mary Eleanor Gough** on 1 Jan 1907. Mary was born on 23 Dec 1883.   Children from this marriage were:

+ 251   M i.   **Harold Dwight Van Vlack** was born on 10 Aug 1907.
+ 252   F ii.   **Eleanor Jeannette Van Vlack** was born on 11 Jun 1909.
+ 253   M iii.   **Franklin Reid Van Vlack** was born on 13 Oct 1910.
+ 254   F iv.   **Ethel Margaret Van Vlack** was born on 3 Feb 1912.
+ 255   M v.   **William Gough Van Vlack** was born on 3 Feb 1914.
+ 256   F vi.   **Catherine Hope Van Vlack** was born on 12 Jun 1916.
+ 257   F vii.   **Dorothy Imogene Van Vlack** was born on 4 Apr 1919.
+ 258   M viii.   **Donald Oliver Van Vlack** was born on 4 Jan 1923.
+ 259   F ix.   **Mary Joan Van Vlack** was born on 30 Mar 1925.
+ 260   F x.   **Carol Lee Van Vlack** was born on 27 Nov 1927.

148. Elbin Bivens was born on 27 Mar 1858 in Northfield, Rice Co., Minnesota.   Elbin married someone.   His child was:

+ 261   F i.   **Frances Bivens**.

149. Guy Henry Bivens was born on 29 Jun 1861 in Northfield, Rice Co., Minnesota and died on 14 May 1867 in Northfield, Rice Co., Minnesota.

150. Benjamin Halsey Bivens was born on 4 Jan 1863 in Northfield, Rice Co., Minnesota and died on 4 Mar 1863 in Northfield, Rice Co., Minnesota.

151. Ervin Lee Lockerby[16] was born on 17 Apr 1860 in Northfield, Rice Co., Minnesota[16] and died in 1918 in Minneapolis, Minnesota.[16]   Ervin married **Alice May Phalen** about 1887 in Rice County, Minn. Alice died on 19 Dec 1946.   Children from this marriage were:

+262   M i.   **Ervin Lockerby** was born on 13 Mar 1889.
+263   F ii.   **Luella Lockerby** was born on 16 Jun 1890.

152. Elizabeth Lockerby[16] was born on 15 Aug 1862 in Northfield, Rice Co., Minnesota[16] and died in Apr 1925 in Minneapolis, Minnesota.[16] Elizabeth married **Charles A. Davis** on 16 Jun 1891. Charles died in 1910. Children from this marriage were:

+264   F i.   **Gennette Clair Davis** was born on 23 Apr 1892 and died in 1943.
+265   M ii.   **Charles Hayden Davis** was born on 18 Oct 1893 and died on 21 May 1951.

153. Dwight Davis Lockerby[16] was born on 24 Jun 1867 in Northfield, Rice Co., Minnesota[16] and died on 8 Aug 1941 in Eau Claire, Wisconsin.[16] Dwight married **Ada Buzzell** in 1893. NO ISSUE

OBITUARY: Eau Claire Newspaper:
Dwight D. Lockerby, 74, former mayor and member of the city council for 24 years died at Luther Hospital, Friday. Mr. Lockerby retired from public life because of ill health, suffering from a throat ailment that grew gradually worse. He was confined to his home for some time and was permitted only a few callers as it was difficult for him to talk. At the age of 18, Lockerby embarked upon a railroad career, entering the employ of the Chicago and Milwaukee railroad as telegraph operator and cashier at Faribault and at Northfield. In 1891, he went over to the then Wisconsin Central as a cashier and bookkeeper at Chippewa Falls, Wisconsin. In 1893, promoted to ticket agent and moved to Eau Claire and had lived here ever since. In 1899, he was promoted to general agent for the line, a position he held until 1914, when friends prevailed upon him to make his first and what proved to be his successful incursion into city politics. He served as city councilman from 1914 to 1932. In 1934, he was elected mayor in a hard fought three cornered race. He served his full six year term as mayor but at the expiration of his term in April, 1940, he declined to become a candidate for re-election, his reason being failing health. Mr. Lockerby's career, to put it briefly, was marked by extended tenures in the lines of endeavor to which he devoted himself, or to which he was called or chosen by the public or by his fraternal associates to write himself.

He served 32 years as secretary of the Masonic lodge to which he belonged epitomized the high points of his life. To whatever he undertook he gave the best he had. As a railroader he was promoted several times, evidence of efficiency and faithful service. When he was prevailed upon to enter public life as a member of the city council, a full time and most responsible office, the fact that he was re-elected time after time evidenced the satisfactory service he had given the public. His 32 years as secretary of his lodge tells its own story. He had been a member of the Masonic order from many yeas. His 32 year tenure of office as secretary of Eau Clair Lodge was a record here and one of the longest in the state.

Fishing and hunting were his hobbies, and he was an adept in both. His fishing was largely confined to trout, and he cast a mean fly and was considered one of the best in this section. Most of his hunting was for chickens and pheasants, and he was an expert with a shotgun.

He was a member of Christ Episcopal Church and had served on the vestry and also as an officer of the diocesan council.

Mr. Lockerby was married twice. His first wife, Miss Ada Buzzell of Chippewa Falls, to who he was married in 1893, died in the twenties. Some years later he married Miss Blanche Nash of Eau Claire, who survives. Dwight D. Lockerby was born in Northfield, Minn, a son of Oscar and Genette Tanner. He was a lad of nine and in school in Northfield on the afternoon of Sept. 7, 1876, the day of the famous Northfield bank robbery, when Jess and Frank James, Cole, Jim and Bob Younger, Bill Chadwell, Charley Pitts, and Clell Miller made their ill-fated raid on the bank. The bank was only three blocks from the school and young Lockerby and the rest of the youngsters in school heard the shooting and yelling that attended the raid, and a few moments later when a messenger brought word to the teacher, Miss Bunker, that her brother, cashier at the bank had been shot, she dismissed school. Lockerby, curious to know what it was all about, ran in the direction of the hubbub and edging his way through the crowd in front of the bank stumbled over the dead body of one of the bandits who had been shot, and then saw the body of cashier Heywood, shot by one of the bandits, carried out of the bank.   Lockerby said his home was on the outskirts of the city and his mother, standing in the yard saw the bandits ride by on horses as they fled from the irate Northfield citizens who had grabbed up guns and revolvers and killed two of the bandits, Bill Chadwell and Clell Miller in short order.

Interment was at Forest Hill Cemetery.   Four hours preceding the funeral the body lay in state at the temple and a steady stream of friends and former associates passed his bier which was banked by many floral offerings from individuals and organizations."

154.   Burt Burr Lockerby[16] was born on 1 Jul 1869 in Northfield, Rice Co., Minnesota,[16] died on 28 Feb 1938 in Rice County, Minn,[16] and was buried in St. Lawrence Cemetery, Faribault, Rice Co., Minnesota.[16]
Burt married **Emma Joachim** on 13 Jul 1896 in Rice County, Minn. Emma was born on 1 Jun 1871 in Thiens, Belgium, died on 26 Jun 1966 in Faribault, Rice Co., MN, and was buried in St. Lawrence Cemetery, Faribault, Rice Co., Minnesota.   Children from this marriage were:

+266	F	i.	**Florence Marie Lockerby**[16] was born on 21 Feb 1899 in Rice County, Minn[16] and died on 26 Aug 1970.[16]
+267	F	ii.	**Marguerito Elizebeth Lockerby**[16] was born on 2 Jun 1901 in Rice County, Minn.[16]
+268	F	iii.	**Grace Lockerby**[16] was born in Rice County, Minn[16] and died on 20 Jul 1973 in Faribault, Rice Co., MN.[16]
+269	M	iv.	**Dwight Richard Lockerby**[16] was born on 21 Sep 1910 in Rice County, Minn[16] and died on 20 Jul 1973.[16]

General Notes: According to the "History of Rice County" 1910 -- "Burt Lockerby grew up in his native place and after finishing his schooling in the common and high schools burned the metal worker's trade at Northfield.   On attaining his majority, he entered the employ of A. L. Carnfel, for whom he worked ten years, being foreman of the shop.   He then worked two years with Mr. John Cassidy at Faribault, and later was eight years foreman in the works of Deverey and Dohohue, after which he established himself in the business to which he has since devoted his attention, and in which he has achieved success. (1906)

Mr. Lockerby is active in fraternal and benevolent Organizations being identified with the B.P.O.E. the Maccabees, and the Yeomen, and also belong to the Commercial Club of Faribault.   In politics he adheres to Democratic principles.   On July 13, 1896, Mr. Lockerby was married to Emma Joachim whose parents came from Belguim in about 1876 and settled on a farm in Rice County."

OBITUARY: Faribault Daily News - Tuesday, March 1, 1938 --
Lockerby Rites to be Thursday.   Funeral services for Burt B. Lockerby, 68, who died Monday morning (Feb 28) at his residence here, 12 Third Avenue, S. W., following a three weeks illness, will be conducted Thursday at 9 a.m. at the Church of the Sacred Heart, the Rev. I. Domestici officiating. Burial will be in the St. Lawrence Cemetery.   Active pallbearers will include Ray Endres, Paul Schroeder, Phil McCarthy, Theodore Grundman, William Caron, Hadley P. Bell, Alfred Ochs and John Foster.   Honorary pallbearers will be Fred Kilkenapp, Godfrey Endres, M. J. Bungarden, Benson Brown, J. P. O'Neil, H. P. Leach, Thomas Donohue and Herbert F. Smallidge.

Mr. Lockerby was born July 1, 1869, at Northfield and attended the public schools of that community.   At an early age he began learning the fundamentals of the Sheet Metal Trade, gaining valuable experience from the late T. M. Carufel in his shop.   Later Mr. Lockerby engaged in the Sheet Metal work in Kenyon and then came to Faribault where for 32 years he operated a shop which became widely known for quality work throughout this community.   He assisted in the construction of scores of Faribault buildings and was recognized as an expert in his chosen profession.   In 1896, he was married to Miss Emma Joachem of Faribault.

A keen enthusiast of baseball, Mr. Lockerby was one of Faribault's most ardent fans.   He strongly boosted local ball clubs, serving as president of the Faribault team and in 1924 managed the club which annexed the championship of its circuit.   He was well posted on major baseball clubs and could quote batting averages and fielding statistics with unerring accuracy.

He was evenly interested in the business development of Faribault and served as a member of the depositors committee of the Citizens National Bank, now under liquidation.

He is survived by his widow, on son, Dwight of Faribault, and two daughters, Mrs. Frank Bofenkamp of Albuquerque, New Mexico, and Florence Lockerby, a school instructor at Hurley, Wisconsin.   A brother, Dwight Lockerby of Eau Claire, Wisconsin, also survives."

OBITUARY: Mrs. Emma Lockerby (1966) --"Mrs. Emma Lockerby, 95, of 12 S. W. Third Avenue Faribault, passed away on Sunday afternoon June 26th at the Pleasant Manor Nursing Home. Funeral services will be held on Wed. morning June 19, at 9 a.m. at the Sacred Heart Catholic Church with the Rev. Donald Westoff, pastor, officiating.   Interment will be at St. Lawrence Cemetery.   Friends and relatives may call at the Kohl Funeral Home from Tuesday afternoon until the hour of service on Wednesday morning.   Mrs. Lockerby is survived by one son, Dwight of Faribault, two daughters, Miss Florence Lockerby of Faribault and Mrs. Frank Bofenkamp."

155.   Benjamin Lockerby[16] was born on 25 Jul 1871 in Northfield, Rice Co., Minnesota,[16] died on 1 Mar 1908 in Minneapolis, Minnesota,[16] and was buried in Old Northfield Cemetery, Pike Co., Minnesota.[16]

General Notes: Northfield Paper 1907 -- "Benjamin Lockerby fall in Minneapolis and Life Now Hangs in Balance." -- As a result of a breaking scaffold Benjamin Lockerby of this city is lying in a hospital in Minneapolis with the barest chance of living.   The accident happened last week while he and some other men were working on a scaffolding in Minneapolis.   The breaking of a plank threw him to the ground as that the plank and one of the men fell on his body.   At first it was thought that Mr. Lockerby had only broken his arm, but after an examination at the hospital to which he was taken, the doctors discovered a dislocation of the vertebrae.   There is no hope of recovery held out by the attending physicians who say there is one chance in a hundred of any benefit being derived through an operation.   Benjamin Lockerby is the son of Mr. and Mrs. Oscar Lockerby of this city and is well known here."

OBITUARY: Northfield Independent, Mar 5, 1908.   "Benjamin F. Lockerby who has for the past year been confined in a hospital in Minneapolis died Sunday morning, March 1 1908.   The body was brought here Monday morning.   Funeral services were held Tuesday.   Interment will be in the Northfield Cemetery.   Mr. Lockerby was born July 1, 1871, about three miles south of this city.   He has been confined in the hospital a year as the result of a broken back sustained by falling from the rafters of an ice house where he was at work.   The deceased leaves a father and mother, Mr. and Mrs. Oscar Lockerby, three brothers, Lee Lockerby of Minneapolis, D. d. Lockerby of Eau Claire, Wisconsin, and Burt Lockerby of Faribault, and a sister, Mrs. C. A. Davis of Minneapolis."

156.   Ida Frances Lockerby was born on 17 Mar 1873 in Northfield, Rice Co., Minnesota and died on 1 Jan 1883 in Northfield, Rice Co., Minnesota.

157.   Charles Edgar Lockerby was born on 25 Nov 1876 in Northfield, Rice Co., Minnesota and died on 30 Jan 1950 in Northfield, Rice Co., Minnesota.   Charles married **Mae Otte** on 7 Jun 1911. The child from this marriage was:

+270   F   i.   **Mary Lockerby** was born on 8 Mar 1914 in Minneapolis, Minnesota and died in Apr 1991 in Minneapolis, Minnesota.

158. **Francis E. Lockerby** was born on 5 Jul 1874 in Northfield, Rice Co., Minnesota, died on 10 Mar 1903 in Minnesota, and was buried in Brownton, Minnesota.

159. **Ermina Bell Lockerby** was born on 7 Dec 1874 in Faribault, Rice Co., MN, died on 21 Mar 1955 in Rosemont, Minnesota, and was buried in Northfield Cemetery, Northfield, Rice Co., Minnesota. Ermina married **Roldon Kingman**. Children from this marriage were:

+271	F	i.	**Marion Jane Kingman** was born in 1905.
+272	F	ii.	**Nellie Kingman**.
+273	M	iii.	**Roldon F. Kingman**.
+274	F	iv.	**Geraldine Kingman**.

General Notes: OBITUARY:
"Funeral services for Ermina Bell Kingman who passed away suddenly on March 21, 1955, at the home of her grandson in Rosemont where she was visiting were held Monday at Bierman's Funeral Home at Northfield. Burial was made in the Northfield Cemetery --- Ermina Bell Lockerby was born Dec 7, 1874, in Rice County. After her marriage she made her home for many years at the old Kingman home, 200 Linden St in Northfield. A few years ago she moved to Minneapolis to live with her daughter, Nellie Palmer. She is survived by four children: Mrs. Earl Cook (Marian) of Farmington; Mrs. A. K. Palmer (Nellie) of Minneapolis; Roldon F. Kingman of Farmington, and Mrs. F. W. Tubb (Geraldine) of Buffalo, New York. Also surviving are six grandchildren, three great-grandchildren, and two sisters, Mrs. Jessie Von Ruden and Dolly Lockerby, both of Faribault, Minn."

160. **Katherine Barton Lockerby** was born on 17 Aug 1880 in Faribault, Rice Co., MN and died on 12 Mar 1968 in St. Paul, Minnesota. Katherine married **H. A. Von Ruden**. The child from this marriage:

+275	M	i.	**Lawrence Von Ruden**.

General Notes: OBITUARY: Katherine Barton Lockerby was born at her parents farm home in Rice County on August 17, 1880. She attended the Northfield High School, following which she was employed for several years with the Singer Company in Faribault. She then made her home in Red Wing for a number of years. Following that she resided in Minneapolis where for many years she had been employed with Holtzermana Imports. Upon Miss Lockerby's retirement she returned to Faribault where she made her home for a number of years. For the past year Miss Lockerby resided at the Minn. Episcopal Church Home in St. Paul. Miss Lockerby passed away at the Midway Hospital in St. Paul on Tuesday evening March 12th following a brief illness. (note: from this point forward the obituary appears to be incorrect so in order to eliminate confusion, I am not including it)

161. **Dolly Lockerby** was born in 1880, died on 15 Mar 1968 in Faribault, Rice Co., MN, and was buried in Maple Lawn Cemetery in Faribault, Minnesota.

General Notes: OBITUARY: "Funeral services for Miss Dolly Lockerby 88, were held at the Parker Funeral Home in Faribault on Friday March 15th at 2 p.m. with the very Rev. Ernest F. Campbell, Dean of the Cathedral of Our Merciful Saviour, officiating. Interment was made in the Maple Lawn Cemetery in Faribault. Music was provided by Mrs. Kenneth Monson, organist. Pallbearers were nephews of Miss Lockerby and included Lawrence Von Ruden and Frank Chappuis of Faribault, Roldon Kingman, Earl Cook and Richmond Cook of Farmington and ----"

162. **Nellie Lockerby** was born on 21 Nov 1885 in Faribault, Rice Co., MN and died on 5 Jan 1887 in Faribault, Rice Co., MN.

163. **Jessie E. Lockerby** was born on 9 Mar 1889 in Faribault, Rice Co., MN and died died young (no mention in obit's).

164. Addie Charles.[2] Addie married **Leon Washburn**, son of **Frederick Washburn** and **Etta Whitmarsh**, on 5 Dec 1900.   Children from this marriage were:

+276   F   i.   **Helen Washburn**.
+277   M   ii.   **Charles Washburn**.

165. Grace Charles.[2] Grace married **Omar Egan** on 31 Aug 1910. Omar was born in 1886 and died in 1929.   Children from this marriage were:

+278   M   i.   **Gene Egan**.
+279   M   ii.   **Donald Egan**.
+280   F   iii. **Barbara Egan**.
+281   M   iv.   **Gordon Egan**.

166. Katharine Charles[2] was born on 23 Dec 1886, died on 22 Apr 1919 in Odessa, Town of Catherine, Schuyler Co., NY, and was buried in 1919 in Laurel Hill Cemetery, Odessa, Schuyler Co., NY. NEVWE MARRIED.

167. Thomas Burr Charles[2] was born on 11 Jan 1890. Thomas graduated from Cornell University and taught in PA. State College.   He was the Professor of Husbandry at N.H. University, Durham, H.H., in 1945.   Thomas married **Harriett Moe** on 28 Aug 1920.

168. Chapman Wood.[2]
169. Robert Wood.[2]
170. Harry Wood.[2]
171. Alta Wood.[2]
172. Buena Wood.[2]
173. Prentiss Burt.[2]
174. William Burt.[2]
175. Frank Burt.[2]
176. Burton Burt.[2]

177. Arnold Lockerby died on 26 Jan 1949 in Rockford, Kent Co., MI[65] and was buried in 1949 in Rockford Cemetery, Kent Co., MI.[65]

178. Findley Lockerby.

General Notes: At the time of his father's death in 1927, Findley was working at the "Thompson-Lockerby Lumber Company" in Grand Rapids, Michigan.

179. Kitty May Lockerby[2] was born on 4 Sep 1875 in Odessa, Town of Catherine, Schuyler Co., NY.[47]

Kitty married **John Bloom Vann**[2] on 4 Sep 1894 in Odessa, Town of Catherine, Schuyler Co., NY.[47] John was born on 12 Mar 1867[2] and died on 9 Dec 1929 in Ithaca, New York.[46]   The child from this marriage:

+282   M   i.   **John Truman Vann**[46] was born on 9 Nov 1908.

180. Truman B Lockerby[2] was born on 5 May 1874 in Odessa, Town of Catherine, Schuyler Co., NY,[46] died on 29 Aug 1891 in Odessa, Town of Catherine, Schuyler Co., NY,[46] and was buried in Laurel Hill Cemetery in Odessa, Town of Catherine, Schuyler Co., NY.

General Notes: Death: Age 17.   Killed by derrick in construction of LVRR

181.   Edith M. Lockerby (twin)[2] was born on 26 Jun 1879 in Odessa, Town of Catherine, Schuyler Co., NY.[47] Edith married **William Francis Lamb**.[47] William died in 1918 in France.[47]   NO ISSUE

182.   Ethel M. Lockerby (twin)[46] was born on 26 Jun 1879 in Odessa, Town of Catherine, Schuyler Co., NY.[47] Ethel married **George Maybee**.[47]   NO ISSUE

183.   Bennajah William Lockerby[71] was born on 22 Oct 1879 in Rockford, Kent Co., MI,[71] died on 18 Aug 1880 in Sand Lake, Kent Co., MI,[71] and was buried in 1880 in Rockford Cemetery, Rockford, Kent Co., MI.[72]

184.   Marshall Samuel Lockerby[73] was born on 27 Dec 1880 in Sand Lake, Kent Co., MI,[74] died on 15 Feb 1949 in St. Ignace, Mackinac Co., MI,[56] and was buried in 1949 in the Catholic Cemetery in St. Ignace, Mackinac Co., MI.

Marshall married **Jessie Dockerty**,[86] daughter of **John Dockerty** and **Lena Corbet**, on 5 Feb 1902 in Newaygo Co., MI.[86] Jessie was born in 1882,[87] died on 5 Sep 1902 in Raber, Michigan,[56] and was buried in 1902 in Whipple Cemetery, Big Rapids, Mecosta Co., MI.[56]   NO ISSUE

185.   Mabel Melvinia Lockerby[75] was born on 26 Sep 1882 in Sand Lake, Kent Co., MI,[76] died on 21 Jan 1978 in Big Rapids, Mecosta Co., MI,[77] and was buried in 1978 in Pine Plains Cemetery, Big Rapids, Mecosta Co., MI.[78]

General Notes: FAMILY HISTORY:

Mable Melvina Lockerby was born September 26, 1882, at Sandlake, Kent County, Michigan.   She was the oldest daughter of Ezekiel and Delphine (Depew) Lockerby, and tradition relates "when her father died on March 22, 1900, a great deal of the responsibility for caring for the family was passed to her for a period of time."   Her mother, Della, it is said, "was so grief-stricken it took her to bed for several weeks and Mabel was left to tend the needs of the family; washing; cooking; etc."   After a time, Mabel became ill and her brother, Mart (Marshall), took her to the doctor.   It was determined she was suffering from over-exhaustion so she was sent to stay with her aunt, Frankie, in Rockford until she recovered.   It was here she met her future husband, Leon Totton.

According to her daughter, Beulah (Totten) Wright, the couple dated a few times and then Mable returned home.   Before she had a chance to speak to her mother about Leon, a letter arrived at the home and Della requested an explanation as to the gentleman who desired to correspond with her daughter.   Mabel explained by stating "Leon was the son of William Totten, and of the same family whom the Lockerby's, Terry's and Depew's had known in New York."   Della approved, and the courtship was allowed to continue.

Before Leon met Mabel, he had been working as a teamster.   His father was known to have been very strict and when Leon decided to seek a job as a teamster, he had to first make arrangements to hire, and pay (!), a 'farm hand' to work in his place on the homestead and help his parents.   This agreement was honored until Leon reached the age of twenty-one.

On January 30, 1901, Leon celebrated his 21st birthday, and the following August (Aug 10, 1901) he and Mabel were united in marriage at the home of her mother, Della, in Keno, Newaygo County, Michigan.   After they married, they traveled by train to Sandlake where they purchased, for the sum of $11.00, all the necessary household furnishings they would need to establish their home.

Leon was a "stumper" which was a well-paid profession; however, his employment required the family to relocate often, so the couple spent the majority of the summer months living out of a tent. When the job moved, so did they!   Mable had a cook stove which she kept in the tent and it is said she did all the cooking for the crews on the job sites.   It is also said, "when she did the dishes, she would re-set the table and cover it with a towel.   One time, when they were staying near a farm, the mistress had a Bantam chicken, and the chicken would find its way into the tent and under the cloth before Mabel would discover it, and before she knew, the chicken would eat all the butter and anything else left there for the next meal."   It is further claimed, "She discovered the cloth moving and realized the chicken was at it again, --so she just reached down, grabbed the cloth with the chicken in it, and wrung its neck!   She proceeded to prepare her catch for dinner, but every time the water would come to a boil, the mistress would come to visit and Mabel would shove the chicken into the oven, and try again when she left.   After several attempts, the bird became dinner and the mistress never asked what happened, -- and Mable never mentioned it."

According to Beulah, when Mable and Leon were expecting their first child (Harry), Mable had taken the buggy and drove by herself over to visit Leon's parents.   When it came time to leave, Leon's mother is reported to have encouraged her to stay a few more hours but would offer no explanation as to her suggestion.   Within a few hours, Harry was born, and later Mabel asked her mother-in-law how she knew, and received the answer, "your face would flush, then pale, then flush and pale."

When the 2nd child was born, (Violet), Leon was ten miles away.   The neighbor took a trotting horse out to get him and upon reaching him, offered to drive his t4eam back and he could take the horse, that way he could reach home faster.   Leon was known to have said, "My team will beat your horse" -- and the race was on!   The team did beat the horse, but not the baby.   It was already born by the time they arrived.

67

Through the next years, six more children blessed the union of Mabel and Leon: Delphine, Paul, Leo, William, Nellie, and Beulah.   The couple bought a farm in Sandlake and built their own home. Mable did a lot of the lathing and when the home was completed, they purchased a windmill which was quite a novelty.   They lived at Sandlake until 1914, at which time they moved to Big Rapids, Mecosta County, Michigan.   John Totten had settled there and had a good farm so they decided to move there also and rented a place which had been a logging camp (Seaman Hills).   Here they raised a few livestock, etc., and were quite successful.

According to Beulah, when they decided to move from Sandlake in November, Mabel and the younger children traveled by train to Big Rapids, and stayed overnight with John Totten.   Harry and Leon brought the wagon with the household goods the next evening.   Tradition tells they left Sandlake about four in the morning and arrived about nine or ten the next night.   It was quite a long haul for the team and after arriving they had to walk the team for quite a while.

Later the family rented a place at Marshfield where the children attended Clear Lake School.   Then they purchased 160 acres of "sandy loam" land covered with pine stumps.   They had to set the stumping machine across the road from the property and stump their way in!   After they were able to clear enough land, they built a small building which served as a temporary shelter for Leon, Harry, and possibly, Vi.   Mable traveled back and forth between the farm and Marshfield which was about five to seven miles.   The younger children stayed in Marshfield during the time the family was clearing the land, but as soon as this could be accomplished, a home was built and the family reunited.

At one time our subjects moved a building on the farm by raising it up, placing planks under it and inserting large logs under the planks.   They used a team of oxen to pull the building forward, inch by inch, pausing to reposition the logs again and again before continuing.   It was moved almost three miles from its original site.

School was held in the Burden Lake School house and the children walked two-miles back and forth through the woods.   When it was time for High School, the children were sent into Big Rapids where they sought room and board and remained until the weekends, returning home for visits with the family.   This was an extra burden on Mabel as during the weekends, she would launder their clothes and prepare special foods for them to take back for their meals during the week.   Della and Paul graduated from High School and went on to Normal College in Mount Pleasant, Michigan.   Bill did not complete his education, and Nellie died of leukemia three months after beginning her freshman year.

After Nellies death, Leon went to work in the woods for a time up by Sandlake and Mable took Beulah and went to the home of her mother, Della, to help with the chores there.   Della was alone then, as Father Bush had died and Olive and Ray were moving to a farm of their own.   They stayed through the winter, and in the spring hired a gentleman to help with the chores until Ezekiel 11 could come home.   They returned to Marshfield and Leo and Mable spent the next years continuing on their busy ways.

In 1951, the couple celebrated their 50th Wedding Anniversary.   At the time of Leon's death in 1959, they had shared 59 years together and raised eight children.   Mabel died January 21, 1978 in Big Rapids, Mecosta County, and is buried beside her husband in Pine Plains Cemetery.

Mabel married **Leon Cornel Totten**[88] on 10 Aug 1901 in Keno, Newaygo Co., MI.[86] Leon was born on 30 Jan 1880 in Watkins-Glen, New York, died on 22 Jun 1959 in Big Rapids, Mecosta Co., MI,[84] and was buried in 1959 in Big Rapids, Mecosta Co., MI.

Children from this marriage were:
+283   M   i.   **Harry Olen Totten**[56] was born on 2 Nov 1903 in Pierson, Montcolm Co, MI,[56] died on 13 Jan 1969 in Grasmere, British Columbia, Canada, and was buried in 1969 in Grasmere, British Columbia, Canada.

+284   F ii.   **Violet Olive Totten**[56] was born on 28 Sep 1905 in Pierson, Montcolm Co, MI.[56]

+285   F iii.   **Delphine Wilvina Totten**[56] was born on 24 Mar 1907 in Pierson, Montcolm Co, MI.[56]

+286   M iv.   **Paul Leon Totten**[56] was born on 3 Feb 1909 in Pierson, Montcolm Co, MI.[56]

+287   M v.   **Leo Carl Totten**[56] was born on 26 Jul 1911 in Sand Lake, Kent Co., MI,[56] died on 21 Feb 1947 in Big Rapids, Mecosta Co., MI,[56] and was buried in 1947 in Big Rapids, Mecosta Co., MI.

+288   M vi.   **William Edwin Totten**[56] was born on 22 Oct 1914 in Pierson, Montcolm Co, MI.[56]

+289   F vii.   **Nellie Mae Totten**[56] was born on 11 May 1920 in Big Rapids, Mecosta Co., MI,[56] died on 11 Apr 1936 in Big Rapids, Mecosta Co., MI,[56] and was buried in 1936 in Big Rapids, Mecosta Co., MI.[56]

+290   F viii. **Beulah Belle Totten**[56] was born on 25 Apr 1925 in Big Rapids, Mecosta Co., MI,[56] died on 3 Sep 1985 in Shelby, MI, and was buried on 6 Sep 1985 in Morley, Mecosta Co., MI.

186.   Ezekiel Terry Lockerby[79] was born on 30 Jul 1884 in Sand Lake, Kent Co., MI,[80] died on 24 Sep 1964 in Evart, Osceola Co., MI,[81] and was buried in 1964 in Whipple Cemetery, Big Rapids, Mecosta Co., MI.[82]

General Notes: FAMILY HISTORY:

Ezekiel was born on July 30, 1884, in Sandlake, Kent County, Michigan, and spent the majority of his youth in Keno, "Lockerby Town" helping his parents with the saw mill and farm chores.   He accompanied his mother, Della, in about 1886/7 to New York and stayed for a time with the Bela Depew family.   Tradition indicates he was "high tempered and a hard worker, and when he drove a team of horses, they would trot highly."

Beulah Totten recalled a story her mother retold regarding an incident which happened one evening while Zeke and her mother, Mabel (Zeke's sister) were returning from town. "Once when Mabel and Zeke were coming home to Keno (Lockerby Town), after dark, Zeke got down off the wagon to open the gate and something came up from out of the bushes next to the stream and frightened the team. The horses bolted and began to run. Zeke grabbed the back of the wagon and held on while Mabel dragged him almost halfway down the lane. Eventually, he was able to pull himself up into the wagon and crawl through to the front and get a grip on the reins and calm the horses." They were never certain exactly what had frightened the team, but always believed it was a bear.

In 1982, Zeke's only surviving sister, Olive, age 94, recalled a time " when they were playing in the front yard of the home and something happy occurred and they laughed til their eyes were wet and the water rolled down their faces." It is good to remember there were "happy times" because, much of Zeke's life after he left the farm, was certainly less then what his childhood dreams may have been for himself.

Ezekiel was sixteen years of age when his father passed away. Not long after his death, "Lockerby Town" was sold and a new home constructed for the family on the adjoining property. We can only assume Ezekiel assisted with the building of the second homestead, and a great deal of the responsibility for the farm and fairly likely rested upon his shoulders during the next few years.

Nine years later, on February 3, 1909, when he was twenty-five years of age, his mother sold him forty acres of land for the sum of $1.00.

NOTE: The property is described as follows: "Comm 7 rods N. of SW. corner of the NW 1/4, Sec. 35, Home Township, thence N to NW corner of the said Sec., E. 80 rods, S to a point 7 rods S of SE corner of said NW 1/4 of NW 1/4 of said Sec., NW'ly to place of beginning..." (Liber 96, p 328, and Liber 96, p. 607, land deeds White Cloud, Michigan)

He was farming the land when on May 18, 1920, in Big Rapids, Michigan, he was united in marriage by S. A. Whitmore, Minister, to: Mrs. Clara Bell (Inman) Coldwell of Grand Rapids, Michigan. His sister, Olive Lockerby, and Wilson Deck, acted as witnesses for the ceremony (VR-M). During the summers, Zeke would work the farm and during the winter months he would work the woods cutting logs. They had one daughter, Reva Estella, born on June 12, 1913. The couple separated about a year later on August 5, 1914, and divorced on August 3, 1915. (VR-Div). Custody of Reva, was granted to her mother and Zeke was to pay $4.00 a month for support.

NOTE: Clara Inman Lockerby died in March of 1920, five years later. Zeke was no longer in Michigan. Reva lived with the Stedman family for a while and then went to live with the Roy Jontz family of Grand Rapids, Michigan.

Three months and three days after the divorce, on November 6, 1915, Ezekiel sold his forty acres of land to Arthur Jernstadt for the sum of $1,300.00 (Liber 113, p 114, White Cloud, Michigan deeds) and left the farm in Michigan, removing to Iowa. He rented a farm in Garner Township, Pottawattamie County, Iowa, and farmed in the evenings and on weekends. During the week he was employed at Scofield Grain Mill. Years later, his son, Marshall, applied for a job at the same mill and the employer recalled Ezekiel's experience and commented, "if you are as hard of a worker as your father was, --- you're hired!"

In correspondence dated December 15, 1935, Ezekiel listed the extent of his personal property in 1925: "free from in cumbrance, 22 head of hogs, 13 of which were breeding sows; 26 sows, 8 in the fattening stage; a boar worth a thousand dollars; 10 head of cattle, 5 of them for milking, 2 two-year old heifers (bred), a full blooded bull, 3 years old, and 2 calves; four head of horses; three of the four first class Harness Wagons; all kinds of tools, and between two to three hundred chickens."

On September 30, 1917, Ezekiel married a second time in Rockport, Missouri (VR-M) to Mrs. Etta Mae (White) Fernley. She was born Jan. 28, 1885, in Jewell County, Kansas, and the daughter of Thomas Foster and Sarah (Moler) White. Etta had been married previously and brought the following children into the marriage: Vera, Laura, Paul and Mary Fernley. To the union of Ezekiel and Etta the following were born: Ezekiel Terry Lockerby "Bud", Marshall Samuel, "Marty", and Bessie Olive.

On April 20, 1925, Ezekiel was indicted and charged with a crime for which he was sentenced to serve twenty-five years in the Iowa State Pen. He remained in the States care until 1936 when, at the age of fifty-two years, he returned to Michigan and stayed on the farm with his aged mother, Della, helping her with the daily chores and responsibilities of the farm. Tradition indicates he would never shave in any month that had an "R" because he believed the warmth of a beard protected his health.

On July, 18, 1946, a local Michigan newspaper reported the following:

"FARMER INJURED AS TEAM BOLTS.
        E. T. Lockerby, 62, of Route 2, Big Rapids, was seriously injured Wednesday afternoon about 5 o'clock, when the team he was driving in the field ran away and dragged him some distance. He suffered bruises and possible internal injuries, according to a report from the sheriff's department today. Lockerby makes his home with his aged mother about two miles northeast of town, and the couple were unable to summon help until this morning, when they attracted the attention of a passerby, who summoned relatives and medical help. The full extent of his injuries were not known this morning, but it was feared he may be seriously injured."

In another item, dated same, it said,

"MECOSTA FARMER INJURED BY TEAM.
Big Rapids -- E. T. Lockerby, 62, a farmer living three miles northeast of here, was being treated Friday for serious injuries resulting when his team bolted in the field and dragged him several hundred feet. Lockerby lives with his mother who was unable to attract the attention of passerby's to send for medical aid until nearly 18 hours after her son had managed to get from the field to his home."

Ezekiel recovered from his experience and continued to reside with his mother until her death on April 8, 1947. Finding himself alone, and at the end of his days, he yearned to see his children once more and traveled to Iowa in the summer of 1947 to visit them. After a brief stay, he returned to Michigan and some years later, on July 22nd, 1951, we find that Judge A. W. Miles, Judge of Probate in Big Rapids, Mecosta County, Michigan, granted guardianship of Ezekiel Lockerby, Mentally Incompetent, age 67 years, to, George Nicholson. He was admitted to the Evart Convalescent Home in Evart, Michigan, and on September 10, 1964, died at the age of 80 years of heart disease. He was laid to rest in Whipple Cemetery in Big Rapids, Michigan.

NOTE: In researching for documents regarding Ezekiel's life, it was discovered that only his mother and sister, Olive, were aware he had three children in Iowa, and their names were not recorded in the family records. Further, the records reflected the union between Ezekiel and Etta was "Common Law Marriage" (evidently they did not know he actually married Etta, --)

Copies of the vital records and Family Journal are in the care of Ezekiel's granddaughter, Marsha Pilger, 807 Madison Ave, Council Bluffs, Iowa, in 2007. Also in her care are the newspaper articles; court records; and letters which ET wrote during his stay in the penitentiary at Ft. Madison, IA.

Ezekiel married **Etta Mae White**,[89] daughter of **Thomas Foster White** and **Sarah Moler**, on 30 Sep 1918 in Rockport, Atchison Co., MO.[90] Etta was born on 28 Jan 1885 in Esbon, Jewell Co., KS,[91] died on 30 Apr 1977 in Council Bluffs, Pottawattamie Co., IA,[92] and was buried in 1977 in Council Bluffs, Pottawattamie Co., IA.[92] Children from this marriage were:

  +291   F i.   **Bessie Olive Lockerby**[56] was born on 10 Jul 1918 in Council Bluffs,
              Pottawattamie Co., IA[56] and died on 27 Oct 1998 in California.

+292   M ii.   **Ezekiel Terry Lockerby**[56] was born on 9 Apr 1921 in Council Bluffs, Pottawattamie Co., IA,[56] died on 19 Sep 1998 in Council Bluffs, Pottawattamie Co., IA, and was buried on 22 Sep 1998 in Council Bluffs, Memorial Park, Pott. Co., Iowa.

+293   M iii.   **Marshall Samuel Lockerby**[56] was born on 31 May 1923 in Council Bluffs, Pottawattamie Co., IA,[56] died on 7 Sep 2010 in Council Bluffs, Pottawattamie Co., IA, and was buried in Walnut Hill Cemetery, Council Bluffs, Iowa.

187.   Olive Adell Lockerby[83] was born on 7 Aug 1888 in White Cloud, Newaygo Co., MI,[83] died on 5 Jan 1985 in Big Rapids, Mecosta Co., MI, and was buried in 1985 in Big Rapids, Mecosta Co., MI.

Keno (Lockerby Town) and we can assume after the death of her father

General Notes: FAMILY HISTORY:

Olive Lockerby was born August 7, 1888, in White Cloud, Newaygo County, Michigan, to parents, Ezekiel and Delphine Depew Lockerby. Although her birth was expected, she arrived early and because she was so tiny it became convenient to carry her on a pillow whenever the family traveled. She spent the majority of her youth growing up in 1900 she helped with the care of the younger children and assumed some of the household duties though just a child of twelve years.

She attended Big Jackson School in Newaygo County and terminated her education on the first day of the fifth grade when her teacher asked her to provide the meaning of "alfoamego" and she was unable to do so. She always stated, "This was the beginning of the end because she had failed to even open her book." The teacher sent her back to the fourth grade and that was enough to discourage Olive. She never bothered to return to school again and tradition indicated, "this was the beginning of trouble between herself and her mother, Della."

Olive left home in her mid-teens, and from this time until she married, she kept house for several families, some of which included her sister, Mable, and Joseph Cousineau. At the age of twenty-four years, she married John Ray Haggman. Ray had been married previously to Sylvia __?__ and had four children. Ray's wife, Sylvia, died in childbirth and two daughters were deceased at the time he and Olive married. Twin sons remained of Ray's family but were separated at the time of the marriage. The frail child was sent to live with an aunt while the second twin remained with Olive and Ray. The frail son died first, and when the second son was approximately two years of age, he died from a fall off a horse drawn wagon.

Ray was a farm hand on numerous places in Newaygo County and the couple made their home on the farms where they worked. On October 11, 1915, their first child, Raymond Freddie, was born. He died when he was nineteen months, two weeks and five days old. The couple then removed to

734 East Vine Street in Kalamazoo, Michigan, and it was here that Gertrude Muriel was born. During this time, Ray was employed as a brakeman in the railroad yards. Later the family moved back to Newaygo County and Emma joined the family circle.

In 1823, the family was located at 1017 Garden Street in Kalamazoo where Ray became a truck driver for A. W. Walche, a distributor of wholesale groceries. This was not a permanent position for Ray and the ensuing years found the family relocating numerous times. In 1935 to 1936, they resided on the family farm of Olive's mother, Della, while she travelled to New York to visit family there. Then they moved to Warren Ave and East Grand Traverse and from 1938 to the fall of 1951 resided at 524 N. Michigan Ave., in Big Rapids.

Finally in the fall of 1951, Ray and Olive bought their first home at 611 Finley Ave. in Big Rapids. It was during this time and up until 1953 that Ray worked for the Lans Coal Company in Big Rapids delivering coal during the Second World War. Then, he worked for the WPA and later the DPW for the city. He also served as a fireman but due to the loss of hearing was removed in 1952. He signed on as a maintenance man and janitor of the Phillip Free Library for less than a year and had a light stroke. In his better moments he would journey down to the old fire station stroke in 1951 that claimed his life. He was taken to the Big Rapids Hospital and a week later, on Feb. 3, 1951, just lacking 18 days of reaching his 65th birthday and retirement, death claimed him. He was laid to rest in Whipple Cemetery.

From the fall of 1936 to early 1940 Olive worked at many jobs herself to assist with the income. She cleaned houses for several wealthy families in Big Rapids and also cleaned for a couple of churches. She was a dishwasher for a couple of restaurants and during the next years stayed home to keep house and help raise her two grandsons.

In her declining years after Ray's death, she continued to share her home with her daughter, Muriel, and her grandsons, but due to her extremely poor health it became necessary to admit her to Greenridge Nursing Center in 1975. Ten years later, on January 5th, 1985, death claimed her and she was placed to rest beside her husband in Whipple Cemetery, Newaygo County, Michigan. Officiating at the 1:00 p.m. services January 8th, was the Rev. Paul Price, and the services were held at the Rogers-Mohnke Funeral Home in Big Rapids.

Throughout her life Olive had been a strong, independent woman, with a very dominating personality such as her mother, Della, had possessed. After the death of her mother, Olive continued in the tradition of recording the family events and happenings in the Journal which her mother had kept during her years. This Journal was in the care of her daughter, Muriel, until her death. The ancestral photographs which had been passed from generation to generation, were given to Mrs. Ronald Pilger, 807 Madison Ave, Council Bluffs, Iowa.

NOTE: Funeral notice and obituary on file.

Olive married **John Ray Haggman**[56] on 24 Dec 1912 in Everett Twp., Newaygo Co., MI.[56] John was born on 21 Feb 1888 in Home Twp, Newaygo Co., Michigan,[56] died on 3 Feb 1953 in Big Rapids, Mecosta Co., MI,[84] and was buried in 1953 in Big Rapids, Mecosta Co., MI. Children from this marriage were:

+294   M i.   **Raymond Freddie Haggman**[56] b. 11 Oct 1915 in Home Twp, Newaygo Co., MI.[56]

+295   F ii.   **Gertrude Muriel Haggman**[56] was born on 15 Apr 1918 in Kalamazoo, MI,[56] died on 20 Jan 1986 in Big Rapids, Mecosta Co., MI, and was buried on 23 Jan 1986 in Big Rapids, Mecosta Co., MI.

+296   F iii.   **Emma Melvina Haggman**[56] b. 13 Mar 1921 in Home Twp, Newaygo Co., MI.[56]

188.   Lena May Lockerby[56] was born on 18 Dec 1889 in White Cloud, Newaygo Co., MI,[56] died on 13 Sep 1977 in Greenville, MI,[84] and was buried in 1977 in Pierson, Montcolm Co, MI.

General Notes: FAMILY HISTORY:

Lena Lockerby was born on December 18, 1889, in Newaygo County, Michigan, to Ezekiel and Delphine Depew Lockerby.   She was sixteen years of age when she married on September 20, 1906, to George Frank Bryant of Pierson, Michigan.   They were married in the living room of the home on George's farm, on Kimball Road, where they lived all their lives.

In 1966, they celebrated their 60th Wedding Anniversary with an Open House at the farm east of Pierson.   It is said that George seldom left the farm except to go hunting, and Lena spent much of her time making quilts and doing various kinds of needlework.   She also enjoyed playing the mouth organ.

Seven children blessed their marriage: Fred, Pearl, Isabelle, Beatrice, Carroll "Bud", Gretchen, Martha, and Kenneth Bryant who was born, and died, January 21, 1922, in Pierson, Michigan and buried in the Pierson Cemetery.

George Bryant was born April 16, 1886, in Pierson, and died November 30, 1972, at the Greenville Memorial Hospital in Greenville, Michigan.   Lena died September 13, 1977, at the same hospital and both are buried in the Pierson Cemetery in Pierson, Montcolm Co., Michigan.

Lena married **George Frank Bryant**[56] on 20 Sep 1906 in Pierson, Montcolm Co, MI.[56] George was born on 16 Apr 1886 in Pierson, Montcolm Co, MI, died on 30 Nov 1972 in Greenville Mem H, Greenville, Michigan, and was buried in 1972 in Pierson, Montcolm Co, MI.   Children from this marriage were:

+ 297   M i.   **Fred Erwin Bryant**[56] was born on 7 Jun 1907 in Pierson, Montcolm Co, MI,[56] died on 28 Aug 1973 in Grand Rapids, Kent Co., MI, and was buried in 1973 in Pierson, Montcolm Co, MI.

+ 298   F ii.   **Pearl Ester Bryant**[56] was born on 13 Feb 1909 in Pierson, Montcolm Co, MI.[56]

+ 299   F iii.   **Isabelle Elizabeth Bryant**[56] b. 19 Jun 1911 in Pierson, Montcolm Co, MI.[56]

+ 300   F iv.   **Beatrice Bryant** was born on 19 Apr 1914 in Pierson, Montcolm Co, MI.

+ 301   F v.   **Gretchen Rebecca Bryant**[56] was born on 6 May 1918 in Pierson, Montcolm Co, MI.

+ 302   M vi.   **Kenneth Bryant**[56] b. 21 Jan 1922 in Pierson, Montcolm Co, MI, died on 21 Jan 1922 in Pierson, Montcolm Co, MI, and was buried in 1922 in Pierson, Montcolm Co, MI.

+303   M vii.   **Carroll George Bryant**[56] was born on 22 Jan 1923 in Pierson, Montcolm Co, MI, died on 15 Aug 1964 in Michigan, and was buried in 1964 in Curtis Cemetery, Big Rapids, Mecosta Co., Michigan.

+304   F viii.   **Martha Bryant**[56] was born on 21 Aug 1924 in Pierson, Montcolm Co, MI,[56] died on 31 Jul 1965 in Pierson, Montcolm Co, MI, and was buried in 1965 in Pierson Cemetery, Pierson, Montcolm Co, Michigan.

Taken on June 22, 1947 in front of the old family home in Bitely, Michigan (Newaygo Co.)
Left to right
<arshall Lockerby, Mable Totten, Olive Haggman, Lena Bryant, Erwin and Herbert.
NOTE: All children of Ezekiel T. and Delphine Depew Lockerby

189. Herbert Bela Lockerby[83] was born on 20 Jul 1891 in Keno, Newaygo Co., MI,[83] died on 6 May 1967 in Grand Rapids, Kent Co., MI,[84] and was buried on 8 May 1967 in Big Rapids, Mecosta Co., MI.

General Notes: FAMILY HISTORY:

Herbert Bela Lockerby was born July 20, 1891, at Keno (Lockerby Town), Newaygo County, Michigan, to parents, Ezekiel and Delphine (Depew) Lockerby. He married on April 2, 1922, to Effie Cousineau. She was born April 2, 1902, in Newaygo County, and died December 13, 1929, same. She was the daughter of Joseph A. and Effa E. (Gordon) Cousineau. Three sons were born to the couple, however, the first two died at birth. One son, Fred Herbert, reached adulthood and married.

After Effie's death, Herbert married a second time to Celia Belle Biller. They married on May 1, 1943. Celia was born January 15, 1898, and died January 13, 1974. Herbert died May 6, 1967, at the Vet's Hospital in Grand Rapids, Michigan. Both are buried in the Pine Plaines Cemetery ("Byers") in Big Rapids, Mecosta County, Michigan.

Herbert was a veteran of World War 2 having served in France, and a member of the Big Rapids D. A. V.

NOTE: Obituary and funeral notice on file.

Herbert married **Effie Cousineau**[56] on 2 Apr 1922 in Michigan.[56] Effie was born on 2 Apr 1902 in Newaygo Co., MI,[56] died on 13 Dec 1929 in Newaygo Co., MI,[56] and was buried in 1929 in Whipple Cemetery, Big Rapids, Mecosta Co., MI.[56] Children from this marriage were:

+305   M i.   **Unnamed Boy (twins) Lockerby**[56] was born on 5 Mar 1926 in Newaygo Co., MI.[56]

+306   M ii.   **Fred Herbert Lockerby**[56] was born on 10 Mar 1929 in Newaygo Co., MI.[56]

190.   Erwin Agustus Lockerby[83] was born on 12 Jul 1898 in Keno, Newaygo Co., MI,[83] died on 21 Nov 1977 in Bitely, Newaygo Co., MI,[84] and was buried in 1977 in Big Rapids, Mecosta Co., MI.

General Notes: FAMILY HISTORY:

Erwin Lockerby was born on July 12, 1898, at Keno (Lockerby Town) Newaygo County, Michigan. He was only two years of age when his father, Ezekiel Terry Lockerby, passed away. He was raised by his mother, Delphine.

On March 8, 1924, he married in Newaygo County to Josie Briggs, the daughter of Ferdhand and Lola (Rhodes) Briggs. They remained on the homestead of Erwin's ancestors and on May 12, 1926, purchased the property from his mother, Delphine (Liber 142, p 71, Deeds in White Cloud, Michigan).

His favorite past time was working in his craft shop. He would carve for hours creating miniature figures of the past generations of milling equipment. He paid special attention to every detail, thus creating a perfect image of his past. Sleds, covered wagons drawn by teams of horses , surreys of every style, and miniature models of all the equipment used by the ancestors. Everything was complete right down to the tiny logs that were carried on the wagons and sleds. One winter he constructed a miniature model of a logging camp, complete with the buildings and furniture. Many of his items can be located throughout the family descendants. While Erwin would carve, Josie would sew and create her own items of special interest. Many of their items were sold at local art shows and craft fairs.

They shared fifty-three years of marriage before death claimed Erwin on November 21, 1977, and had three children: Dan, Betty and Jean. Erwin was laid to rest in Whipple Cemetery in Big Rapids, Mecosta County, Michigan.

Erwin married **Josie Wave Briggs**,[56] daughter of **Ferdinand Briggs** and **Lola Rhoades**, on 8 Mar 1924 in Newaygo Co., MI.[56] Josie was born on 20 Feb 1908 in White Cloud, Newaygo Co., MI,[56] died on 31 Oct 2004 in Newaygo Co., MI,[93] and was buried in Whipple Cemetery, Big Rapids, Newaygo Co., MI.
Children from this marriage were:

+307   M i.   **Dan Arnold Lockerby**[56] was born on 2 Dec 1924 in Muskegon, Michigan.[56]

+308   F ii.   **Betty Rea Lockerby**[56] was born on 21 Oct 1926 in Muskegon, Michigan.[56]

+309   F iii.   **Jean Rosella Lockerby**[56] was born on 23 Aug 1932 in Muskegon, Michigan.[56]

191.   Basher Childs. Died young
192.   Ida Childs.
193.   Eva Childs.

194.   Adda Terry was born in Veteran, Chemung Co., New York.   Adda married **William S. Gardner**, son of **Mitchell Gardner** and **Sarah Barnes**, in 1897 in Veteran, Chemung Co., New York.

195.   Ella Terry was born on 19 Jul 1879 in Veteran, Chemung Co., New York.   Ella married **Arthur Lattin**, son of **Henry Lattin** and **Matilda Beardsley**, on 27 Nov 1895. Arthur was born on 3 Jun 1872 in Big Flats, New York, died in 1937 in Catharine, Schuyler Co., NY, and was buried in 1937.
Children from this marriage were:

+310	F	i.	**Hazel Lattin** was born on 2 Oct 1896 in Catharine, Schuyler Co., NY.
+311	F	ii.	**Ethel Lattin** was born on 8 Oct 1897 in Catharine, Schuyler Co., NY.
+312	M	iii.	**Albert Arthur Lattin** was born on 3 Mar 1907 in Catharine, Schuyler Co., NY.

196.   Lottie Terry was born in Veteran, Chemung Co., New York. Lottie married **S. Banfield**.
Children from this marriage were:

+313	M	i.	**Tomas Banfield**.
+314	M	ii.	**Glen Banfield**.
+315	M	iii.	**Douglas Banfield**.

197.   Mary Terry was born in Veteran, Chemung Co., New York.

198.   Ida Ann Crowe.   Ida married **H. Danbury**.   Children from this marriage were:

+316	M	i.	**Wesley Danbury**.
+317	M	ii.	**Hubert Danbury**.

199.   William Crowe. William married **Lula Russell**.   The child from this marriage was:

+318	M	i.	**James Russell**.

200.   Harry Shelton. Died young
201.   Lee Shelton. Lee married **Maude Carpenter**.
202.   May Leaton[13] was born in 1875 in Illinois.[13]
203.   Alice Grace Leaton[13] was born in Sep 1878 in Illinois.[13]
204.   Louise Leaton[13] was born in Sep 1890 in Illinois.[13]
205.   Paul L. Corbin[13] was born in Sep 1875 in Illinois.[13]
206.   James R. Corbin[13] was born in Jul 1877 in Illinois.[13]
207.   Clara R. Corbin[13] was born in Nov 1879 in Illinois.[13]
208.   Laurie Corbin[13] was born in Mar 1885 in Illinois.[13]
209.   Edward L. Corbin[13] was born in Mar 1888 in Illinois.[13]
210.   Annie L. Corbin[13] was born in Jun 1890 in Illinois.[13]
211.   Alice H. Corbin[13] was born in Mar 1892 in Illinois.[13]
212.   Blanche Guthrie[13] was born in 1873 in Illinois.[13]
213.   Lucy L. Guthrie[13] was born in 1876 in Illinois.[13]

214.   Avis Lockerby[13] was born on 28 Aug 1882 in Racine, Wisconsin[13] and died on 10 Apr 1967 in Orlando, Florida.[13]   Avis married **William Bonner Richards**[13] on 17 Aug 1909 in Racine, Wisconsin.[13] William was born on 28 Apr 1877 in Racine, Wisconsin.[13] Children from this marriage were:

+319	M	i.	**William Legro Richards**[13] was born on 17 Mar 1914.[13]
+320	F	ii.	**Rachel Richards**[13] was born on 24 Sep 1917.[13]

General Notes: Avis graduated in 1909 from the University of Minnesota. Her husband, William Richards, graduated from the University of Wisconsin and became a Professor of Agriculture at the College of North Dakota.

215. William Lockerby[13] was born in Sep 1875 in Minnesota.[13] William married **Mary**.[13] The child from this marriage was:

+ 321   M i.   **Harrison Salisbury Lockerby**[13] was born on 2 Sep 1877 in Blue Earth, Minnesota[13] and died on 17 Sep 1877 in Blue Earth, Minnesota.[13]

General Notes: William served in the Spanish American War between 29 April and the 5th of November, 1898. He was a printer for the Chicago Daily News.

216. Charles Lockerby[13] was born in Feb 1880 in South Dakota[13] and died in Apr 1939 in Chicago, Cook Co., IL.[13] Charles married someone. His child was:

+ 322   F i.   **Margaret Lockerby**.[13]

217. Samuel Lockerby[13] b. 1882 in South Dakota[13] and died on 20 Apr 1899 in Mapleton, Minnesota.[13]

218. Maude Lockerby[13] b. 1887 in Medford, WI[13] and died on 20 Nov 1896 in Mapleton, Minnesota.[13]

219. Ethel A. Lockerby[13] was born in May 1884 in North Dakota[13] and died on 18 Mar 1956 in Kasota, Le Sueur Co., Minnesota.[13] Ethel married **Adolph Mueller**.[13] Adolph was born on 3 Nov 1881 in Minnesota[13] and died on 12 Mar 1974 in Kasota, Le Sueur Co., Minnesota.[13] Children:

+ 323   M i.   **Kenneth Lockerby Mueller**[13] was born on 25 Nov 1911 in Minnesota[13] and died on 3 Sep 1978 in Blue Earth, Minnesota.[13]
+ 324   F ii.   **Dorothy Mueller**[13] was born in 1916 in Minnesota.[13]

220. Bessie Alice Lockerby[13] was born on 18 Apr 1886 in North Dakota[13] and died on 7 Jun 1977 in Kanabec, Minnesota.[13] Bessie married **Ira Van Gorden**.[13] Children from this marriage were:

+ 325   M i.   **Donald Van Gorden**.[13]
+ 326   M ii.   **Earl Van Gorden**[13] was born on 21 Sep 1916[13] and died on 12 Sep 1981 in Hennepin Co., Minnesota.[13]
+ 327   M iii.   **James L. Van Gorden**[13] was born on 29 Jun 1923[13] and died on 1 Sep 1993 in Isanti, Minnesota.[13]

221. Rosco M. Conklin[13] was born in Jun 1879.[13]

222. Elmer Conklin[13] was born in May 1883.[13]

223. Hazel E. Conklin[13] was born in Oct 1888.[13]

224. Carl McCurdy Conklin[13] was born on 12 Feb 1892 in Southbend, Minnesota[13] and died on 3 Apr 1979 in Minneapolis, Minnesota.[13] Carl married **Thersia Mary Ruhland**. Thersia was born on 3 Sep 1891 in Mankato, Blue Earth Co., MN and died on 1 Mar 1987 in Minneapolis, Minnesota. Children from this marriage were:

+ 328   F i.   **Violet Conklin**.
+ 329   M ii.   **George Elmer Conklin** was born on 24 Nov 1914 and died on 4 Nov 1988.
+ 330   M iii.   **Jerome K. Conklin** was born on 15 Feb 1919 and died on 17 Nov 1919.

+331	F iv.	**Hazel Lucille Conklin** was born on 10 Jun 1920 in Redondo Beach, CA.
+332	M v.	**Leonard M. Conklin** was born on 8 Aug 1921 and died on 3 Sep 1936.
+333	M vi.	**Ralph M. Conklin** was born on 25 Aug 1922 and died on 12 May 1951.
+334	F vii.	**Genevieve M. Conklin** was born on 16 Apr 1924 and died in Feb 1976.
+335	F viii.	**Margaret Conklin** was born on 9 Mar 1929.

225. Jay Douglas Lockerby[13] was born on 29 Apr 1887 in Sleepy Eye, MN[13] and died on 11 Jun 1957 in Lewiston, ID.[13] Jay married **Hazel Seavey**[13] on 22 Aug 1921 in St. Cloud, Minnesota.[13] Hazel was born in 1887 in Minnesota[13] and died in Lewiston, ID.[13]

General Notes: Jay Douglas Lockerby moved to Spokane, Washington, and resided there from 1910-1921. He then moved to Sandpoint and in 1922 was residing in Lewiston, Idaho.

He served in the U. S. Army in World War 1 and was attached as a Gunner with the 146th Regiment of the 66th Artillery. He was wounded in action and received a Purple Heart.

He was a conductor for the Camas Prairie Railroad Company and retired from here in 1948.

226. Ellsworth Elmer Lockerby[13] was born in Apr 1890 in Sleepy Eye, MN[13] and died in 1938 in Cypress Lawn, Colma Co., CA.[13] Ellsworth married **Randalla Bickford**[13] in San Mateo, California. Randalla was born in 1896 in Iowa[13] and died in California.[13] Children from this marriage were:

+336	M i.	**Ellsworth Bickford Lockerby**[13] was born on 13 Sep 1914 in Carlinville, IL,[13] died on 18 Mar 1996 in San Mateo, California,[13] and was buried in St. John's Cemetery, San Mateo, CA.[13]
+337	F ii.	**Dorothy Frances Lockerby**[13] was born in 1918 in California.[13]
+338	F iii.	**Geneva Lockerby**[13] was born in 1925.[13]

General Notes: Ellsworth Elmer Lockerby was living in San Francisco, CA., around the time of his mother's death in 1926.

227. Frances Leonard Lockerby[13] was born on 31 Jan 1893 in Preston, MN[13] and died on 10 Oct 1963 in Delano, Minnesota.[13] Frances married **Meda Albina Packer**,[13] daughter of **James Packer** and **Margaret Gilmer**, on 5 Sep 1916.[13] Meda was born on 19 Dec 1892 in Winsnted, Minnesota[13] and died on 4 Sep 1974 in Minneapolis, Minnesota.[13] Children from this marriage were:

| +339 | M i. | **Jay Douglas Lockerby**[13] was born on 15 Aug 1918 in Ellsworth, WI,[13] died on 5 Dec 1989 in St Paul, Minnesota,[13] and was buried on 8 Dec 1989 in Woodville, WI.[13] |
| +340 | F ii. | **Betty Jeanne Lockerby**[13] was born on 1 Jan 1921 in Ellsworth, WI.[13] |

228. Margaret Louise Lockerby[13] was born on 6 Jan 1896 in Preston, MN[13] and died on 15 Feb 1958 in Winthrop, Sibley Co., MN.[13] Margaret married **Clarence Lind**[13] on 5 Sep 1924 in Winthrop, Sibley Co., MN.[13] Children from this marriage were:

+341	M i.	**James Lind**[13] was born on 23 Jun 1928 in Winthrop, Sibley Co., MN.[13]
+342	M ii.	**John M. Lind**[13] was born on 21 Jun 1930 in Winthrop, Sibley Co., MN.[13]
+343	F iii.	**Mary Margaret Lind**[13] was born on 8 Feb 1932 in Winthrop, Sibley Co., MN.[13]

229. Frank McCarthy Lockerby[13] was born on 28 Dec 1899 in Illinois[13] and died on 24 Feb 1969 in Tacoma, WA.[13] Frank married **Lucille**.[13] Lucille was born in 1899 in Washington[13] and died on 19 Jun 1990 in Tacoma, WA.[13] Children from this marriage were:

| +344 | F | i. | **Lucille Lockerby**[13] was born in 1924 in Washington.[13] |
| +345 | F | ii. | **Joan Lockerby**[13] was born in 1929 in Washington.[13] |

General Notes: Frank graduated from the University of Washington and was the Editor of the Tacoma News Tribune.

230. Desiah Lockerby[13] was born in 1901 in North Dakota[13] and died on 3 Jun 1991 in Seattle, WA.[13]

General Notes: Desiah was a librarian in the Seattle Public Library in Washington.

231. Jessie A. Dean[13] was born in 1868 in Wisconsin.[13]

232. Robert H. Dean[13] was born in 1870 in Wisconsin.[13]

233. Albert Waterman[13] was born in Mar 1867 in Wisconsin.[13] Albert married **Annie M.**.[13] Annie was born in 1867 in Minnesota.[13] Children from this marriage were:

+346	F	i.	**Abbie Waterman**[13] was born in May 1889 in Wisconsin.[13]
+347	F	ii.	**Gretchen Waterman**[13] was born in Apr 1891 in Wisconsin.[13]
+348	F	iii.	**Eleanor Waterman**[13] was born in Mar 1894 in Wisconsin.[13]
+349	F	iv.	**Isabelle Waterman**[13] was born in Aug 1896 in Wisconsin.[13]
+350	M	v.	**Francis Waterman**[13] was born in Dec 1899 in Wisconsin.[13]

234. Alice M. Waterman[13] was born in 1870 in Wisconsin.[13]

235. Grace E. Waterman[13] was born in 1877 in Wisconsin.[13]

236. Marian L. Waterman[13] was born in Aug 1885 in Wisconsin.[13]

237. Blanche Morley[13] was born in Aug in Michigan.[13]

Seventh Generation

238. William Mallory was born about 1878 in Hector, NY and died in 1899 in Hector, NY.

239. Alice Smith. Alice married **Herbert Lyon**.   Children from this marriage were:

+351   M i.   **Maynard Lyon** was born on 7 May 1893.
+352   M ii.   **Jesse Gordon Lyon** was born on 19 Sep 1896.

240. Helen M. Smith.
241. Mildred E. Hunter was born on 18 Jul 1887 and died on 29 Apr 1942.

242. Mary Alice Hunter was born on 28 Jul 1891. Mary married **Henry William Kaufman** on 17 Sep 1913. Henry was born on 3 Jun 1891. Children from this marriage were:

+353   F i.   **Gretchen Kaufman** was born on 25 Jul 1914.
+354   M ii.   **Henry William Kaufman** was born on 3 Jul 1916.
+355   F iii.   **Jean Louise Kaufman** was born on 5 Jul 1924.

243. Hubert Beardsley.   Hubert married **Rose Britten** on 9 Dec 1909 in Odessa, Town of Catherine, Schuyler Co., NY.

General Notes: Hubert Beardsley operated a nursery of shrubs and ornamental trees in Odessa, New York.   NO ISSUE

244. Ada Brown.   Ada married **Duane L. Brown**.   Children from this marriage were:

+356   F i.   **Aline Brown**.
+357   M ii.   **Wilbur Brown**.

General Notes: Ada and her husband Duane resided in Odessa, New York.   They owned a coal yard on Depot Hill.

245. Walter Brown.
246. Harry Catlin.

247. Myrtle Louisa Birch was born on 7 Jan 1903 in Minnesota.   Myrtle married **Carl Theodore Hansen**. Carl was born on 26 Jan 1881 in Wisconsin and died on 25 May 1966 in South Dakota. The child from this marriage was:

+358   M i.   **Carl Richard Hansen** was born on 28 Jul 1927 in Iowa.

248. Earl Van Vlack was born on 21 May 1888.   Earl married **Mildred Sparks** on 16 Oct 1917. Mildred died on 26 May 1935. The child from this marriage was:

+359   F i.   **Ardythe Mae Van Vlack** was born on 7 Aug 1918.

249. Floyd Howell Van Vlack was born on 27 Aug 1891. Floyd married **Opal Wasson** on 27 Dec 1930.

250. Eva Marie Van Vlack. Eva married **Lloyd L. Gibson** on 16 Aug 1926. Lloyd was born on 14 Mar 1899. The child from this marriage was:

+360   M i.   **James Van Gibson** was born on 18 Mar 1937.

251. **Harold Dwight Van Vlack** b.10 Aug 1907. Harold married **Helen Shulta** in Dec 1937. NO ISSUE

252. **Eleanor Jeannette Van Vlack** was born on 11 Jun 1909. Eleanor married **Stanley W. Smith** in Waterloo, Iowa.   Children from this marriage were:

+361	F	i.	**Patricia Smith**.
+362	F	ii.	**Mary Janice Smith**.
+363	M	iii.	**Marshall Smith** was born on 5 Dec 1945.
+364	F	iv.	**Rebecca Lee Smith** was born on 16 Aug 1947.
+365	F	v.	**Eleanor June Smith** was born on 23 Jun 1950.

253. **Franklin Reid Van Vlack** was born on 13 Oct 1910. Franklin married **Ethel Marie Tadlock** in 1927 in Kahoka, MO.   Children from this marriage were:

+366	F	i.	**Peggy Reidena Van Vlack**.
+367	F	ii.	**Kristine Marie Van Vlack** died at birth.
+368	M	iii.	**David Van Vlack** was born on 8 Jul 1946.

254. **Ethel Margaret Van Vlack** was born on 3 Feb 1912. Ethel married **Roger H. Stine** in Yucca Valley, CA.   Children from this marriage were:

+369	M	i.	**Richard Howard Stine** was born in 1932.
+370	M	ii.	**David Oliver Stine** was born in 1936.
+371	M	iii.	**Steven Van Vlack Stine**.
+372	M	iv.	**Stanley Reid Stine**.

255. **William Gough Van Vlack** was born on 3 Feb 1914. William married **Irma Lucille Cowles** on 9 Jul 1936 in Manchester, Iowa. Children from this marriage were:

+373	F	i.	**Linda Lou Van Vlack** was born on 18 Jun 1941.
+374	F	ii.	**Judith Ann Van Vlack** was born on 5 Nov 1943.

256. **Catherine Hope Van Vlack** was born on 12 Jun 1916. Catherine married **Claire Joseph Jahnke** on 15 Nov 1937.
Children from this marriage were:

+375	F	i.	**Sally Ann Jahnke** was born on 15 Jan 1945.
+376	M	ii.	**Joseph Claire Jahnke** was born on 25 Sep 1947.

257. **Dorothy Imogene Van Vlack** was born on 4 Apr 1919. Dorothy married **Ancil E. Wallingford** on 22 Feb 1942 in Paso Robles, Califonia.   Children from this marriage were:

+377	M	i.	**Steven Ancil Wallingford** was born on 30 May 1945 in Des Moines, Polk Co., Iowa.
+378	M	ii.	**William Edward Wallingford** was born on 19 Oct 1948 in Yakima, Washington.

258. **Donald Oliver Van Vlack** was born on 4 Jan 1923. Donald married **Dorothy Gail Asher** on 21 Nov 1946.   Children from this marriage were:

+379	F	i.	**Kristine Marie Van Vlack** was born on 8 Dec 1947.
+380	F	ii.	**Barbara Jo Van Vlack** was born on 14 Aug 1950.
+381	F	iii.	**Patti Jean Van Vlack** was born on 25 Mar 1954.

259. **Mary Joan Van Vlack** was born on 30 Mar 1925. Mary married **Olliver C. Amick** on 3 Jun 1943.
The child from this marriage was:

+382   F i.   **Cynthia Marie Amick** was born on 26 Feb 1947.

260.   Carol Lee Van Vlack was born on 27 Nov 1927. Carol married **William Joe Jackson** on 28 Nov 1946. The child from this marriage was:

+383   F i.   **Mary Anadell Jackson** was born on 19 Jan 1952 in Fairfield, Iowa.

261.   Frances Bivens.

262.   Ervin Lockerby was born on 13 Mar 1889.

263.   Luella Lockerby was born on 16 Jun 1890. Luella married **William Mehrens**.

264.   Gennette Clair Davis was born on 23 Apr 1892 and died in 1943.

265.   Charles Hayden Davis was born on 18 Oct 1893 and died on 21 May 1951.

266.   Florence Marie Lockerby[16] was born on 21 Feb 1899 in Rice County, Minn[16] and died on 26 Aug 1970.[16] She was a school teacher at Hurley, Wisc

267.   Marguerito Elizebeth Lockerby[16] was born on 2 Jun 1901 in Rice County, Minn.[16] Marguerito married **Frank Bofenkamp**.

268.   Grace Lockerby[16] b. Rice County, Minn[16] and died on 20 Jul 1973 in Faribault, Rice Co., MN.[16]

269.   Dwight Richard Lockerby[16] was born on 21 Sep 1910 in Rice County, Minn[16] and died on 20 Jul 1973.[16] Dwight married **Ruth Ann Louise Witzke** on 23 Sep 1937. Ruth was born on 3 Mar 1918.
Children from this marriage were:

+384   F i.   **Nora Delight Lockerby**[16] born on 8 Mar 1942 in Faribault, Rice Co., MN.[16]
+385   M ii.   **Dwight R. Lockerby** was born on 9 Dec 1945.

270.   Mary Lockerby was born on 8 Mar 1914 in Minneapolis, Minnesota and died in Apr 1991 in Minneapolis, Minnesota. Mary married **Balow**.   Children from this marriage were:

+386   M i.   **John Balow**.
+387   F ii.   **Rosemary Balow** was born on 8 Jun 1944.

General Notes: I communicated with Mary (Lockerby) Balow for many years regarding our common heritage.   In 1986, she was 72 years of age.   She died in April 1991.

271.   Marion Jane Kingman was born in 1905. Marion married **Earl A Cook**. Earl was born in 1903.   The child from this marriage was:

+388   M i.   **Alan F. Cook** was born in 1928.

272.   Nellie Kingman. Nellie married **A. K. Palmer**.

273.   Roldon F. Kingman.

274.   Geraldine Kingman. Geraldine married **F. W. Tubb**.

275.   Lawrence Von Ruden.

276. Helen Washburn. Helen married **Galvin Walker**. Children from this marriage were:

+389   F i.   **Elizabeth Walker.**
+390   M ii.   **Lester Leon Walker.**

277. Charles Washburn. Charles married **Eleanor Robinson**, daughter of **A. J. Robinson** and **Unknown**. Children from this marriage were:

+391   F i.   **Katherine Ann Washburn.**
+392   M ii.   **John Washburn.**

278. Gene Egan.
279. Donald Egan.
280. Barbara Egan.
281. Gordon Egan.

282. John Truman Vann[46] was born on 9 Nov 1908. John married **Cora Elizabeth Martin** on 3 Feb 1937.[47] Cora was born on 24 Feb 1917.The child from this marriage was:

+393   M i.   **Ernest Arthur Vann** was born on 16 Oct 1936.

283. Harry Olen Totten[56] was born on 2 Nov 1903 in Pierson, Montcolm Co, MI,[56] died on 13 Jan 1969 in Grasmere, British Columbia, Canada, and was buried in 1969 in Grasmere, British Columbia, Canada.

General Notes: FAMILY HISTORY:

Harry Olen Totten was born November 2, 1903, at the home of his grandparents, Mr. and Mrs. William Totten, in Pierson, Montcolm County, Michigan.   He lived with his parents, Leon and Mabel M. Lockerby Totten, at Sandlake, Michigan, until 1914, when at the age of eleven, they moved to Big Rapids.   Tradition indicates they moved in November and he and his father drove the team of horses and wagon load of household furnishings from Sandlake to Big Rapids, leaving around four in the morning and arriving about ten o'clock the next evening.

He later moved to Marshfield, Michigan, where he helped his parents clear the land where they were to spend the remaining years of their life.   At the age of fourteen, he went to work in the woods with his father and became a teamster.   In order for him to work beside his father, and not jeopardize his father's employment, he had to assume the nickname of "Jeff" and work as his father's brother rather than his son.

At the age of eighteen, he left home and traveled west where he met and later married, Harriett Elizabeth "Bessie" Sinclair in 1928/9 in Cranbrook, British Columbia.   She was one quarter Indian and held her Indian rights with the Canadian Government.   He became a Canadian citizen and bought property at Rock Lake, Elco, British Columbia, and ran a small resort there.

When World War 11 broke out, he enlisted in the Canadian Army and served for four years.   He was stationed in England during the Blitz and while there, took a brief vacation into Scotland and visited the ancestral village of the Totten family, "Tottenham Village."

After his return, the Libby Dam in Libby, Montana, was built across the Kootenai River and the backwaters flooded portions of the land that Harry and Bessie owned, as well as, parts of the land owned by their brother, Paul.

In later life, Harry developed cancer of the Kidneys which on January 13, 1969, claimed his life.   He is buried in Grassmere Cemetery in Grassmere, British Columbia, Canada.

Bessie sold the ranch and lived with her son, Robert James, and ten years later, on October 19, 1979, she died and was buried beside her husband.

REF: Beulah Totten Wright

Birth: born at the home of his grandparents, M/M William Totten in Pierson, Michigan.

Migration: b. Pierson, Michigan; lived in Sandlake, Michigan until 1914 when he removed w/pts to Big Rapids, Michigan.   Later moved to Marshfield, Michigan; at age 18 went west and in ca. 1928/9 took up residence in Cranbrook, Brittish Columbia, Canada, and then bought property at Rock Lake, Elco, B.C. and ran a small resort there.   Shortly after WW2 he removed to Grassmere, B.C., Canada

Personal data: became a Canadian citizen.   Became a teamster at age 14 yrs.   Later owned a ranch in Canada.   Death: Cancer of the kidneys.   Burial: Grassmere Cemetery, Grassmere, British Columbia, Canada

Harry married **Harriett Elizabeth Sinclair** about 1928. Harriett was born on 2 Jan 1906, died on 19 Oct 1979, and was buried in Grasmere, British Columbia, Canada.   Children from this marriage were:

+394	M	i.	**Harry Lloyd Totten** was born on 3 May 1930.
+395	M	ii.	**Robert James Totten** was born on 25 Mar 1934.
+396	F	iii.	**Shirley Lorna Totten** was born on 29 May 1935.
+397	F	iv.	**Genevieve Mabel Totten** was born on 20 Oct 1937.

284.   Violet Olive Totten[56] was born on 28 Sep 1905 in Pierson, Montcolm Co, MI.[56]

General Notes: FAMILY HISTORY: REF: Beulah Totten Wright

Violet was born September 28, 1905, in Pierson, Michigan.   She grew up on the family farm in Michigan and attended Clear Lake and Burden Lake Elementary Schools completing eight years of education.   In later life, she decided to attend Farris Institute, which was a private college (now a State College).   Upon graduating, she went to Grand Rapids, Michigan where she became a secretary.

On August 10, 1928, she was joined in marriage to Bernard Glen Brower in Auston (Austin?) Township and then moved to their home in Grand Rapids, Michigan.   Over the next years the following children were born to them: Kathleen Marie and Marilyn May.

Violet married **Bernard Glen Brower**[56] on 10 Aug 1928 in Big Rapids, Mecosta Co., MI.[56] Bernard was born in Oct 1905, died on 30 Apr 1976, and was buried in 1976.   Children from this marriage were:

+398	F	i.	**Kathleen Marie Brower**[56] b. 15 Apr 1929 in Grand Rapids, Kent Co., MI.[56]
+399	F	ii.	**Marilyn May Brower**[56] was born on 28 Feb 1932 in Grand Rapids, Kent Co., MI.[56]

285.   Delphine Wilvina Totten[56] was born on 24 Mar 1907 in Pierson, Montcolm Co, MI.[56]

Delphine married **John B. Zandstra**[56] on 16 May 1930 in Indiana.[56] John was born on 1 Jan 1907 in Oak Glen, Illinois.   Children from this marriage were:

+400	M	i.	**Burdette H. Zandstra**[56] was born on 25 Sep 1931 in Highland, Indiana.[56]
+401	M	ii.	**John Paul Zandstra**[56] was born on 12 Oct 1934 in Munster, Indiana.[56]

+402	M iii.	**Jerry Allen Zandstra**[56] was born on 12 May 1939 in Hammond, Indiana.
+403	F iv.	**Elaine Zandstra**[56] was born on 15 Mar 1942 in Hammond, Indiana.[56]
+404	F v.	**Eunice Zandstra** was born on 19 Jan 1945 in Hammond, Indiana.[56]

General Notes: Birth: Delphine was raised on the family farm of her parents. Education: Attended Clear Lake and Burden Lake Elementary Schools. High School in Big Rapids, Mecosta Co., Michigan; Normal College in Mount Pleasant, Michigan. Degree in Education.

Marriage: Married John Zandstra May 16, 1930. He was one of sixteen children and was born January 1, 1907 in Oak Glen, Illinois. His parents were born in Holland. John's family was established in the truck farming business. He later became a manager for a local Dairy which was owned by his brother-in-law and remained here until retirement. Residence: Indiana

286.   Paul Leon Totten[56] was born on 3 Feb 1909 in Pierson, Montcolm Co, MI.[56] Paul married **Wilda Betty Truaz** on 12 Oct 1933. Wilda was born on 15 Feb 1907. Children from this marriage were:

+405	F i.	**Betty Annette Totten** was born on 31 Oct 1934.
+406	M ii.	**Paul Leon Totten Jr.** was born on 28 Jan 1936.
+407	M iii.	**Walter Patrick Totten** was born on 17 Mar 1940.

General Notes: Birth: Raised on the family farm in Pierson, Michigan Education: Clear Lake and Burden Lake Elementary Schools. Big Rapids High School. Normal College in Mount Pleasant, Michigan. Degree in Education. Profession: Teacher and farmer. Residence: Moved to British Columbia, Canada. Later removed to Rexford, Montana, and then to Eureka, Montana.

287.   Leo Carl Totten[56] was born on 26 Jul 1911 in Sand Lake, Kent Co., MI,[56] died on 21 Feb 1947 in Big Rapids, Mecosta Co., MI,[56] and was buried in 1947 in Big Rapids, Mecosta Co., MI. Leo married **Eleonor Richardson** on 27 Sep 1934. Children from this marriage were:

+408	M i.	**David Keith Totten** was born on 2 Aug 1935.
+409	M ii.	**Donald Leo Totten** was born on 1 Feb 1937.
+410	F iii.	**Karen Margaret Totten** was born on 20 Aug 1941.
+411	M iv.	**Christopher Wayne Totten** was born on 1 Jun 1947.

General Notes: Funeral Notice: Serviced held at Martinson-Rogers Funeral Home, March 24, 1947, Big Rapids, at 1:00 p.m. Officiating, Walter Foster. Bearers: William Totten, Walter Wright, Jon Zandstra, Glen Bower, Harland Rood, Frank We3ntland. Burial: Pine Plains Cemetery, Big Rapids, Mecosta Co., Michigan

288.   William Edwin Totten[56] was born on 22 Oct 1914 in Pierson, Montcolm Co, MI.[56] William married **Lavonne Edna Lee** in 1935. Children from this marriage were:

+412	M i.	**Duane Edwin Totten** was born in Feb 1937 in Big Rapids, Mecosta Co., MI.
+413	M ii.	**Dewey Lee Totten** was born in Apr 1943 in Big Rapids, Mecosta Co., MI.
+414	F iii.	**Donna Lou Totten** was born in Oct 1944 in Big Rapids, Mecosta Co., MI.
+415	F iv.	**Susan Mae Totten** was born in Mar 1952 in Big Rapids, Mecosta Co., MI.
+416	F v.	**Billie Jean Totten** was born in May 1953 in Big Rapids, Mecosta Co., MI.

General Notes: Birth: born on the farm in Pierson, Michigan. Residence: Pierson, Montcolm Co., Michigan on the farm of his parents where he raises livestock. Profession: was employed by the Pipeline Company and worked in numerous states including; North Carolina, Indiana, Ohio, North Dakota, etc. Became a farmer.

289.   Nellie Mae Totten[56] was born on 11 May 1920 in Big Rapids, Mecosta Co., MI,[56] died on 11 Apr 1936 in Big Rapids, Mecosta Co., MI,[56] and was buried in 1936 Pine Plains Cemetery in Big Rapids, Mecosta Co., MI.[56] Death: died at age 15 yrs, 11 months of Leukemia

290.   Beulah Belle Totten[56] was born on 25 Apr 1925 in Big Rapids, Mecosta Co., MI,[56] died on 3 Sep 1985 in Shelby, MI, and was buried on 6 Sep 1985 in Morley, Mecosta Co., MI.

General Notes: FAMILY HISTORY:

Beulah was born on April 25, 1925, in Big Rapids, Michigan.   She was the last born child of Leon and Mabel Lockerby Totten, and like the rest of the family, grew up on the family farm and attended the local schools of Clear Lake and Burden Lake Elementary.   She graduated, in a class of nine students, in 1943, from the Mecosta High School, and in May of 1983, attended her 40th class Reunion.

Between her Sophomore and Junior years, she attended Bible Camp under the American Sunday School Union at Brethren, Michigan, and the following summer, met her future husband, Walter. They courted during her senior year of high school and in May of 1943, were united in marriage by Rev. George P. Stanford in the living room of his parent's home in Newaygo County, Michigan.

According to Beulah, "Walt was working for a farmer getting $50.00 a month, their house, milk, and a garden spot, when Walt was called to service in the United States Army.   She decided to have a party for him and roast a suppling pig and claimed that cooking it on her wood stove was quite an experience!"   Walt was sent to Camp Robert's in California for basic training and in April was transferred to Camp Beal in Sacramento.   Beulah went on the bus to meet him and rented quarters for them for $28.00 a month.   She stated that the conditions under which they lived "were quite primitive!"

When Walt went overseas, Beulah took a brief vacation up the coast going into Canada to visit her brother, Harry, before returning home.   She spent the winter with her sister, Dee, and the following spring went to work for the American Sunday School Union teaching Bible School.   She was later employed by te local factory which was making the Honeysuckle Line of under garments for Sears. During this time, Walt was stationed in England and France and while there went into Belgium and Germany as part of the "Army of Occupation" after Peace was declared.   He was discharged on April 1, 1946, with the rank of Corporal after serving in Battery A. 753D, Field Artillery Battalion.

He returned to Michigan and he and Beulah bought a small trailer where they lived until Walt Jr. was about to be born.   At that time they moved in with Beulah's mother, Mabel, and later they bought property North of Big Rapids.   Eventually they purchased 40 acres of land west of Morley, Michigan.   They lived in the garage for a time and later purchased an older home, constructed with square nails, which they had moved, by truck, seven and a half miles from its original site to their property.   After the house was in place, a foundation was constructed under it and they began to remodel.

Walt's job asd an electrician offered them the opportunity to travel, and after the children were grown, Beulah joined him.   Travelling from state to state offered her the opportunity to expand her interests in hunting and stone collecting, as well as, many other fields.   She enjoyed pressing flowers, working on crafts of various natures, canning her own garden products, drying her own fruits and vegetable, and being active in church.

She could be compared to the pioneer women of the ancestors as she could adapt to almost any circumstance; cooking on an old wood burning stove, or a modern gas range; tramping through the woods hunting her own game, or shopping the most modern markets; carrying her own water for miles, or having the convenience of running water at her fingertips.

Walt and Beulah had six children together and prided themselves in knowing they not only shared a close family of love, but were great friends as well.   Beulah Totten Wright died September 3, 1985, and was laid to rest in the Aetna Cemetery in Morley, Michigan.   The following is a copy of her obituary:

BEULAH B. WRIGHT

"Howard City -- Mrs. Beulah B. Wright, 60, of Morley, died Tuesday at the Lakeshore Community Hospital in Shelby.   She was born April 25, 1925, near Big Rapids.   She lived her entire life in the Morley and Big Rapids area. For many years she was a sewing machine operator for Wolverine World Wide.   Surviving are her husband, Walt; three sons, Walter of California, Wayne of Morley, and Warren of West Germany; three daughters, Mrs. William (Ann) Brischke of Shelby, Mrs. Robert (Carolyn) Ego of Hart, and Mrs. Dennis (Doris) Freeland of Casnovia; 20 grandchildren; two brothers, Paul Totten of Montana, and William Totten of Big Rapids; two sisters, Mrs. David (Violet) LaFerney of Flint and Mrs. John (Dee) Zandstra of Big Rapids.

Services will be at 1:00 p.m. Friday at the First Baptist Church of Howard City with the Rev. Karl Pike officiating. Burial will be in Aetna Cemetery in Morley.   Friends may call at the Germain Funeral Home in Howard City."

Education: Clear Lake and Burden Lake Elementary Schools.   Mecosta High School in Big Rapids.   Bible Camp under the American Sunday School Union at Bretheran, Michigan.

Marriage: Met her husband at the Am. Sunday School Camp in Bretheran, Michigan.

Residence: Morley, Michigan.

Burial: Aetna Cemetery, Morley, Mecosta Co., Michigan

Beulah married **Walter Cornel Wright**,[56] son of **Frank Wright** and **Inez Graves**, on 8 May 1943 in Atena, Newaygo Co., Michigan. Walter was born on 4 Sep 1923 in Mecosta Co., MI, died on 9 Sep 2000 in Mount Pleasant, Iowa, and was buried on 15 Sep 2000 in Morley, Mecosta Co., MI. Children from this marriage were:

+417	M	i.	**Walter Cornel Wright**[94] born 17 Feb 1947 in Big Rapids, Mecosta Co., MI.[94]
+418	M	ii.	**Wayne Edward Wright**[94] b. 25 Aug 1949 in Big Rapids, Mecosta Co., MI.[94]
+419	F	iii.	**Anna Belle Wright**[94] was born on 30 Sep 1950 in Big Rapids, Mecosta Co., MI.
+420	F	iv.	**Carylon Louise Wright**[94] born on 8 Sep 1953 in Big Rapids, Mecosta Co., MI.
+421	F	v.	**Doris Jean Wright**[94] born on 26 Mar 1954 in Big Rapids, Mecosta Co., MI.
+422	M	vi.	**Warren E. Wright**[94] was born on 14 Mar 1956 in Big Rapids, Mecosta Co., MI.

291.   Bessie Olive Lockerby[56] was born on 10 Jul 1918 in Council Bluffs, Pottawattamie Co., IA[56] and died on 27 Oct 1998 in California.

General Notes: FAMILY HISTORY:

Bessie Olive Lockerby was born July 10, 1918 in Council Bluffs, Iowa and was the only daughter of Ezekiel and Ella Mae (White) Lockerby.   She was the oldest child of her father and spent her early years growing up in Council Bluffs attending Longfellow Elementary.   In 1936, at the age of 18, she married Clair Minor.   Clair had served in the U.S. Army and was among those detained as a prisoner of war in WW 11 with the 168th Division of Company L. from Council Bluffs.   He was in a prison camp in Germany.

On December 14, 1951, Bessie married Albert Hollins.   He had two children from his previous marriage; Albert Jr. "Sunny" and Ilene, and with Bessie's three children, they were kept quite busy.   Our subject enjoyed being able to work in her garden and can her own produce.

She died in 29 Palms, California on October 27, 1988.

OBITUARY:

Twenty-nine Palms, California -- "Memorial service for Bessie Olive Hollins, 80, of Twenty-nine Palms, California, a former Council Bluffs resident, will be held Nov 1 at 7:30 p.m. at the Church of the Nazarene in 29 Palms with the Rev. Charles Swicker officiating.

Mrs. Hollins died Oct 27 at her home. She was a homemaker and a member of the Church of the Nazarene in 29 Palms. Survivors include two daughters, Anita Root of 29 Palms and Beverly Ally of Council Bluffs; a son, Craig Miner, of Shelby; a brother, Marty Lockerby, of Walnut; eight grandchildren, one great-grandchild, nieces and nephews.

Burial will be private. Wiefels & Sons Funeral Home in 29 Palms is in charge of arrangements."

Bessie married **Clair Miner** in 1936.

Children from this marriage were:
+423　F　i.　　**Juanita Miner** born on 9 Jan 1938 in Council Bluffs, Pottawattamie Co., IA.
+424　F　ii.　　**Gloria Miner** was born from 1938 to 1939 in Council Bluffs, Pottawattamie Co., IA, died in 1942 in Council Bluffs, Pottawattamie Co., IA, and was buried in 1942 in Council Bluffs, Pottawattamie Co., IA.
+425　F　iii.　**Beverly Kay Miner** born 6 Feb 1941 in Council Bluffs, Pottawattamie Co., IA.
+426　M　iv.　**Craig William Miner** b. 26 Mar 1945 in Council Bluffs, Pottawattamie Co., IA.

292.　Ezekiel Terry Lockerby[56] was born on 9 Apr 1921 in Council Bluffs, Pottawattamie Co., IA,[56] died on 19 Sep 1998 in Council Bluffs, Pottawattamie Co., IA, and was buried on 22 Sep 1998 in Council Bluffs, Memorial Park, Pott. Co., Iowa.

General Notes: Military Service:　US Army 2nd Battalion of the 168the Infantry Division of L. Company which was transferred to the 133 Division out of Sioux City, Iowa, and sent to Europe in WW 2.　The 133rd lift in Feb. 1942 and traveled to Halifax, Nova Scotia, where they joined several convoys and continued on to Ireland.　They remained in Ireland from March to Dec. of 1942 and then crossed the Irish Sea into Scotland and travelled by train into Eng.　They were in England for about two weeks, spending Christmas in Liverpool Harbor aboard ship.　In early 1943 the unit was transferred to Africa to enter combat.　Bud was wounded by machine gun fire on April 9, 1943, (his birthday) and after recuperating was sent to Italy (Sept 1943). He was wounded again while in Italy and hospitalized. He returned to the U.S. in March of 1944, aboard a hospital ship and on April 29, 1944, was discharged from active service. Received a Purple Heart and a Sharpshooter Award.

Profession: worked for the Union Pacific Railroad and retired from there after 32 years of service on April 30, 1982.

Died at home on 19 Sept 1998. McCurdy Funeral Home. Military Honors by VFW Post 737. 18 Grandchildren, 14 Great-Grandchildren. Burial in Westlawn Section of Cedar Lawn Cemetery in lot 146. (VR-Cem)

!MARRIAGE: Vital Record of Marriage #54032 Pott Co., Iowa, to Ethel A. Lockerby

OBITUARY: Daily Nonpareil: 04/06/2004

Ethel Annabelle (Fales) Lockerby, 78, of Council Bluffs died April 2.

She was born March 29, 1926, in Omaha to Sam and Ethel Fales. She was a member of Harvest Temple Church of God.

Mrs. Lockerby was preceded in death by her husband, Ezekiel, and two brothers.

Survivors include daughters, Sharon Story and husband, James, of Council Bluffs; Susie Buse and husband, Jim, of Council Bluffs, Gloria Tesch and husband, Larry, of Council Bluffs; son, Terry Lockerby and wife, Terri, of Shenandoah; 24 grandchildren; 34 great-grandchildren; three great-great-grandchildren.

Visitation with the family will be today from 7 to 8 p.m. at McCurdy Funeral Home. The funeral will be Wednesday at 11 a.m. at Harvest Temple Church of God (700 S. Seventh St.) with Pastor Claude Maddox officiating. Burial will be in Memorial Park Cemetery.

Ezekiel married **Ethel Annabell Fales**, daughter of **Samuel Alfred Fales** and **Ethel Ellen Clear**, on 7 Sep 1944 in Council Bluffs, Pottawattamie Co., IA. Ethel was born on 29 Mar 1926 in Omaha, Douglas Co., NE and died on 2 Apr 2004 in Council Bluffs, Pottawattamie Co., IA.

Children from this marriage were:

+427	F	i.	**Sharon Ann Lockerby** b 23 Jul 1945 Council Bluffs, Pottawattamie Co., IA.
+428	F	ii.	**Susan Elaine Lockerby** b 7 May 1948 Council Bluffs, Pottawattamie Co., IA.
+429	F	iii.	**Gloria Jean Lockerby** b 27 May 1951 Council Bluffs, Pottawattamie Co., IA.
+430	M	iv.	**Terry Leroy Lockerby** b 14 Oct 1956 in Council Bluffs, Pottawattamie Co., IA.

293. Marshall Samuel Lockerby[56] was born on 31 May 1923 in Council Bluffs, Pottawattamie Co., IA,[56] died on 7 Sep 2010 in Council Bluffs, Pottawattamie Co., IA, and was buried in Walnut Hill Cemetery, Council Bluffs, Iowa.

General Notes: FAMILY HISTORY:

Marshall Samuel Lockerby was born May 31,1923 and was the youngest son of Ezekiel Terry and Etta Mae (White) Lockerby. He spent his early years growing up in Council Bluffs and attended McMillen and Longfellow Elementary Schools completing eight grades of education.

At the age of eighteen, he married Betty Alice Williams, the daughter of James Walter and Alta Vesta (Guin) Williams. She was born August 25, 1924, in Council Bluffs, Iowa. The couple were married April 20, 1942, in Papillion, Sarpy County, Nebraska, and to this union two children were born, Monte Lee "Biff" and Marsha Lynn.

After their marriage Marty worked for a local grain elevator where is father, Ezekiel, had been employed. Then he went to work for the City Transit Company and drove a bus in Council Bluffs until approximately 1951 when he decided to go to work for the government building the Air Force Base in Thule, Greenland.

In 1952, the job completed, he returned home to Co Bluffs and helped with the efforts to avoid the Missouri River Flood by packing sandbags. During the next few years, the family traveled to Texas and Cheyene, Wyo, where Marty gained employment on construction sites.

On Christmas Eve, 1953, the family returned to Council Bluffs, and Marty later went to work for Micklin Home Improvement Company. After about two years, he decided to strike out on his own and established the Lockerby Construction Company. For his remaining years, he continued to build and remodel homes throughout the community and was the first contractor to build a "split level" residence in the city. The company was dissolved in 1981 and Marty went to work as the Maintenance Supervisor for the City of Council Bluffs where he remained until his retirement.

The couple then moved to Walnut, Pottawattamie County, Iowa, where they continued to reside for the next twenty-one years.

On December 5th, 2008, Marty and Betty moved back to Council Bluffs, Iowa, to be nearer to their family and medical help because their health was failing. On January 15th, 2009, Betty was diagnosed with stage four lung cancer, and died on June 1st, 2009. She was cremated and laid to rest in Walnut Hill Cemetery. Marshall continued to reside in CB until his death in 2010 on September 7th. His cremated remains were laid to rest beside his wife.

Marshall and Betty Williams Lockerby

Marshall married **Betty Alice Williams**, daughter of **James Walter Williams** and **Alta Vesta Guin**, on 20 Apr 1942 in Papillion, Sarpy Co, Nebraska.[95] Betty was born on 25 Aug 1924 in Council Bluffs, Pottawattamie Co., IA, died on 1 Jun 2009 in Council Bluffs, Pottawattamie Co., IA, and was buried on 9 Jun 2009 in Walnut Hill Cemetery, Council Bluffs, Iowa.   Children from this marriage were:

> +431   M i.   **Monte Lee Lockerby** was born on 7 Oct 1942 in Council Bluffs, Pottawattamie Co., IA, died on 4 Oct 2012 in Council Bluffs, Pott. Co., Iowa, and was buried in Walnut Hill Cemetery, Council Bluffs, Iowa.
> +432   F ii.   **Marsha Lynn Lockerby** born 10 Jun 1944 in Council Bluffs, Pottawattamie Co., IA.

294.   Raymond Freddie Haggman[56] was born on 11 Oct 1915 in Home Twp, Newaygo Co., Michigan.[56]

295.   Gertrude Muriel Haggman[56] was born on 15 Apr 1918 in Kalamazoo, MI,[56] died of Cancer on 20 Jan 1986 in Big Rapids, Mecosta Co., MI, and was buried on 23 Jan 1986 in Big Rapids, Mecosta Co., MI. Burial: Whipple Cemetery, Big Rapids, Mecosta Co., Mi.

General Notes: FAMILY HISTORY:

Muriel was born April 15, 1918, in Kalamazoo, Michigan.   Her parents were John and Olive (Lockerby) Ray.   She attended Edison Grade School and Washington Jr. High School terminating her education while in the tenth grade of Lincoln High School.

She moved with her family to Big Rapids and there gained employment bagging fruits and food commodities for the county welfare, and also working fore the NYAQ as a check girl for swimmers at Loomis Pool.

She married Thomas J. Whalen, the son of Peter and Mary (Williams) Whalen on August 24, 1940, at the home of her parents, 524 N. Michigan Ave., Big Rapids, and Michigan.   They moved to a home north of Big Rapids on 19 mile road and a year later moved northeast of Paris, Michigan.   After remaining here for a short time, they moved into the home of Muriel's parents where they were residing when their first son, Raymond Peter, was born in 1941.   Their second son, Neddie Frank, was born four years later.   Muriel and Tom divorced in 1951 and she moved to her parents' home at 611 Finley Ave., in Big Rapids.   She remained here until her death in January 1986.

Gertrude married **Thomas J. Whalen**,[56] son of **Peter Whalen** and **Mary Williams**, on 24 Aug 1940 in Big Rapids, Mecosta Co., MI.[56] Thomas was born on 19 Aug 1910 and died in Jul 1963. Children from this marriage were:

> +433   M i.   **Raymond Peter Whalen**[56] b. 2 Aug 1941 in Big Rapids, Mecosta Co., MI.[56]
> +434   M ii.   **Nedie Frank Whalen**[56] born on 26 May 1945 in Big Rapids, Mecosta Co., MI.[56]

296.   Emma Melvina Haggman[56] was born on 13 Mar 1921 in Home Twp, Newaygo Co., Michigan.[56] Emma married **L. Clint Helsel**[56] in Jan 1944.[56]

297.   Fred Erwin Bryant[56] was born on 7 Jun 1907 in Pierson, Montcolm Co, MI,[56] died on 28 Aug 1973 in Grand Rapids, Kent Co., MI, and was buried in Pierson Cemetery in 1973 in Pierson, Montcolm Co, MI.
Fred married **Mary Maxim**[56] on 24 Jun 1929.[56] Children from this marriage were:

> +435   M i.   **Jerald Bryant**[56] was born on 15 Sep 1930 in Pierson, Montcolm Co, MI.[56]

+436	M ii.	**James Bryant**[56] was born on 27 Nov 1932 in Pierson, Montcolm Co, MI, died on 22 Feb 1952, and was buried in 1952 in Pierson Cemetery, Pierson, Montcolm Co, Michigan.
+437	M iii.	**Edwin Bryant** was born in Pierson, Montcolm Co, MI.
+438	F iv.	**Mazel Bryant** was born in Pierson, Montcolm Co, MI.
+439	F v.	**Doris Bryant** was born in Pierson, Montcolm Co, MI.
+440	F vi.	**Cathy Bryant** was born in Pierson, Montcolm Co, MI.

General Notes: Beulah Totten said he married Mary Ruppert.

298. Pearl Ester Bryant[56] was born on 13 Feb 1909 in Pierson, Montcolm Co, MI.[56]   Pearl married **Roy Brisbin Sr.**. Roy was born on 22 May 1888, died on 24 Sep 1978 in Sand Lake, Kent Co., MI, and was buried in 1978 in Sand Lake Cemetery, Sand Lake, Michigan.   Children from this marriage were:

+441	F i.	**Joy Brisbin**.[56]
+442	F ii.	**Pride Brisbin**[56] was born in 1932.[56]
+443	M iii.	**Roy Brisbin Jr.**[56]

General Notes: Della Depew Lockerby's journal states Pearl Ester Bryant married Roy Brisbin but does not give the date.

299. Isabelle Elizabeth Bryant[56] was born on 19 Jun 1911 in Pierson, Montcolm Co, MI.[56] Isabelle married **William Laird Hoover** on 27 Dec 1942. William was born on 14 Feb 1913, died on 26 Jan 1964, and was buried in 1964 in Spencer Mills Cemetery, Cedar Springs, Michigan. Children from this marriage were:

+444	F i.	**Geraldine Hoover**.
+445	M ii.	**William L. Hoover Jr.**

300. Beatrice Bryant was born on 19 Apr 1914 in Pierson, Montcolm Co, MI.   Beatrice married **Russell Poulsen**. Russell was born on 30 Jul 1916, died on 29 Jan 1956, and was buried in 1956 in Trufant Cemetery, Trufant, Michigan.   Children from this marriage were:

+446	F i.	**Diane Poulsen**.
+447	M ii.	**Gary Poulsen**.

301. Gretchen Rebecca Bryant[56] was born on 6 May 1918 in Pierson, Montcolm Co, MI. Gretchen married **Lloyd Jay Weeks**,[56] son of **Burrell Weeks** and **Loretta**, on 14 Sep 1940. Lloyd was born on 30 Jul 1916.   Children from this marriage were:

+448	M i.	**Lloyd George Weeks**[56] was born on 18 Apr 1943 in Pierson, Montcolm Co, MI,[56] died on 1 Dec 1950, and was buried on 3 Dec 1950 in Elmwood Cemetery, Cedar Springs, Michigan.
+449	M ii.	**Larry Weeks**[56] was born on 6 Oct 1947 in Grand Rapids, Kent Co., MI.[56]
+450	F iii.	**Louise Weeks** was born on 6 Sep 1950 in Grand Rapids, Kent Co., MI.

302. Kenneth Bryant[56] was born on 21 Jan 1922 in Pierson, Montcolm Co, MI, died on 21 Jan 1922 in Pierson, Montcolm Co, MI, and was buried in Burial Pierson Cemetery in Pierson, Montcolm Co, MI.

303. Carroll George Bryant[56] was born on 22 Jan 1923 in Pierson, Montcolm Co, MI, died on 15 Aug 1964 in Michigan, and was buried in 1964 in Curtis Cemetery, Big Rapids, Mecosta Co., Michigan.
Carroll married **Stella Frederick** on 1 Jan 1942. Children from this marriage were:

+451	F	i.	**Sharon Bryant** was born in Oct 1942.[56]
+452	F	ii.	**Peggy Anne Bryant** was born on 3 Feb 1945.
+453	F	iii.	**Velma Bryant**.
+454	F	iv.	**Verna Bryant**.
+455	M	v.	**Jack Bryant**.
+456	F	vi.	**Jill Bryant**.

General Notes: Burial: Curtis Cemetery Funeral notices states: Services at Rogers Funeral Home in Big Rapids, Michigan at 2:30 p.m. August 17, 1964. Officiating was Rev. James Dalton. Final Resting Place; Curtis Cemetery. Bearers: Fredrick Paetke, George Dann, August Bradley, Carl Paetke, Harold Ludtke, and Harold Roland.

304. Martha Bryant[56] was born on 21 Aug 1924 in Pierson, Montcolm Co, MI,[56] died on 31 Jul 1965 in Pierson, Montcolm Co, MI, and was buried in 1965 in Pierson Cemetery, Pierson, Montcolm Co, Michigan.

General Notes: Funeral Notice: Services held at Walsh-Bliss Funeral Home Wed, Aug 4, 1965, at 1:30 jp.m. Officiating Rev. Ronald Workman. Bearers: Jerold Bryant, Edwin Bryant, Roy Bisbinn, Jr., Lloyd Weeks, Raymond Tatro, William Hoover. Burial: Pierson Cemetery

305. Unnamed Boy (twins) Lockerby[56] was born on 5 Mar 1926 in Newaygo Co., MI.[56]

306. Fred Herbert Lockerby[56] was born on 10 Mar 1929 in Newaygo Co., MI.[56]

307. Dan Arnold Lockerby[56] was born on 2 Dec 1924 in Muskegon, Michigan.[56]

Dan married **June Cousineau** on 22 Feb 1946. June was born on 23 Jun 1925, died on 21 Nov 1981 in Bitely, Mecosta Co., MI, and was buried in 1981 in Big Rapids, Mecosta Co., MI. Children from this marriage were:

+457	M	i.	**Mark Lockerby** was born on 10 Dec 1958 in Big Rapids, Mecosta Co., MI.
+458	M	ii.	**Vance Lockerby** was born on 30 Nov 1957 in Big Rapids, Mecosta Co., MI.
+459	F	iii.	**Maryjo Lockerby** was born on 2 Oct 1951 in Big Rapids, Mecosta Co., MI.

308. Betty Rea Lockerby[56] was born on 21 Oct 1926 in Muskegon, Michigan.[56] Betty married **Pete Loren Baird**,[56] son of **John Erwin Baird** and **Unknown**, on 30 Aug 1944 in Goldeberg, NC.[56] Children from this marriage were:

+460	M	i.	**Gary Lynn Baird**[56] was born on 30 Oct 1945 in Big Rapids, Mecosta Co., MI.[56]
+461	F	ii.	**Gloria Jean Baird**[56] was born on 15 Jul 1947 in Big Rapids, Mecosta Co., MI.[56]
+462	M	iii.	**John Erwin Baird**[56] was born on 20 Aug 1948 in Big Rapids, Mecosta Co., MI.[56]
+463	M	iv.	**Glen Ivan Baird** was born on 22 Dec 1949 in Big Rapids, Mecosta Co., MI.
+464	F	v.	**Kathi Sue Baird** was born on 1 Apr 1954 in Big Rapids, Mecosta Co., MI.
+465	F	vi.	**Shelley Kaye Baird** was born on 13 Jan 1966 in Orange Park, Florida.
+466	M	vii.	**David William Baird** was born on 19 Jan 1968 in Orange Park, Florida.

309. Jean Rosella Lockerby[56] was born on 23 Aug 1932 in Muskegon, Michigan.[56] Jean married **Richard Baxter** on 16 Jun 1951. Children from this marriage were:

+467	M	i.	**Bradley Baxter** was born on 16 Jun 1952.
+468	M	ii.	**Brian Baxter** was born on 21 Jan 1954.
+469	F	iii.	**Kim Baxter** was born on 31 Dec 1957.

+470   F   iv.   **Colette Baxter** was born on 7 Jul 1963.

310.   Hazel Lattin was born on 2 Oct 1896 in Catharine, Schuyler Co., NY.   Hazel married **George T. Lattin**. George was born in 1879, died in 1937 in Catharine, Schuyler Co., NY, and was buried in 1937 in Highland Mitchell Cem, Catherine, Schuyler Co, New York.   Children from this marriage were:

+471   F   i.   **Edith Lattin** was born on 8 May 1916 and died in 1942.
+472   F   ii.   **Ellen Lattin** was born on 16 Sep 1918.
+473   M   iii.   **Clyde George Lattin** was born on 5 Nov 1919.

311.   Ethel Lattin was born on 8 Oct 1897 in Catharine, Schuyler Co., NY.   Ethel married **Charles Brink**.   Children from this marriage were:

+474   F   i.   **Eleanor Ella Brink** was born on 24 Nov 1916 in Catharine, Schuyler Co., NY.
+475   F   ii.   **Grace Brink**.

312.   Albert Arthur Lattin was born on 3 Mar 1907 in Catharine, Schuyler Co., NY.   Albert married **Marjorie Dewey**, daughter of **Harry Dewey** and **Lottie Isabelle**.

313.   Tomas Banfield.

314.   Glen Banfield.

315.   Douglas Banfield.

316.   Wesley Danbury.

317.   Hubert Danbury.

318.   James Russell.

319.   William Legro Richards[13] b.17 Mar 1914.[13] Md **Sara Beavers**[13] born on 17 Apr 1924.[13]

320.   Rachel Richards[13] was born on 24 Sep 1917.[13] Rachel married **C. M. Jenks** on 22 Dec 1954.

321.   Harrison Salisbury Lockerby[13] was born on 2 Sep 1877 in Blue Earth, Minnesota[13] and died on 17 Sep 1877 in Blue Earth, Minnesota.[13]

322.   Margaret Lockerby.[13]

323.   Kenneth Lockerby Mueller[13] was born on 25 Nov 1911 in Minnesota[13] and died on 3 Sep 1978 in Blue Earth, Minnesota.[13]   Kenneth married **Lucille McQueen**.[13]

324.   Dorothy Mueller[13] was born in 1916 in Minnesota.[13]

325.   Donald Van Gorden.[13]

326.   Earl Van Gorden[13] was born on 21 Sep 1916[13] and died on 12 Sep 1981 in Hennepin Co., Minnesota.[13]

327.   James L. Van Gorden[13] was born on 29 Jun 1923[13] and died on 1 Sep 1993 in Isanti, Minnesota.[13]

328.   Violet Conklin.

329. George Elmer Conklin was born on 24 Nov 1914 and died on 4 Nov 1988.

330. Jerome K. Conklin was born on 15 Feb 1919 and died on 17 Nov 1919.

331. Hazel Lucille Conklin was born on 10 Jun 1920 in Redondo Beach, CA. Hazel married **John Adam Dvorsky**. John was born on 1 Jan 1920 and died on 19 Mar 1993 in Minneapolis, Minnesota. Children from this marriage were:

+476	M i.	**John Richard Dvorsky** was born on 24 Nov 1939 in Minneapolis, Minnesota.
+477	M ii.	**Terry Emil Dvorsky** was born on 7 Feb 1942 in Minneapolis, Minnesota.
+478	M iii.	**Ralph Bruce Dvorsky** was born on 27 Sep 1944 in Minneapolis, Minnesota.

332. Leonard M. Conklin was born on 8 Aug 1921 and died on 3 Sep 1936.

333. Ralph M. Conklin was born on 25 Aug 1922 and died on 12 May 1951.

334. Genevieve M. Conklin was born on 16 Apr 1924 and died in Feb 1976.

335. Margaret Conklin was born on 9 Mar 1929.

336. Ellsworth Bickford Lockerby[13] was born on 13 Sep 1914 in Carlinville, IL,[13] died on 18 Mar 1996 in San Mateo, California,[13] and was buried in St. John's Cemetery, San Mateo, CA.[13]

Ellsworth married **Levon B. Rice**.[13] Levon was born on 10 Jan 1919 in Iowa[13] and died on 11 Feb 1991 in San Mateo, California.[13] Children from this marriage were:

| +479 | M i. | **Robert Ellsworth Lockerby**[13] was born on 17 Nov 1956[13] and died on 27 Aug 1994 in Marin Co., CA.[13] |
| +480 | M ii. | **Shawn Lockerby**[13] was born in 1964.[13] |

337. Dorothy Frances Lockerby[13] was born in 1918 in California.[13] Dorothy married **Henry Samons**[13] in San Francisco, CA. Henry was born on 27 Mar 1911[13] and died on 20 Nov 1994 in Brownsville, Yuba Co., CA.[13] Children from this marriage were:

+481	F i.	**Beverly Ann Samons**[13] was born on 20 Jul 1938 in San Francisco, CA.[13]
+482	F ii.	**Judith Randella Samons**[13] was born on 9 Nov 1939 in San Francisco, CA.[13]
+483	F iii.	**Shirley Louise Samons**[13] was born on 12 Dec 1942 in San Francisco, CA.[13]

338. Geneva Lockerby[13] was born in 1925.[13]

339. Jay Douglas Lockerby[13] was born on 15 Aug 1918 in Ellsworth, WI,[13] died on 5 Dec 1989 in St Paul, Minnesota,[13] and was buried on 8 Dec 1989 in Woodville, WI.[13] Jay married **Marion Louise Gullickson**,[13] daughter of **Alfred Gullickson** and **Esther Johnson**, on 22 Dec 1941 in Las Vegas, NV.[13] Marion was born on 20 Jul 1919 in Forsyth, Montana[13] and died on 5 Nov 2004 in Woodville, WI.[13]
Children from this marriage were:

+484	M i.	**Michael Jay Lockerby**[13] was born on 29 Jul 1944 in Palm Springs, CA.[13]
+485	M ii.	**Hugh Alan Lockerby**[13] was born on 15 Mar 1948 in Red Wing, MN.[13]
+486	M iii.	**Frank Ellsworth Lockerby**[13] was born on 30 Nov 1949 in Red Wing, MN.[13]

General Notes: Jay Douglas Lockerby was educated at Bloomer High School in Bloomer, Wisconsin, and received a B. S. at the University of Wisconsin and an M. S. at the University of Minnesota. He served in the Army Air Corps in World War 2 and later became an Industrial Arts Teacher in Salem, Oregon, at South Salem High School. His wife, Marian Gullickson attended Woodville High School graduating in 1937 and went on to attend the University of Wisconsin attaining a B.S. in Home Economics Education in 1941.

340. Betty Jeanne Lockerby[13] was born on 1 Jan 1921 in Ellsworth, WI.[13]

General Notes: Graduated from the University of Minnesota with a B. S. in Library Science and was employed by the City of Minneapolis, Minnesota as a Librarian.

341. James Lind[13] was born on 23 Jun 1928 in Winthrop, Sibley Co., MN.[13] James married **Patricia Larson**.[13] Children from this marriage were:

+487	F	i.	**Rebecca Ann Lind**[13] was born on 23 Feb 1952.[13]
+488	F	ii.	**Cynthia Anne Lind**[13] was born on 15 Mar 1957.[13]
+489	F	iii.	**Pamela Louise Lind**[13] was born on 15 Aug 1958.[13]

342. John M. Lind[13] was born on 21 Jun 1930 in Winthrop, Sibley Co., MN.[13] John married **Mayona Sickmann** on 12 Feb 1955.[13] Children from this marriage were:

+490	M	i.	**Scott John Lind**[13] was born on 13 Aug 1957.[13]
+491	F	ii.	**Sandra Jean Lind**[13] was born on 13 Jun 1959.[13]
+492	M	iii.	**Daniel Jay Lind**[13] was born on 13 Sep 1965.[13]

343. Mary Margaret Lind[13] was born on 8 Feb 1932 in Winthrop, Sibley Co., MN.[13] Mary married **Donald Pioske**[13] on 13 Jun 1953.[13] Donald died on 27 Jul 1985 in Le Sueur Co., MN.[13] Children from this marriage were:

+493	F	i.	**Gail Kay Pioske**[13] was born on 8 Mar 1955 in New Ulm, MN.[13]
+494	M	ii.	**Steven Donald Pioske**[13] was born on 10 Jun 1956 in New Ulm, MN.[13]
+495	F	iii.	**Kerry Sue Pioske**[13] was born on 25 Dec 1958 in St. Peter, MN.[13]
+496	F	iv.	**Lynn Margaret Pioske**[13] was born on 6 Jul 1960 in Le Sueur Co., MN.[13]
+497	F	v.	**Janice Lynn Pioske**[13] was born on 29 Aug 1963 in Le Sueur Co., MN.[13]
+498	M	vi.	**Gregg Allen Pioske**[13] was born on 11 Jan 1967 in Le Sueur Co., MN.[13]
+499	F	vii.	**Lori Sue Pioske**[13] was born on 13 Nov 1968 in Le Sueur Co., MN.[13]
+500	M	viii.	**Gary Steven Pioske**[13] was born on 10 Apr 1971 in Le Sueur Co., MN.[13]

344. Lucille Lockerby[13] was born in 1924 in Washington.[13] Lucille married **Earl F. Luebker**.[13]

345. Joan Lockerby[13] was born in 1929 in Washington.[13] Joan married **A. W. Haslett**.[13]

346. Abbie Waterman[13] was born in May 1889 in Wisconsin.[13]

347. Gretchen Waterman[13] was born in Apr 1891 in Wisconsin.[13]

348. Eleanor Waterman[13] was born in Mar 1894 in Wisconsin.[13]

349. Isabelle Waterman[13] was born in Aug 1896 in Wisconsin.[13]

350. Francis Waterman[13] was born in Dec 1899 in Wisconsin.[13]

Eighth Generation

351. Maynard Lyon was born on 7 May 1893.

352. Jesse Gordon Lyon was born on 19 Sep 1896.

353. Gretchen Kaufman was born on 25 Jul 1914.

354. Henry William Kaufman was born on 3 Jul 1916.

355. Jean Louise Kaufman was born on 5 Jul 1924.

356. Aline Brown. Aline married **George Heineck**. The child from this marriage was:
Aline and her husband George Heineck resided at Rochester, New York and had two children but only one is recorded here.

+ 501   M i.   **Duane Heineck**.

357. Wilbur Brown. Wilbur married **Ruth Rexford**. Wilbur moved to Oregon and had four children.

358. Carl Richard Hansen was born on 28 Jul 1927 in Iowa. Carl married **Martha Elisebeth Sorensen**. Martha was born on 15 Jan 1931 in Minnesota. Children from this marriage were:

+ 502   M i.   **Carl Richard Hansen** was born on 21 Jul 1954 in Minnesota.
+ 503   F ii.   **Teri Lyn Hansen** was born on 1 Dec 1955 in Minnesota.
+ 504   M iii.   **Douglas Kirk Hansen** was born on 28 Jan 1957 in Minnesota.

359. Ardythe Mae Van Vlack born on 7 Aug 1918. She married **David B. Townsend Jr.** 30 Mar 1941.

360. James Van Gibson was born on 18 Mar 1937.

361. Patricia Smith. Patricia married **Ronald Lakey**.

362. Mary Janice Smith. Mary married **Keith Callies** in 1948. Children from this marriage were:

+ 505   F i.   **Kathy Lynn Callies** was born in 1949.
+ 506   M ii.   **Kevan Callies** was born in 1951.

363. Marshall Smith was born on 5 Dec 1945.

364. Rebecca Lee Smith was born on 16 Aug 1947.

365. Eleanor June Smith was born on 23 Jun 1950.

366. Peggy Reidena Van Vlack.

367. Kristine Marie Van Vlack died at birth.

368. David Van Vlack was born on 8 Jul 1946.

369. Richard Howard Stine was born in 1932. Richard served in the U. S. Navy for four years. He married **Sandra**. The child from this marriage:

+507   F i.   **Mary Ellen Stine** was born on 8 Oct 1955.

370. David Oliver Stine was born in 1936.   David attended California State College and was a member of the Air Force Reserves.

371. Steven Van Vlack Stine.

372. Stanley Reid Stine.

373. Linda Lou Van Vlack was born on 18 Jun 1941.

374. Judith Ann Van Vlack was born on 5 Nov 1943.

375. Sally Ann Jahnke was born on 15 Jan 1945.

376. Joseph Claire Jahnke was born on 25 Sep 1947.

377. Steven Ancil Wallingford was born on 30 May 1945 in Des Moines, Polk Co., Iowa.

378. William Edward Wallingford was born on 19 Oct 1948 in Yakima, Washington.

379. Kristine Marie Van Vlack was born on 8 Dec 1947.

380. Barbara Jo Van Vlack was born on 14 Aug 1950.

381. Patti Jean Van Vlack was born on 25 Mar 1954.

382. Cynthia Marie Amick was born on 26 Feb 1947.

383. Mary Anadell Jackson was born on 19 Jan 1952 in Fairfield, Iowa.

384. Nora Delight Lockerby[16] was born on 8 Mar 1942 in Faribault, Rice Co., MN.[16]   Nora married **Linn Dean Gustafson**,[16] son of **Gustaf Helmar Gustafson** and **Ethel Ellen Goff**, on 29 Aug 1964 in Faribault, Rice Co., MN.[16] Linn was born on 5 Jan 1941 in Monmouth, Illinois.[16] Children from this marriage were:

+508   F i.   **Amy Sue Gustafson**[16] was born on 14 Sep 1966 in Faribault, Rice Co., MN.[16]
+509   F ii.   **Jennifer Elise Gustafson**[16] b. 5 Apr 1969 in Weisbaden, Hesse, W. Germany.[16]
+510   F iii.   **Gretchen Suzanne Gustafson**[16] was born on 16 Aug 1973 in Colorado Springs, El Paso, Colorado.[16]

385. Dwight R. Lockerby was born on 9 Dec 1945. Dwight married **Aleanne M. Glynn** on 24 Jul 1970.   Children from this marriage were:

+511   M i.   **Saul Dwight Lockerby** was born on 21 Jul 1973.
+512   F ii.   **Kristan Suzan Lockerby** was born on 25 Mar 1976.

386. John Balow.

387. Rosemary Balow was born on 8 Jun 1944.

General Notes: Mary Balow (October 19, 1986 correspondance) said she had four children: ages 37, 42, 46, and 48.   John and Rosemary (she married a BECK) were living in San Jose, California

388. Alan F. Cook was born in 1928. Alan married **Jean Thor**. Jean was born in 1930.

389. Elizabeth Walker.

390. Lester Leon Walker.

391. Katherine Ann Washburn.

392. John Washburn.

393. Ernest Arthur Vann was born on 16 Oct 1936. Went to Camp Dix, New Jersey

394. Harry Lloyd Totten was born on 3 May 1930.   Harry married **Bernice Girvin** on 1 May 1954. Bernice was born on 23 Oct 1934 in Coeur D'Alene, Idaho.   Children from this marriage were:

+513	F	i.	**Linda Marie Totten** was born on 31 Oct 1955.
+514	F	ii.	**Catherine Ann Totten.**
+515	F	iii.	**Karen Leah Totten.**

395. Robert James Totten was born on 25 Mar 1934. Robert married **Heather Patricia Rodckwell** in 1975 in Cranbrook, British Columbia, Canada. Children from this marriage were:

+516	M	i.	**James Totten** was born on 28 Jun 1976.
+517	F	ii.	**Melody Lea Totten** was born on 29 Sep 1977.

396. Shirley Lorna Totten was born on 29 May 1935. Shirley married **Norman Farmiloe Green** on 23 May 1955 in Coeur D'Alene, Idaho. Children from this marriage were:

+518	F	i.	**Joyce Audry Green** was born on 3 Jan 1956.
+519	M	ii.	**Robert Norman Farmiloe Green** was born on 21 Feb 1959.
+520	M	iii.	**David James Farmiloe Green** was born on 15 Sep 1962.

397. Genevieve Mabel Totten was born on 20 Oct 1937. Genevieve married **Warren Gleason** on 19 Dec 1954 in Coeur D'Alene, Idaho. Children from this marriage were:

+521	M	i.	**Lawrence Warren Gleason** was born on 14 Jul 1955.
+522	F	ii.	**Lorna Faye Gleason** was born on 5 Sep 1957.
+523	M	iii.	**Terrance Leslie Gleason** was born on 25 Apr 1959.
+524	F	iv.	**Kelly Gleason** was born on 9 Dec 1960.
+525	F	v.	**Shawna Gaye Gleason** was born on 30 Jul 1963.

398. Kathleen Marie Brower[56] was born on 15 Apr 1929 in Grand Rapids, Kent Co., MI.[56] Kathleen married **Clyde E. Lee.**   Children from this marriage were:

+526	F	i.	**Cheryl Kay Lee** was born on 29 Apr 1954.
+527	M	ii.	**Jon Timothy Lee** was born on 8 Feb 1958.

399. Marilyn May Brower[56] was born on 28 Feb 1932 in Grand Rapids, Kent Co., MI.[56] Marilyn married **Richard Van Dyke,**[56] son of **Unknown** and **Unknown.**   Children from this marriage were:

+528	M	i.	**Richard Allen Van Dyke** was born on 24 Apr 1952 and died in 1976.
+529	M	ii.	**Michael Glen Van Dyke** was born on 5 Jul 1955.
+530	F	iii.	**Vickie Marie Van Dyke.**
+531	M	iv.	**Timoth Lee Van Dyke.**

400. Burdette H. Zandstra[56] was born on 25 Sep 1931 in Highland, Indiana.[56]   Burdette married **Eileen Joyce Haasksma** on 10 Jun 1955. Eileen was born on 2 Feb 1936 in Chicago, Cook Co., IL. Children from this marriage were:

+532	F	i.	**Karen Lynn Zandstra** was born on 16 Apr 1956 in Hammond, Indiana.
+533	M	ii.	**Frederick John Zandstra** was born on 25 Jun 1957 in Hammond, Indiana.
+534	F	iii.	**Victoria Dawn Zandstra** was born on 21 Mar 1959 in Hammond, Indiana.
+535	F	iv.	**Cheryl Marie Zandstra** was born on 27 Dec 1962 in Hammond, Indiana.
+536	F	v.	**Sandra Jean Zandstra** was born on 28 May 1966 in Hammond, Indiana.

401.   John Paul Zandstra[56] was born on 12 Oct 1934 in Munster, Indiana.[56]   John married **Barbara Jean Alters** on 12 Nov 1954. Barbara was born on 12 Feb 1934 in Hammond, Indiana. Children from this marriage were:

+537	M	i.	**Daniel William Zandstra** was born on 22 Apr 1957 in Hammond, Indiana.
+538	F	ii.	**Patricia Jean Zandstra** was born on 8 Jun 1958 in Hammond, Indiana.
+539	M	iii.	**John Bartel Zandstra** was born on 30 Jul 1961 in Hammond, Indiana.
+540	M	iv.	**Jerry Zandstra** was born on 20 May 1964 in Hammond, Indiana.

402.   Jerry Allen Zandstra[56] was born on 12 May 1939 in Hammond, Indiana.   Jerry married **Jacqueline Gay Lagester** on 31 Aug 1962. Jacqueline was born on 27 Oct 1942 in Hammond, Indiana.   Children from this marriage were:

+541	F	i.	**Anita Marie Zandstra** born on 29 Jan 1964 in Grand Rapids, Kent Co., MI.
+542	M	ii.	**Daryl Zandstra** was born on 23 Mar 1967 in Patterson, New Jersey.

403.   Elaine Zandstra[56] was born on 15 Mar 1942 in Hammond, Indiana.[56]   Elaine married **John William Ooms** on 11 Nov 1960. John was born on 21 Jul 1941 in Hammond, Indiana.   Children from this marriage were:

+543	M	i.	**William John Ooms** was born on 27 Jul 1961 in Valparaiso, Indiana.
+544	M	ii.	**Russel Dean Ooms** was born on 9 Jul 1962 in Valparaiso, Indiana.
+545	M	iii.	**Randall Scott Ooms** was born on 3 Oct 1963 in Valparaiso, Indiana.
+546	F	iv.	**Eunice Kay Ooms** was born on 19 Oct 1967 in Hammond, Indiana.
+547	M	v.	**Andrew Jay Ooms** was born on 27 Feb 1971 in Wausau, Wisconsin.

404.   Eunice Zandstra was born on 19 Jan 1945 in Hammond, Indiana.[56]   Eunice married **George Mossel** on 27 Aug 1965. George was born on 2 Apr 1945 in South Holland, Illinois. Children from this marriage were:

+548	M	i.	**Robert George Mossel** was born on 6 Jan 1971 in Ann Arbor, Michgian.
+549	M	ii.	**Todd Calvin Mossel** was born on 18 Jul 1974 in Wausau, Wisconsin.
+550	M	iii.	**John Edward Mossel** born on 10 Apr 1977 in Grand Rapids, Kent Co., MI.

405.   Betty Annette Totten was born on 31 Oct 1934.   Betty married **Colin Roy Sinclair**, son of **Colin Sinclair** and **Alice**, on 4 Apr 1953 in Newgate, British Columbia, Canada. Colin was born on 24 Dec 1933.   Children from this marriage were:

+551	F	i.	**Annette Arlene Sinclair** was born on 30 Mar 1954.
+552	M	ii.	**Gordon Roy Sinclair** was born on 6 Jun 1955.
+553	M	iii.	**Colin Robert Sinclair** was born on 14 Nov 1957 and died on 30 Nov 1957.
+554	M	iv.	**Colin Fraser Sinclair** was born on 27 Nov 1961.
+555	F	v.	**Annelle Rowena Sinclair** was born on 1 Feb 1963.

406.   Paul Leon Totten Jr. was born on 28 Jan 1936. Paul married **Sandra Joy Hunter** on 29 Aug 1958 in San Francisco, CA. Sandra was born in Jun 1940.   Children from this marriage were:

+556	M	i.	**Robert Totten** was born on 21 Jun 1959.
+557	M	ii.	**Keith Lee Totten** was born on 20 Jun 1961.

407.   Walter Patrick Totten was born on 17 Mar 1940. Walter married **Panela Nancy Chambless** on 4 Sep 1964. Panela was born on 3 Mar 1933.   Children from this marriage were:

+558	M	i.	**Matthew Vincent Fraidenburg Totten** was born on 11 Jun 1958.
+559	F	ii.	**Karen Lynn Fraidenburg Totten**.

408.   David Keith Totten was born on 2 Aug 1935. David married **Normagene Elaine Deal** on 11 Aug 1960. Children from this marriage were:

+560	M	i.	**David Lee Totten** was born on 28 Dec 1959.
+561	F	ii.	**Diana Dee Totten** was born on 28 Dec 1959.
+562	F	iii.	**Naoma Ruth Totten** was born on 21 Jul 1961.

409.   Donald Leo Totten was born on 1 Feb 1937.   Donald married **Joan Enile Marsh**, daughter of **Harold A. Marsh** and **Violet Nix**, on 28 Mar 1958. Joan was born on 28 Mar 1938 in Reed City, Michigan.   Children from this marriage were:

+563	M	i.	**Douglas Leon Totten** was born on 6 Mar 1961 in Plymouth, Indiana.
+564	M	ii.	**Jeffrey Eric Totten** was born on 3 Mar 1963 in Reed City, Michigan.

410.   Karen Margaret Totten was born on 20 Aug 1941. Karen married **Ronald Freiberg**, son of **Edward Freiberg** and **Lela**, on 10 Jun 1961. Children from this marriage were:

+565	F	i.	**Gretchen Freiberg** was born on 15 May 1964.
+566	M	ii.	**Gregory Freiberg** was born on 13 Feb 1966.
+567	F	iii.	**Jennifer Freiberg** was born on 22 Sep 1968.
+568	M	iv.	**Joel Freiberg** was born on 23 Oct 1972.

411.   Christopher Wayne Totten was born on 1 Jun 1947. Christopher married **Janet Morris**, daughter of **Y. O. Morris** and **Unknown**.

412.   Duane Edwin Totten was born in Feb 1937 in Big Rapids, Mecosta Co., MI.   Duane married **Janet Louise Kilbourne** in Jun 1956. Janet was born in 1935 in "of Stanwood, Michigan". Children from this marriage were:

+569	M	i.	**Marc Edwin Totten** was born in Aug 1959 in Grand Rapids, Kent Co., MI.
+570	F	ii.	**Michelle Louise Totten** born in May 1962 in Big Rapids, Mecosta Co., MI.

413.   Dewey Lee Totten was born in Apr 1943 in Big Rapids, Mecosta Co., MI.   Dewey married **Gloria Louise Schmit** in Jun 1963. Gloria was born in "of Minot, North Dakota".   Children from this marriage were:

+571	F	i.	**Lisa Kay Totten** was born in Jan 1967 in Big Rapids, Mecosta Co., MI.
+572	M	ii.	**Kevin Lynn Totten** was born in May 1969 in Big Rapids, Mecosta Co., MI.
+573	F	iii.	**April Lee Totten** was born in Jun 1972 in Lakeview, Montcalm County, Michigan.
+574	F	iv.	**Jolene Lynnette Totten** was born in 1975 in Lakeview, Montcalm County, Michigan.

414.   Donna Lou Totten was born in Oct 1944 in Big Rapids, Mecosta Co., MI.   Donna married **Charence John Churchill** on 29 Jun 1963 in Methodist Church, Reed City, Michigan.   Children from this marriage were:

+575	M	i.	**David John Churchill** was born in Dec 1964 in Reed City, Michigan.
+576	F	ii.	**Doreen robin Churchill** was born in May 1966 in Reed City, Michigan.

415. Susan Mae Totten was born in Mar 1952 in Big Rapids, Mecosta Co., MI. Susan married **Rodney Thurston Bressler** in Mar 1970. Rodney was born in "of Adrain, Michigan). Children from this marriage were:

   +577   M i.   **Jeffery Duane Bressler** was born in Oct 1971 in Adrain, Michigan.
   +578   M ii.   **Benjamin William Bressler** was born in Aug 1974 in Adrain, Michigan.
   +579   M iii.   **Daniel Thurston Bressler** was born in May 1977 in Adrain, Michigan.

416. Billie Jean Totten was born in May 1953 in Big Rapids, Mecosta Co., MI.

417. Walter Cornel Wright[94] was born on 17 Feb 1947 in Big Rapids, Mecosta Co., MI.[94] Walter married **Rebeca Marie Arndt**.

General Notes: Military: United States Army Feb 17, 1966, in Hq & Co. A. 123rd Maint Bn lst Armed Div, Fort Hoot, Texas, Fourth US Army.   Stationed for a time in Vietnam.

418. Wayne Edward Wright[94] was born on 25 Aug 1949 in Big Rapids, Mecosta Co., MI.[94]   Wayne married **Sandra Miles**, daughter of **Samuel Miles** and **Jean**, on 29 Apr 1972. Sandra was born on 20 Mar 1950.   Children from this marriage were:

   +580   F i.   **Lisa Marie Wright** was born on 15 Aug 1969 in Lakeview, Montcalm County, Michigan.
   +581   F ii.   **Beulah Jean Wright** was born on 28 Apr 1973 in Lakeview, Montcalm County, Michigan.
   +582   M iii.   **Wayne Edward Wright Jr.** was born on 22 Jan 1976 in Lakeview, Montcalm County, Michigan.
   +583   M iv.   **Henry Jay Wright** was born on 17 Feb 1982 in Lakeview, Montcalm County, Michigan.

General Notes: Military: Enlisted in the US Army on Nov 20, 1967 in Co. B. 864th Engr Bn.   Served in Vietnam

419. Anna Belle Wright[94] was born on 30 Sep 1950 in Big Rapids, Mecosta Co., MI.   Anna married **Loren "Ben" Bennett Kelsey** on 26 Dec 1970. Children from this marriage were:

   +584   M i.   **Loren Bennett Kelsey Jr.** was born on 16 Feb 1972 in Big Rapids, Mecosta Co., MI.
   +585   F ii.   **Nina Ann Kelsey** was born on 23 Oct 1973 in Virginia.

General Notes: Birth: born with a "VALE" over her face
Military Service: Enlisted in the US Army and served as an X-Ray Tech
Profession: Ultra-Sound Equipment operator at the local hospital in Shelby, Michigan (1993)

420. Carylon Louise Wright[94] was born on 8 Sep 1953 in Big Rapids, Mecosta Co., MI.   Carylon married **Ronald Dale Towns**, son of **Dale Towns** and **Joyce Stilson**, on 15 Jan 1972. Children from this marriage were:

   +586   F i.   **Carol Lynn Towns** was born on 20 Aug 1972 in Big Rapids, Mecosta Co., MI.
   +587   F ii.   **Janice Erma Towns** was born on 3 Oct 1975 in Big Rapids, Mecosta Co., MI.

421. Doris Jean Wright[94] was born on 26 Mar 1954 in Big Rapids, Mecosta Co., MI.   Doris married **Dennis Alan Freeland**, son of **Melvin Freeland Jr.** and **Evelyn Austin**, on 26 Mar 1972. Dennis was born on 26 Sep 1952.   Children from this marriage were:

   +588   M i.   **Dennis Alan Freeland II** was born on 17 Sep 1972 in Big Rapids, Mecosta Co., MI.

+589	F ii.	**Jennifer Misty Freeland** was born on 28 Feb 1976 in Grand Rapids, Kent Co., MI.
+590	M iii.	**Lance Edward Freeland** born on 29 Aug 1978 in Grand Rapids, Kent Co., MI.

422. Warren E. Wright[94] was born on 14 Mar 1956 in Big Rapids, Mecosta Co., MI. Warren married **Barbara Ann Freiberg**, daughter of **Tom Freiberg** and **Starn**, on 25 Dec 1976. Barbara was born on 22 Apr 1960. Children from this marriage were:

+591	M i.	**Gregory Warren Wright** was born on 11 May 1977 in Big Rapids, Mecosta Co., MI.
+592	F ii.	**Cami Jo Wright** was born on 26 Sep 1979 in Witchi Falls, Texas.

General Notes: Military Service: US Army (E-6 C. Company 44th Signal Battalion.)

423. Juanita Miner was born on 9 Jan 1938 in Council Bluffs, Pottawattamie Co., IA. Juanita married **Rex Root**. The child from this marriage was:

+593	M i.	**Eric Matthew Root** was born on 5 Mar 1971.

424. Gloria Miner was born from 1938 to 1939 in Council Bluffs, Pottawattamie Co., IA, died in 1942 in Council Bluffs, Pottawattamie Co., IA, and was buried in 1942 in Council Bluffs, Pottawattamie Co., IA.

425. Beverly Kay Miner was born on 6 Feb 1941 in Council Bluffs, Pottawattamie Co., IA. Beverly married **Ronald Harry Basch** on 1 Nov 1958 in Council Bluffs, Pottawattamie Co., IA. Ronald was born on 16 Jul 1938 in Logan, Harrison County, Iowa. Children from this marriage were:

+594	F i.	**Rhonda Kay Basch** born on 13 Jul 1959 in Missouri Valley, Harrison Co., IA.
+595	F ii.	**Connie Sue Basch** born 31 Jul 1961 in Council Bluffs, Pottawattamie Co., IA.
+596	F iii.	**Annette Gay Basch** b. 13 May 1963 in Council Bluffs, Pottawattamie Co., IA.
+597	M iv.	**Joseph Henry Basch** b. 27 Oct 1966 in Council Bluffs, Pottawattamie Co., IA.

426. Craig William Miner was born on 26 Mar 1945 in Council Bluffs, Pottawattamie Co., IA. Craig married **Ester**. Children from this marriage were:

+598	F i.	**Michelle Miner** was born on 29 Jan 1975 in California.
+599	F ii.	**Theresa Miner**.
+600	M iii.	**Jeffrey Miner** was born on 25 Jan 1981.

427. Sharon Ann Lockerby was born on 23 Jul 1945 in Council Bluffs, Pottawattamie Co., IA. Sharon married **Joseph Peter Wyatt** on 10 Sep 1963 in Council Bluffs, Pottawattamie Co., IA. Joseph was born on 24 Aug 1940 in Council Bluffs, Pottawattamie Co., IA. Children from this marriage were:

+601	F i.	**Vicki Kaye Wyatt** b. 4 Jun 1965 in Council Bluffs, Pottawattamie Co., IA.
+602	F ii.	**Julie Ann Wyatt** b.7 Jun 1967 in Council Bluffs, Pottawattamie Co., IA.

NOTE: She married 2nd to James Storey and had another daughter, Jamie.

428. Susan Elaine Lockerby was born on 7 May 1948 in Council Bluffs, Pottawattamie Co., IA. Susan married **Micahel Richard Ahrens**. Children from this marriage were:

+603	F i.	**Penny Sue Ahrens** b. 25 Jan 1968 in Council Bluffs, Pottawattamie Co., IA.
+604	M ii.	**Michael Richard Ahrens Jr.** was born on 25 Feb 1970 in Council Bluffs, Pottawattamie Co., IA.

429. Gloria Jean Lockerby was born on 27 May 1951 in Council Bluffs, Pottawattamie Co., IA.

Gloria married **Robert Sales**, son of **Herbert Sales** and **Gertrude McIntosh**, on 28 Jan 1970 in Council Bluffs, Pottawattamie Co., IA.   Children from this marriage were:

+605   F   i.   **Amy Mae Sales** b. 26 Jun 1973 in Council Bluffs, Pottawattamie Co., IA.
+606   F   ii.   **April Mae Sales** b. 26 Jun 1973 in Council Bluffs, Pottawattamie Co., IA.
+607   M   iii.   **Robert Joe Sales Jr.** b. 21 May 1970 in Council Bluffs, Pottawattamie Co., IA.
+608   F   iv.   **Angela Marie Sales** was born on 25 May 1976 in Omaha, Douglas Co., NE.
+609   F   v.   **Amanda Jo Sales** born on 16 Nov 1981 in Council Bluffs, Pottawattamie Co., IA.

430.   Terry Leroy Lockerby was born on 14 Oct 1956 in Council Bluffs, Pottawattamie Co., IA. Terry married **Rhonda Richardson**.   The child from this marriage was:

+610   M   i.   **Terry LeRoy Lockerby Jr** was born on 14 Feb 1977 in Council Bluffs, Pottawattamie Co., IA.

Monte "Biff" Lockerby and Marsha Lynn Lockerby

431.   Monte Lee Lockerby was born on 7 Oct 1942 in Council Bluffs, Pottawattamie Co., IA, died on 4 Oct 2012 in Council Bluffs, Pott. Co., Iowa, and was buried in Walnut Hill Cemetery, Council Bluffs, Iowa.

General Notes: FAMILY HISTORY:

Monte Lee Lockerby "Biff" was granted eternal rest on October 4th, 2012, following an extensive battle with congestive heart failure.   He was born on October 7, 1942, to Marshall Samuel and Betty Alice (Williams) Lockerby.

On October 18, 1963, he married Sandra Thomas in Council Bluffs, Iowa, and had one child, Patricia Ann, born March 12, 1964.

Biff excelled in Track and Field in High School and received the Honorary Baton from Drake University for winning or placing in ten track events during his senior year.   He became a "Light Weight" boxer and was the Midwest Golden Gloves Champion in 1967, advanced to the National Championships in Kansas City, Missouri, and placed second.   He was invited to participate in the 1968 Olympics but declined.

During his early years, he worked for the family-owned business of Lockerby Construction and in this capacity built, or refurbished, numerous homes in the Council Bluffs Community.   After his father retired, he gained employment with the Council Bluffs School System as a carpenter and retired from there in 2000 following a massive heart attack.

Biff was likely best known for his strong love and loyalty to family and friends, his wonderful sense of humor, his love of classic cars and his impersonations of Elvis Presley.   He lived life with a real zest and enjoyed almost 70 years before being called to rest,

He was preceded in death by his parents and many dear friends.   He is survived by his special love, Vickie Colpitts; sister, Marsha Pilger and husband, Ronald; daughter, Patricia (Lockerby) Brown; three grandchildren: Anthony (and wife, Rachel) Hernandez; Nathan Mount; Kelsey Brown, and one great grandchild: Noah Hernandez; and nieces, nephews and numerous cousins and friends.

Celebration of Life services held at Cutler Funeral Home October 8, 2012.   His cremated remains were buried with his parents in Walnut Hill Cemetery.

Monte married **Sandra Ann Thomas**, daughter of **Douglas Thomas** and **Verna Kelson**, on 18 Oct 1963 in Council Bluffs, Pottawattamie Co., IA. Sandra was born on 19 Oct 1944 in Council Bluffs, Pottawattamie Co., IA.   The child from this marriage was:

+611   F i.   **Patricia Ann Lockerby**   b. 12 Mar 1964 in Council Bluffs, Pottawattamie Co., IA.

432.   Marsha Lynn Lockerby was born on 10 Jun 1944 in Council Bluffs, Pottawattamie Co., IA. Marsha married **Ronald Gene Pilger** on 17 Jul 1965 in Council Bluffs, Pottawattamie Co., IA.[96] Ronald was born on 29 Sep 1943 in Council Bluffs, Pottawattamie Co., IA.   Children from this marriage were:

+612   M i.   **Timothy Scott Pilger** was born on 13 Dec 1968 in Dennison, , Crawford Co., Iowa.
+613   M ii.   **Andrew Gene Pilger** was born on 9 Mar 1974 in Omaha, Douglas Co., NE.

General Notes: FAMILY HISTORY:

Marsha Lynn Lockerby was born June 10, 1944, in Council Bluffs, Iowa, to parents, Marshall Samuel and Betty Alice (Williams) Lockerby. She attended Elementary school in Council Bluffs, and in 1962 Graduated from Thomas Jefferson High School. She continued her education by attending Bellevue University in Bellevue, Nebraska, and Victors Comp. College in Omaha, Nebraska, and gained employment with Northwestern Bell Telephone Company in Omaha and remained there for eight years.

She met her husband, Ronald Gene Pilger, at Thomas Jefferson High School and married him at Timothy Lutheran Church, in Council Bluffs, on July 17, 1965. Ron was the son of Perry Waldo Emerson and Hattie Mary Elizabeth (Malzahn) Pilger. He was born September 29, 1943, at the home of his parents in Council Bluffs.

Ron graduated from T.J. in 1961 and enlisted in the United States Navy on July 7th, the same year. He took his basic training in San Diego, California and attended Boiler Tech School at the Great Lakes Naval Training Center in Chicago, Illinois. He was later transferred the U.S.S. Hopewell which was a destroyer in the 7th Fleet. and in 1964/5, was in the Tonkin Gulf off the shore of Vietnam. On February 12, 1965, he was given an Honorable discharge from the Navy and returned to Council Bluffs.

In 1969, the couple adopted their first son, Timothy Scott Pilger (b. Dec 13, 1968), from the Christian Home Association in CB, and on March 9th, 1974, their second son, Andrew Gene Pilger, was born. This second adoption was through a private source. Both boys were baptized in the Lutheran Church; Timothy was baptized by Pastor Richard Nagler, at Timothy Lutheran Church, and Andrew was baptized by Pastor Hartfield at St. Paul's Lutheran Church.

Ronald is employed as a Sheet Metal Journeyman for local number 3, and works for Hemple Sheet Metal, in Omaha, Nebraska. He retired in October 2003. Marsha later became employed at U. S. Bank in Council Bluffs. She retired from US Bank in 2001 and became the Office Manager for Kouri Management and Oakland Properties Corporation.

Marsha is a charter member of various chapters of Beta Sigma Phi Sorority and a lifetime member of this organization. She served seven years as President of the Pottawattamie County (IA) Genealogical Society and is a proud member of the Daughter's of the American Revolution; the Society of Mayflower Descendants; The National Huguenot Society, and the Ancient and Honorable Artillery Company. She has been the editor of the Genealogical Society Quarterly for the past seven years and has written numerous family history books; compiled one book of Poetry entitled "Reflections" and another entitled, "Hourglass" and as of 2022 has published five non-fiction books with more to come. These are available through Barnes and Nobles and Amazon.com.

433. Raymond Peter Whalen[56] was born on 2 Aug 1941 in Big Rapids, Mecosta Co., MI.[56]

434. Nedie Frank Whalen[56] was born on 26 May 1945 in Big Rapids, Mecosta Co., MI.[56]

435. Jerald Bryant[56] was born on 15 Sep 1930 in Pierson, Montcolm Co, MI.[56]

436. James Bryant[56] was born on 27 Nov 1932 in Pierson, Montcolm Co, MI, died on 22 Feb 1952, and was buried in 1952 in Pierson Cemetery, Pierson, Montcolm Co, Michigan.

437. Edwin Bryant was born in Pierson, Montcolm Co, MI. Edwin married someone. His children were:

+614	F	i.	**Mazel Bryant** was born in Pierson, Montcolm Co, MI.
+615	F	ii.	**Doris Bryant** was born in Pierson, Montcolm Co, MI.
+616	F	iii.	**Cathy Bryant** was born in Pierson, Montcolm Co, MI.

438. **Mazel Bryant** was born in Pierson, Montcolm Co, MI.

439. **Doris Bryant** was born in Pierson, Montcolm Co, MI.

440. **Cathy Bryant** was born in Pierson, Montcolm Co, MI.

441. **Joy Brisbin**.[56]

442. **Pride Brisbin**[56] was born in 1932.[56]

443. **Roy Brisbin Jr.**[56] (Notes: Delphine Depew Lockerby's journal gives his date of marriage as: "September 22, 1956" but does not list his wife's name.)

444. **Geraldine Hoover**.

445. **William L. Hoover Jr.**

446. **Diane Poulsen**.

447. **Gary Poulsen**.

448. **Lloyd George Weeks**[56] was born on 18 Apr 1943 in Pierson, Montcolm Co, MI,[56] died on 1 Dec 1950, and was buried on 3 Dec 1950 in Elmwood Cemetery, Cedar Springs, Michigan.

General Notes: Funeral Notice states the services were held at the First Baptist Church Dec 3, 1950, at 2:30 p.m.   Officiating was Rev. H. O. Van Gilder, Jr.   Pallbearers were: Bob Ploeg, Dick Morris, Gene DeGraaf, Frank Austin.   Burial in Elmwood Cemetery

449. **Larry Weeks**[56] was born on 6 Oct 1947 in Grand Rapids, Kent Co., MI.[56] Larry married **Sara Walsh**. Sara was born in Grand Rapids, Kent Co., MI.   Children from this marriage were:

+617   M i.   **Jason Guy Weeks** was born on 3 Mar 1970 in Philidelphia, Pennsylvania.
+618   F ii.   **Brooke Weeks** was born on 14 Jun 1971.

450. **Louise Weeks** was born on 6 Sep 1950 in Grand Rapids, Kent Co., MI. Louise married **Thomas Leathers** on 1 Apr 1972. Thomas was born in "of Warren, Pennsylvania".

451. **Sharon Bryant** was born in Oct 1942.[56]

452. **Peggy Anne Bryant** was born on 3 Feb 1945.   Peggy married **Glenn Arthur Gould**. Glenn was born on 15 Aug 1943.   Children from this marriage were:

+619   F i.   **Brenda Anne Gould** was born on 17 Aug 1964.
+620   F ii.   **Bianca Louise Gould** was born on 8 Apr 1967.

453. **Velma Bryant**.

454. **Verna Bryant**.

455. **Jack Bryant**.

456. **Jill Bryant**.

457. **Mark Lockerby** was born on 10 Dec 1958 in Big Rapids, Mecosta Co., MI.   Co-Owner of Lockerby Sawmill in Bitely, Michigan.   Mark married **Charlotte Willis**, daughter of **Leon Willis** and **Helen**, on 18 Oct 1980. Charlotte was born on 12 Jan 1956 in Douglasville, Cobb Co., Georgia.

458. Vance Lockerby was born on 30 Nov 1957 in Big Rapids, Mecosta Co., MI. Co-Owner of Lockerby Sawmill in Bitely, Michigan. Vance married **Charlotte Luthy**, daughter of **Ervin Fredrick Luthy** and **Joyce Elaine Meyers**, on 1 Nov 1975. Charlotte was born on 5 Mar 1957. Children from this marriage were:

+621   M i.   **Jacob Lockerby** was born on 17 Apr 1977 in Grand Rapids, Kent Co., MI.
+622   F ii.   **Danielle Lee Lockerby** born on 20 Aug 1980 in Grand Rapids, Kent Co., MI.
+623   M iii.   **Joshua Luthy Lockerby** b. 25 Aug 1982 in Grand Rapids, Kent Co., MI.

459. Maryjo Lockerby was born on 2 Oct 1951 in Big Rapids, Mecosta Co., MI. Maryjo married **Robert Bongard**, son of **Robert Richard Bongard** and **Phyllis Linteuth**, on 17 Oct 1981. Robert was born on 25 Nov 1955. The child from this marriage was:

+624   F i.   **Jennifer June Bongard** born on 2 Jun 1983 in Grand Rapids, Kent Co., MI.

460. Gary Lynn Baird[56] was born on 30 Oct 1945 in Big Rapids, Mecosta Co., MI.[56]

Gary married **Nikki Bolyjack**, daughter of **Mr. Bolyjack Bolyjack** and **Unknown**, on 10 Feb 1968 in Fairbanks, Alaska. Nikki was born on 15 Feb 1947. Children from this marriage were:

+625   M i.   **Bradley Baird** was born on 5 Oct 1973 in Orlando, Florida.
+626   F ii.   **Shann Baird** was born on 25 Dec 1976 in Miami, Florida.

461. Gloria Jean Baird[56] was born on 15 Jul 1947 in Big Rapids, Mecosta Co., MI.[56] Gloria married **Barry Wood**, son of **Ben Wood** and **Virginia**, on 5 Jun 1976 in Georgia. Barry was born on 18 Nov 1946 in Lawrence, Massachusetts. Children from this marriage were:

+627   M i.   **Ben Wood** was born on 24 Dec 1967 in Jacksonville, Florida.
+628   F ii.   **Jenney Wood** was born on 29 Aug 1973 in Charleston, SC.

462. John Erwin Baird[56] was born on 20 Aug 1948 in Big Rapids, Mecosta Co., MI.[56] John married **Syble Jones**. Syble was born in Georgia.

463. Glen Ivan Baird was born on 22 Dec 1949 in Big Rapids, Mecosta Co., MI. Glen married **Desiree Warch** on 28 Feb 1976 in Jacksonville, Florida. Desiree was born on 16 Dec 1955 in Los Angeles, CA. The child from this marriage was:

+629   M i.   **Nicholas Christopher Baird** was born on 25 Jul 1981 in Jacksonville, Florida.

464. Kathi Sue Baird was born on 1 Apr 1954 in Big Rapids, Mecosta Co., MI. Kathi married **William Howard**, son of **Richard Howard** and **Jean**, on 2 Jun 1973 in Jacksonville, Florida. William was born on 27 Jan 1951 in Philidelphia, Pennsylvania. Children from this marriage were:

+630   M i.   **Bradley Michael Howard** was born on 8 Nov 1979 in Jacksonville, Florida.
+631   M ii.   **Craig Willliam Howard** was born on 1 May 1975 in Jacksonville, Florida.

465. Shelley Kaye Baird was born on 13 Jan 1966 in Orange Park, Florida.

466. David William Baird was born on 19 Jan 1968 in Orange Park, Florida.

467. Bradley Baxter was born on 16 Jun 1952. Bradley married **Gloria Kiehl**. Gloria was born on 14 Feb 1954. The child from this marriage was:

+632   F i.   **Ashley Nicole Baxter** was born on 10 Aug 1982.

468. Brian Baxter was born on 21 Jan 1954. Brian married someone. His children were:

| +633 | M i. | **Zacary Brian Baxter** was born in 1978. |
| +634 | M ii. | **Kyle Baxter** was born on 17 Dec 1979. |

469. **Kim Baxter** was born on 31 Dec 1957. Kim married **Randy Adams**. Randy was born on 20 Feb 1955. Children from this marriage were:

| +635 | M i. | **Allin Dean Adams** was born on 7 Jan 1975. |
| +636 | F ii. | **Brandy Jean Adams** was born on 11 May 1977. |

470. **Colette Baxter** was born on 7 Jul 1963.

471. **Edith Lattin** was born on 8 May 1916 and died in 1942. Edith married **John Carley**. John was born in "of Catherine, Schuyler Co., NY".

472. **Ellen Lattin** was born on 16 Sep 1918.

473. **Clyde George Lattin** was born on 5 Nov 1919. Clyde married **Clara Hoffman**, daughter of **Joseph Hoffman** and **Alice Drake**, on 5 Dec 1941. Clara was born in "of Catherine, Schuyler Co., NY".

474. **Eleanor Ella Brink** born on 24 Nov 1916 in Catharine, Schuyler Co., NY. Eleanor married **Brown**.

475. **Grace Brink**.

476. **John Richard Dvorsky** was born on 24 Nov 1939 in Minneapolis, Minnesota. John married **Linda Rikas**. Linda was born on 31 Jan 1944 in London, England. Children from this marriage were:

| +637 | F i. | **Kimberly Michelle Dvorsky** was born on 14 Nov 1968 in Los Angeles, CA. |
| +638 | M ii. | **John Ralph Dvorsky** was born on 31 Oct 1970 in Los Angeles, CA. |

477. **Terry Emil Dvorsky** was born on 7 Feb 1942 in Minneapolis, Minnesota.

478. **Ralph Bruce Dvorsky** was born on 27 Sep 1944 in Minneapolis, Minnesota.

Ralph married **Kristine Ross**. Kristine was born on 18 Oct 1946 in Minneapolis, Minnesota. The child from this marriage was:

| +639 | M i. | **Ralph Emil Dvorsky** was born on 30 Apr 1963 in Minneapolis, Minnesota. |

479. **Robert Ellsworth Lockerby**[13] born on 17 Nov 1956[13] and died on 27 Aug 1994 in Marin Co., CA.[13]

480. **Shawn Lockerby**[13] was born in 1964.[13]

481. **Beverly Ann Samons**[13] was born on 20 Jul 1938 in San Francisco, CA.[13] Beverly married **Norris**.[13] Children from this marriage were:

+640	M i.	**Richard Norris**[13] was born in 1958.[13]
+641	M ii.	**Robert Norris**[13] was born in 1960.[13]
+642	F iii.	**Julie Norris**[13] was born in 1962.[13]

482. **Judith Randella Samons**[13] was born on 9 Nov 1939 in San Francisco, CA.[13] Judith married **Young**.[13] Children from this marriage were:

+643	M	i.	**Wayne Young**[13] was born in 1958.[13]
+644	F	ii.	**Janelle Young**[13] was born in 1965.[13]
+645	F	iii.	**Colleen Young**[13] was born in 1968.[13]

483.   Shirley Louise Samons[13] was born on 12 Dec 1942 in San Francisco, CA.[13]   Shirley married **Fetterman**.[13] Children from this marriage were:

| +646 | M | i. | **Eric Fetterman**[13] was born in 1964.[13] |
| +647 | M | ii. | **Curt Fetterman**[13] was born in 1966.[13] |

484.   Michael Jay Lockerby[13] was born on 29 Jul 1944 in Palm Springs, CA.[13]   Michael married **Mae Ellen Plumb**[13] on 10 Jun 1967 in Bremerton, WA.[13]   Children from this marriage were:

| +648 | F | i. | **Joy Michelle Lockerby**[13] was born on 14 Jul 1971 in Valley City, North Dakota.[13] |
| +649 | M | ii. | **Jonathan Michael Lockerby**[13] born on 27 Jul 1973 in Valley City, North Dakota.[13] |

General Notes: Attended the Pacific Lutheran University, Luther Seminary in St. Paul, MN and became a ELCA Lutheran Minister in Kenyon, MN

485.   Hugh Alan Lockerby[13] was born on 15 Mar 1948 in Red Wing, MN.[13] Hugh married **Diana Jane Vernon**,[13] daughter of **Bernard Vernon** and **Margery Davis**, on 13 Mar 1971 in Weirton, West Virginia.[13] Diana was born on 13 Nov 1949 in Waynesboro, Virginia.[13]   Children from this marriage were:

| +650 | M | i. | **Hugh Dale Lockerby**[13] was born on 9 Aug 1975 in Menomonie, WI.[13] |
| +651 | F | ii. | **Sonja Jane Lockerby**[13] was born on 13 Apr 1981 in Menomonie, WI.[13] |

General Notes: Hugh Alan Lockerby and his wife, Diana Jane Vernon, both graduated from the University of Wisconsin in Stout.   He attained his B.S. in Industrial Arts Education and she received a B. S. in Home Economics Education.   Between 1968 and 1972, Hugh served in the U.S. Navy and is a Vietnam Veteran.   He is a Technology Education Instructor at Baldwin-Woodville High School in Wisconsin.

486.   Frank Ellsworth Lockerby[13] was born on 30 Nov 1949 in Red Wing, MN.[13]   Frank married **Cindi Houg**[13] on 21 Jun 1975 in Menomonie, WI.[13] Cindi was born on 31 Oct 1951 in New Richmond, WI.[13]   Children from this marriage were:

| +652 | M | i. | **Dustin Robert Lockerby**[13] was born on 20 Jul 1981 in Beaver Dam, WI.[13] |
| +653 | M | ii. | **Drew Ellsworth Lockerby**[13] was born on 15 Oct 1982 in Beaver Dam, WI.[13] |

General Notes: Frank and his wife, Cindi, both graduated from the University of Wisconsin at Stout, Menomonie, Wisconsin.   After they both earned their B.S. degrees, Cindi went on to acquire her M.S.   Frank served in the Vietnam War with the U.S. Navy between 1968 and 1972.   They were last known to be living in Waukesha, WI.

487.   Rebecca Ann Lind[13] was born on 23 Feb 1952.[13] Rebecca married **Bruce Monke**[13] on 29 Dec 1973.[13] Children from this marriage were:

| +654 | M | i. | **Geoffrey Kyle Monke**[13] born on 22 Feb 1982[13] and died on 27 May 1982.[13] |

+655   F ii.   **Lindsay Mae Monke (Twin)**[13] was born on 3 Jun 1983.[13]
+656   F iii.   **Kelsey Anne Monke (Twin)**[13] was born on 3 Jun 1983.[13]

488.   Cynthia Anne Lind[13] was born on 15 Mar 1957.[13]

489.   Pamela Louise Lind[13] was born on 15 Aug 1958.[13] Pamela married **Randall Johnson**[13] on 28 Jan 1984.[13] The child from this marriage was:

+657   M i.   **Ryan James Johnson**[13] was born on 31 Aug 1985.[13]

490.   Scott John Lind[13] was born on 13 Aug 1957.[13]

491.   Sandra Jean Lind[13] was born on 13 Jun 1959.[13]

492.   Daniel Jay Lind[13] was born on 13 Sep 1965.[13]

493.   Gail Kay Pioske[13] was born on 8 Mar 1955 in New Ulm, MN.[13] Gail married **James Fitzpatrick**[13] on 25 Jan 1975.[13] Children from this marriage were:

+658   M i.   **Ryan Fitzpatrick**[13] was born on 16 Aug 1976.[13]
+659   M ii.   **Brandon Fitzpatrick**[13] was born on 24 Aug 1978.[13]
+660   F iii. **Misty Fitzpatrick**[13] was born on 22 Jul 1984.[13]

494.   Steven Donald Pioske[13] was born on 10 Jun 1956 in New Ulm, MN.[13] Steven married **Carrie Barnes**[13] on 11 Jun 1983.[13] The child from this marriage was:

+661   F i.   **Ann Pioske**[13] was born on 29 Jun 1984.[13]

495.   Kerry Sue Pioske[13] was born on 25 Dec 1958 in St. Peter, MN.[13] Kerry married **Mark Crislip**[13] on 6 Sep 1986.[13]

496.   Lynn Margaret Pioske[13] was born on 6 Jul 1960 in Le Sueur Co., MN.[13] Lynn married **Rodney Tollefson**[13] on 14 Aug 1982.[13] The child from this marriage was:

+662   M i.   **Benjamin Tollefson**[13] was born on 11 Jul 1984.[13]

497.   Janice Lynn Pioske[13] was born on 29 Aug 1963 in Le Sueur Co., MN.[13] Janice married **Robert Kellermeier**[13] on 25 May 1985.[13]

498.   Gregg Allen Pioske[13] was born on 11 Jan 1967 in Le Sueur Co., MN.[13]

499.   Lori Sue Pioske[13] was born on 13 Nov 1968 in Le Sueur Co., MN.[13]

500.   Gary Steven Pioske[13] was born on 10 Apr 1971 in Le Sueur Co., MN.[13]

Ninth Generation

501. Duane Heineck.

502. Carl Richard Hansen was born on 21 Jul 1954 in Minnesota.

503. Teri Lyn Hansen was born on 1 Dec 1955 in Minnesota.

504. Douglas Kirk Hansen was born on 28 Jan 1957 in Minnesota.

505. Kathy Lynn Callies was born in 1949.

506. Kevan Callies was born in 1951.

507. Mary Ellen Stine was born on 8 Oct 1955.

508. Amy Sue Gustafson[16] was born on 14 Sep 1966 in Faribault, Rice Co., MN.[16]

509. Jennifer Elise Gustafson[16] was born on 5 Apr 1969 in Weisbaden, Hesse, W. Germany.[16]

510. Gretchen Suzanne Gustafson[16] b. 16 Aug 1973 in Colorado Springs, , El Paso, Colorado.[16]

511. Saul Dwight Lockerby was born on 21 Jul 1973.

512. Kristan Suzan Lockerby was born on 25 Mar 1976.

513. Linda Marie Totten was born on 31 Oct 1955.

514. Catherine Ann Totten.

515. Karen Leah Totten.

516. James Totten was born on 28 Jun 1976.

517. Melody Lea Totten was born on 29 Sep 1977.

518. Joyce Audry Green was born on 3 Jan 1956.   Joyce married **Narcisse Blood** on 7 Jan 1978. Narcisse was born on 13 May 1954.

519. Robert Norman Farmiloe Green was born on 21 Feb 1959.

520. David James Farmiloe Green was born on 15 Sep 1962.

521. Lawrence Warren Gleason was born on 14 Jul 1955.

522. Lorna Faye Gleason was born on 5 Sep 1957.

523. Terrance Leslie Gleason was born on 25 Apr 1959.

524. Kelly Gleason was born on 9 Dec 1960. Kelly married someone.   Her child was:

+663   M i.   **Michael Warren Gleason** was born on 21 Sep 1978.

525. Shawna Gaye Gleason was born on 30 Jul 1963.

526. **Cheryl Kay Lee** was born on 29 Apr 1954.

527. **Jon Timothy Lee** was born on 8 Feb 1958.

528. **Richard Allen Van Dyke** was born on 24 Apr 1952 and died in 1976. Richard married **Wanda**. The child from this marriage was:

+664   M i.   **Richard Glen Van Dyke**.

529. **Michael Glen Van Dyke** was born on 5 Jul 1955. Michael married **Erlene**. The child from this marriage was:

+665   M i.   **Robert Russell Van Dyke**.

530. **Vickie Marie Van Dyke**.

531. **Timoth Lee Van Dyke**.

532. **Karen Lynn Zandstra** was born on 16 Apr 1956 in Hammond, Indiana. Karen married **Melvin Scheerings** on 17 Oct 1975. Melvin was born on 7 Jun 1956 in Hammond, Indiana. Children from this marriage were:

+666   F i.   **Melanie Kay Scheerings** was born on 16 Jul 1978 in Seattle, WA.
+667   F ii.   **Dayna Marie Scheerings** was born on 10 Jul 1979 in Hammond, Indiana.
+668   F iii.   **Julie Yoon Scheerings** was born on 21 Oct 1981 in Seoul, Korea.

533. **Frederick John Zandstra** was born on 25 Jun 1957 in Hammond, Indiana. Frederick married **Sue Nichoer** on 21 Oct 1978. Sue was born on 28 Oct 1958 in Fremont, Michigan.

534. **Victoria Dawn Zandstra** was born on 21 Mar 1959 in Hammond, Indiana.

535. **Cheryl Marie Zandstra** was born on 27 Dec 1962 in Hammond, Indiana.

536. **Sandra Jean Zandstra** was born on 28 May 1966 in Hammond, Indiana.

537. **Daniel William Zandstra** was born on 22 Apr 1957 in Hammond, Indiana. Daniel married **Debbie Groen** on 6 Oct 1978. Debbie was born on 27 Jan 1957 in Hammond, Indiana. The child from this marriage was:

+669   F i.   **Dana Renee Zandstra** was born on 8 Aug 1982 in Hammond, Indiana.

538. **Patricia Jean Zandstra** was born on 8 Jun 1958 in Hammond, Indiana. Patricia married **Wayne Alan Klein** on 4 Nov 1977.

539. **John Bartel Zandstra** was born on 30 Jul 1961 in Hammond, Indiana.

540. **Jerry Zandstra** was born on 20 May 1964 in Hammond, Indiana.

541. **Anita Marie Zandstra** was born on 29 Jan 1964 in Grand Rapids, Kent Co., MI.

542. **Daryl Zandstra** was born on 23 Mar 1967 in Patterson, New Jersey.

543. **William John Ooms** was born on 27 Jul 1961 in Valparaiso, Indiana. William married **Ronda Parish** on 12 Jun 1982. Ronda was born in May 1958 in Wisconsin.

544. **Russel Dean Ooms** was born on 9 Jul 1962 in Valparaiso, Indiana.

545. **Randall Scott Ooms** was born on 3 Oct 1963 in Valparaiso, Indiana.

546. Eunice Kay Ooms was born on 19 Oct 1967 in Hammond, Indiana.

547. Andrew Jay Ooms was born on 27 Feb 1971 in Wausau, Wisconsin.

548. Robert George Mossel was born on 6 Jan 1971 in Ann Arbor, Michgian.

549. Todd Calvin Mossel was born on 18 Jul 1974 in Wausau, Wisconsin.

550. John Edward Mossel was born on 10 Apr 1977 in Grand Rapids, Kent Co., MI.

551. Annette Arlene Sinclair was born on 30 Mar 1954. Annette married **Harold Alexander Cowell** on 31 Oct 1970 in Grasmere, British Columbia, Canada. Harold was born on 8 Jun 1945. Children from this marriage were:

+670   M i.   **Ben Alexander Cowell** was born on 14 Feb 1972.
+671   M ii.   **Carl Albert Cowell** was born on 23 Aug 1975.

552. Gordon Roy Sinclair was born on 6 Jun 1955. Gordon married **Linda Faye Boulter** on 27 Jan 1978 in Wihitehorse, Yukon. Linda was born on 23 Mar 1956. The child from this marriage was:

+672   F i.   **Betsy Danica Sinclair** was born on 19 Jan 1983.

553. Colin Robert Sinclair was born on 14 Nov 1957 and died on 30 Nov 1957.

554. Colin Fraser Sinclair was born on 27 Nov 1961. Colin married **Marla Merle Marer** on 27 Nov 1982 in Grasmere, British Columbia, Canada. Marla was born on 13 Mar 1966.

555. Annelle Rowena Sinclair was born on 1 Feb 1963. Annelle married **Brian Russell Gallagher** on 30 Apr 1982 in Elco, Grasmere, British Columbia, Canada. Brian was born on 10 Dec 1959.

556. Robert Totten was born on 21 Jun 1959.

557. Keith Lee Totten was born on 20 Jun 1961.

General Notes: When Sandra Joy Hunter and Paul Leon Totten Jr. were divorced, the children, Robert and Keith, were adopted by Sandra's 2nd Husband and raised in the Mormon faith.

558. Matthew Vincent Fraidenburg Totten was born on 11 Jun 1958. Matthew married **Donna Kraupa**. Donna was born on 11 May 1960. Children from this marriage were:

+673   F i.   **Rachel Dawn Totten** was born on 25 Nov 1977.
+674   M ii.   **Matthew Vincent Totten Jr.** was born on 25 Feb 1981.
+675   F iii.   **Emily Ann Totten** was born on 25 Aug 1985.

559. Karen Lynn Fraidenburg Totten. Karen married **Stuart Wilson** on 10 Dec 1982. Children from this marriage were:

+676   M i.   **Marc Wilson.**
+677   F ii.   **Bonnie Wilson.**
+678   F iii.   **Kami Jo Wilson.**
+679   M iv.   **Sspencer Wilson.**

560. David Lee Totten was born on 28 Dec 1959.

561. Diana Dee Totten was born on 28 Dec 1959. Diana married **Stephen Waldorf** on 21 Jul 1979. The child from this marriage was:

+680   F i.   **Jillmarie Erin Waldorf** was born on 19 Jan 1982.

562. Naoma Ruth Totten was born on 21 Jul 1961. Naoma married **Tim Smith** on 11 Sep 1979 in Dalles, Georgia.

563. Douglas Leon Totten was born on 6 Mar 1961 in Plymouth, Indiana.

564. Jeffrey Eric Totten was born on 3 Mar 1963 in Reed City, Michigan.

565. Gretchen Freiberg was born on 15 May 1964.

566. Gregory Freiberg was born on 13 Feb 1966.

567. Jennifer Freiberg was born on 22 Sep 1968.

568. Joel Freiberg was born on 23 Oct 1972.

569. Marc Edwin Totten was born in Aug 1959 in Grand Rapids, Kent Co., MI.

Marc married **Brenda Lee Ucrike** in Oct 1978. Brenda was born in "of Sand Lake, Michigan".

Children from this marriage were:
    +681   M i.   **Mitch Edwin Totten** was born in Aug 1959 in Greenville, MI.
    +682   M ii.   **Michael Stewart Totten** was born in Oct 1981 in Greenville, MI.
    +683   M iii.   **Matthew Marc Totten** was born in Sep 1982 in Greenville, MI.

570. Michelle Louise Totten was born in May 1962 in Big Rapids, Mecosta Co., MI. Michelle married **David Zwiers** in Jun 1980. David was born in "of Hudsonville, Michigan".   The child from this marriage was:

    +684   M i.   **Derek David Zwiers** was born in Sep 1981 in Grand Rapids, Kent Co., MI.

571. Lisa Kay Totten was born in Jan 1967 in Big Rapids, Mecosta Co., MI.

572. Kevin Lynn Totten was born in May 1969 in Big Rapids, Mecosta Co., MI.

573. April Lee Totten was born in Jun 1972 in Lakeview, Montcalm County, Michigan.

574. Jolene Lynnette Totten was born in 1975 in Lakeview, Montcalm County, Michigan.

575. David John Churchill was born in Dec 1964 in Reed City, Michigan.

576. Doreen robin Churchill was born in May 1966 in Reed City, Michigan.

577. Jeffery Duane Bressler was born in Oct 1971 in Adrain, Michigan.

578. Benjamin William Bressler was born in Aug 1974 in Adrain, Michigan.

579. Daniel Thurston Bressler was born in May 1977 in Adrain, Michigan.

580. Lisa Marie Wright was born on 15 Aug 1969 in Lakeview, Montcalm County, Michigan. Lisa married **Troy Simpson** on 18 Nov 1990 in Michigan.   Children from this marriage were:

    +685   M i.   **Christopher Simpson** was born on 12 Mar 1989.
    +686   M ii.   **Chad Simpson** was born on 12 Apr 1990.

581. Beulah Jean Wright was born on 28 Apr 1973 in Lakeview, Montcalm County, Michigan.

582. Wayne Edward Wright Jr. was born on 22 Jan 1976 in Lakeview, Montcalm County, Michigan.

583. Henry Jay Wright was born on 17 Feb 1982 in Lakeview, Montcalm County, Michigan.

584. Loren Bennett Kelsey Jr. was born on 16 Feb 1972 in Big Rapids, Mecosta Co., MI.

585. Nina Ann Kelsey was born on 23 Oct 1973 in Virginia.

586. Carol Lynn Towns was born on 20 Aug 1972 in Big Rapids, Mecosta Co., MI.

587. Janice Erma Towns was born on 3 Oct 1975 in Big Rapids, Mecosta Co., MI.

588. Dennis Alan Freeland II was born on 17 Sep 1972 in Big Rapids, Mecosta Co., MI.

589. Jennifer Misty Freeland was born on 28 Feb 1976 in Grand Rapids, Kent Co., MI.

590. Lance Edward Freeland was born on 29 Aug 1978 in Grand Rapids, Kent Co., MI.

591. Gregory Warren Wright was born on 11 May 1977 in Big Rapids, Mecosta Co., MI.

592. Cami Jo Wright was born on 26 Sep 1979 in Witchi Falls, Texas.

593. Eric Matthew Root was born on 5 Mar 1971.

594. Rhonda Kay Basch was born on 13 Jul 1959 in Missouri Valley, Harrison Co., IA. Rhonda married **Kevin Lee Stokes** on 21 Aug 1981 in Council Bluffs, Pottawattamie Co., IA. Kevin was born on 7 Aug 1962.   Children from this marriage were:

> +687   M i.   **Chad Lee Stokes** b. 1 Nov 1981 in Council Bluffs, Pottawattamie Co., IA.
> +688   F ii.   **Kimberly Ann Stokes** b. 3 Jun 1983 in Council Bluffs, Pottawattamie Co., IA.

595. Connie Sue Basch was born on 31 Jul 1961 in Council Bluffs, Pottawattamie Co., IA. Connie married **Kerry Lee Robb** on 4 Aug 1978 in Council Bluffs, Pottawattamie Co., IA. Kerry was born on 11 Sep 1959.   The child from this marriage was:

> +689   M i.   **Christopher Shane Robb** b. 9 Feb 1978 Council Bluffs, Pottawattamie Co., IA.

596. Annette Gay Basch was born on 13 May 1963 in Council Bluffs, Pottawattamie Co., IA.

597. Joseph Henry Basch was born on 27 Oct 1966 in Council Bluffs, Pottawattamie Co., IA.

598. Michelle Miner was born on 29 Jan 1975 in California.

599. Theresa Miner.

600. Jeffrey Miner was born on 25 Jan 1981.

601. Vicki Kaye Wyatt was born on 4 Jun 1965 in Council Bluffs, Pottawattamie Co., IA.

602. Julie Ann Wyatt was born on 7 Jun 1967 in Council Bluffs, Pottawattamie Co., IA. Had child:

> +690   F i.   **Heather Wyatt**.

603. Penny Sue Ahrens was born on 25 Jan 1968 in Council Bluffs, Pottawattamie Co., IA.

604. **Michael Richard Ahrens Jr.** born on 25 Feb 1970 in Council Bluffs, Pottawattamie Co., IA.

605. **Amy Mae Sales** was born on 26 Jun 1973 in Council Bluffs, Pottawattamie Co., IA.

606. **April Mae Sales** was born on 26 Jun 1973 in Council Bluffs, Pottawattamie Co., IA.

607. **Robert Joe Sales Jr.** was born on 21 May 1970 in Council Bluffs, Pottawattamie Co., IA.

608. **Angela Marie Sales** was born on 25 May 1976 in Omaha, Douglas Co., NE.

609. **Amanda Jo Sales** was born on 16 Nov 1981 in Council Bluffs, Pottawattamie Co., IA.

610. **Terry LeRoy Lockerby Jr** was born on 14 Feb 1977 in Council Bluffs, Pottawattamie Co., IA.

611. **Patricia Ann Lockerby** was born on 12 Mar 1964 in Council Bluffs, Pottawattamie Co., IA. Patricia married **Manuel Hernandez** in 1985 in Hawaii. The child from this marriage was:

+691   M i.   **Anthony Hernandez** was born in Jan 1986 in Hawaii.

Note: Patty married two more times: 2nd to Jeffrey Mount and had Nathan Mount born in Auora, Colorado, November 23, 1990. 3rd to Martin Brown and had Kelsey born December 2004 (?)

612. **Timothy Scott Pilger** was born on 13 Dec 1968 in Dennison, , Crawford Co., Iowa. Timothy married **Joyce Ann Hickman** on 17 Sep 1994 in Council Bluffs, Pottawattamie Co., IA. Joyce was born on 1 Feb 1960 in Hawthorne, Los Angeles Co., California. They divorced December 1999. NO ISSUE. Timothy married 2nd to Thomas Oglesby November 27, 2016, in Lansing, Kansas.

General Notes: VR-B and adoption papers. Adopted at 16 months from the Christian Home in Council Bluffs, Iowa. Graduated Abraham Lincoln High School in CB, May 1987. Attended Iowa Western Com. College and received an associate degree in Computer Science. Attended Iowa State University for one year. Married at St. John's Lutheran Church by Pastor Daniel Herring. Wedding colors: Blue and White with a Multi-Disney theme. Best man, Andrew G. Pilger, brother. Matron of Honor, Gayle Hickman, sister of the bride.

613. **Andrew Gene Pilger** was born on 9 Mar 1974 in Omaha, Douglas Co., NE. Christening: St. Paul's Lutheran Church. Andrew and **Catherine Hobbins**, daughter of **Timothy Hobbins** and **Sherry Martin**, Not Married. Catherine was born on 11 Dec 1976 in Council Bluffs, Pottawattamie Co., IA. Children from this union were:

+692   M i.   **Tate Donovan Pilger** b. 23 Nov 2000 in Council Bluffs, Pottawattamie Co., IA.
+693   F ii.   **Annabella Grace Pilger** b. 11 May 2005 Omaha, Douglas Co., NE.
+694   F iii.   **Lucy Lynn Pilger** was born on 23 Aug 2011 in Omaha, Douglas Co., NE.

614. **Mazel Bryant** was born in Pierson, Montcolm Co, MI.

615. **Doris Bryant** was born in Pierson, Montcolm Co, MI.

616. **Cathy Bryant** was born in Pierson, Montcolm Co, MI.

617. **Jason Guy Weeks** was born on 3 Mar 1970 in Philidelphia, Pennsyvannia.

618. **Brooke Weeks** was born on 14 Jun 1971.

619. **Brenda Anne Gould** was born on 17 Aug 1964. Brenda married **Duane Arthur Weed** on 6 Jun 1987. Duane was born on 28 Oct 1961. Children from this marriage were:

+695   F i.   **Rachel Anne Weed** was born on 21 Sep 1990.

+696　　　M ii.　　　**Bryan Arthur Weed** was born on 26 Jun 1993.

620.　Bianca Louise Gould was born on 8 Apr 1967. Bianca married **Glen Mitchell Hackbardt** on 28 Jul 2001. Glen was born on 2 Aug 1967.　Children from this marriage were:

+697　　　M i.　　　**Nathaniel Glen Hackbardt** was born on 9 May 2002.
+698　　　M ii.　　　**Benjamin Isaac Hackbardt** was born on 20 May 2004.
+699　　　M iii.　　　**Jacob Lee Hackbardt** was born on 11 Sep 2005.

621.　Jacob Lockerby was born on 17 Apr 1977 in Grand Rapids, Kent Co., MI.

622.　Danielle Lee Lockerby was born on 20 Aug 1980 in Grand Rapids, Kent Co., MI.

623.　Joshua Luthy Lockerby was born on 25 Aug 1982 in Grand Rapids, Kent Co., MI.

624.　Jennifer June Bongard was born on 2 Jun 1983 in Grand Rapids, Kent Co., MI.

625.　Bradley Baird was born on 5 Oct 1973 in Orlando, Florida.

626.　Shann Baird was born on 25 Dec 1976 in Miami, Florida.

627.　Ben Wood was born on 24 Dec 1967 in Jacksonville, Florida.

628.　Jenney Wood was born on 29 Aug 1973 in Charleston, SC.

629.　Nicholas Christopher Baird was born on 25 Jul 1981 in Jacksonville, Florida.

630.　Bradley Michael Howard was born on 8 Nov 1979 in Jacksonville, Florida.

631.　Craig Willliam Howard was born on 1 May 1975 in Jacksonville, Florida.

632.　Ashley Nicole Baxter was born on 10 Aug 1982.

633.　Zacary Brian Baxter was born in 1978.

634.　Kyle Baxter was born on 17 Dec 1979.

635.　Allin Dean Adams was born on 7 Jan 1975.

636.　Brandy Jean Adams was born on 11 May 1977.

637.　Kimberly Michelle Dvorsky was born on 14 Nov 1968 in Los Angeles, CA. Kimberly married **David Dean Sandvig**. David was born on 3 May 1968 in Burbank, CA.　Children from this marriage were:

+700　　　M i.　　　**Cody Dean Sandvig** was born on 21 Jan 1995 in Los Angeles, CA.
+701　　　M ii.　　　**Shane Michael Sandvig** was born on 25 Aug 1997 in Los Angeles, CA.

638.　John Ralph Dvorsky was born on 31 Oct 1970 in Los Angeles, CA.

639.　Ralph Emil Dvorsky was born on 30 Apr 1963 in Minneapolis, Minnesota.　Ralph married **Christina Kathleen Wright**. Christina was born on 20 Dec 1965 in Glendale, CA. Children from this marriage were:

+702　　　M i.　　　**Preston Tyler Riehl Dvorsky** was born on 20 Nov 1984 in Los Angeles, CA.
+703　　　F ii.　　　**Katie Elizabeth Dvorsky** was born on 23 Jan 1995 in Los Angeles, CA.

640.　Richard Norris[13] was born in 1958.[13]

641. **Robert Norris**[13] was born in 1960.[13]

642. **Julie Norris**[13] was born in 1962.[13]

643. **Wayne Young**[13] was born in 1958.[13]

644. **Janelle Young**[13] was born in 1965.[13]

645. **Colleen Young**[13] was born in 1968.[13]

646. **Eric Fetterman**[13] was born in 1964.[13]

647. **Curt Fetterman**[13] was born in 1966.[13]

648. **Joy Michelle Lockerby**[13] was born on 14 Jul 1971 in Valley City, North Dakota.[13]

649. **Jonathan Michael Lockerby**[13] was born on 27 Jul 1973 in Valley City, North Dakota.[13]

650. **Hugh Dale Lockerby**[13] was born on 9 Aug 1975 in Menomonie, WI.[13]

General Notes: Hugh Dale Lockerby graduated from Winona State University in Minnesota in 1987 and in 1988 became a Police Officer. He is currently serving as a Detective in the Violent Crimes Unit at the Scottsdale Police Department in Arizona.

651. **Sonja Jane Lockerby**[13] was born on 13 Apr 1981 in Menomonie, WI.[13]

652. **Dustin Robert Lockerby**[13] was born on 20 Jul 1981 in Beaver Dam, WI.[13]

653. **Drew Ellsworth Lockerby**[13] was born on 15 Oct 1982 in Beaver Dam, WI.[13]

654. **Geoffrey Kyle Monke**[13] was born on 22 Feb 1982[13] and died on 27 May 1982.[13]

655. **Lindsay Mae Monke (Twin)**[13] was born on 3 Jun 1983.[13]

656. **Kelsey Anne Monke (Twin)**[13] was born on 3 Jun 1983.[13]

657. **Ryan James Johnson**[13] was born on 31 Aug 1985.[13]

658. **Ryan Fitzpatrick**[13] was born on 16 Aug 1976.[13]

659. **Brandon Fitzpatrick**[13] was born on 24 Aug 1978.[13]

660. **Misty Fitzpatrick**[13] was born on 22 Jul 1984.[13]

661. **Ann Pioske**[13] was born on 29 Jun 1984.[13]

662. **Benjamin Tollefson**[13] was born on 11 Jul 1984.[13]

Tenth Generation

663. **Michael Warren Gleason** was born on 21 Sep 1978.

664. **Richard Glen Van Dyke**.

665. **Robert Russell Van Dyke**.

666. **Melanie Kay Scheerings** was born on 16 Jul 1978 in Seattle, WA.

667. **Dayna Marie Scheerings** was born on 10 Jul 1979 in Hammond, Indiana.

668. **Julie Yoon Scheerings** was born on 21 Oct 1981 in Seoul, Korea.

669. **Dana Renee Zandstra** was born on 8 Aug 1982 in Hammond, Indiana.

670. **Ben Alexander Cowell** was born on 14 Feb 1972.

671. **Carl Albert Cowell** was born on 23 Aug 1975.

672. **Betsy Danica Sinclair** was born on 19 Jan 1983.

673. **Rachel Dawn Totten** was born on 25 Nov 1977.

674. **Matthew Vincent Totten Jr.** was born on 25 Feb 1981.

675. **Emily Ann Totten** was born on 25 Aug 1985.

676. **Marc Wilson**.

677. **Bonnie Wilson**.

678. **Kami Jo Wilson**.

679. **Sspencer Wilson**.

680. **Jillmarie Erin Waldorf** was born on 19 Jan 1982.

681. **Mitch Edwin Totten** was born in Aug 1959 in Greenville, MI.

682. **Michael Stewart Totten** was born in Oct 1981 in Greenville, MI.

683. **Matthew Marc Totten** was born in Sep 1982 in Greenville, MI.

684. **Derek David Zwiers** was born in Sep 1981 in Grand Rapids, Kent Co., MI.

685. **Christopher Simpson** was born on 12 Mar 1989.

686. **Chad Simpson** was born on 12 Apr 1990.

687. **Chad Lee Stokes** was born on 1 Nov 1981 in Council Bluffs, Pottawattamie Co., IA.

688. **Kimberly Ann Stokes** was born on 3 Jun 1983 in Council Bluffs, Pottawattamie Co., IA.

689. **Christopher Shane Robb** was born on 9 Feb 1978 in Council Bluffs, Pottawattamie Co., IA.

690. **Heather Wyatt**.

691. **Anthony Hernandez** was born in Jan 1986 in Hawaii.

692. **Tate Donovan Pilger** was born on 23 Nov 2000 in Council Bluffs, Pottawattamie Co., IA.

693. **Annabella Grace Pilger** was born on 11 May 2005 in Council Bluffs, Pottawattamie Co., IA.

694. **Lucy Lynn Pilger** was born on 23 Aug 2011 in Omaha, Douglas Co., NE.

695. **Rachel Anne Weed** was born on 21 Sep 1990.

696. **Bryan Arthur Weed** was born on 26 Jun 1993.

697. **Nathaniel Glen Hackbardt** was born on 9 May 2002.

698. **Benjamin Isaac Hackbardt** was born on 20 May 2004.

699. **Jacob Lee Hackbardt** was born on 11 Sep 2005.

700. **Cody Dean Sandvig** was born on 21 Jan 1995 in Los Angeles, CA.

701. **Shane Michael Sandvig** was born on 25 Aug 1997 in Los Angeles, CA.

702. **Preston Tyler Riehl Dvorsky** was born on 20 Nov 1984 in Los Angeles, CA.

703. **Katie Elizabeth Dvorsky** was born on 23 Jan 1995 in Los Angeles, CA.

Addendum (1)

Reva Estella Lockerby was the daughter of Ezekiel Terry Lockerby and his wife, Clara Inman.   Reva was born on 12 June 1912 in Home Twp. Newaygo Co., Michigan and died 23 April 1968 in Grant, Newaygo Co., Michigan at the age of 55 years.

In 2007, I had contact with Trent Carpenter, a grandson of Reva.   He provided the photo above and told me the following:

"Reva was adopted by the Jontz family and raised by them.   She only completed eleven grades of school.   She had bad health and died at the age of 55 years."
Trent further informed me that, "When her mother, Clara Bell Inman Lockerby Stedman, Reva lived with Mr. Stedman who later married, and his wife was said to have mistreated Reva and one day while she was at school the authorities came and got her.   She was evidently being whipped with a strap and the teacher saw the bruises.   She was removed from the Stedman home and placed with the Jontz family.   It is said that her adopted Jontz mother was the sister to the adopted mother of President Gerald Ford.   Reva died at age 55.   In her later years she had diabetes."

Reva married Robert Carpenter on 5 Jan 1933, son of Claude Carpenter and Zoe Holden.   They had the following children:

1) Elnora Zoe Carpenter b. 11 May 1934
2) Roberta Gene Carpenter b, 7 April 1936 and died 20 Aug 1996
3) Daniel Leigh Carpenter (twin) b. 15 Sept 1943
4)
5) Douglas Roy Carpenter (twin) b. 15 Sept 1943

   Douglas married and had child:

   1.   Trent Carpenter

PHOTO GALLARY

Left to right-standing: Ezekiel Terry Lockerby 3rd, Bessie Olive Lockerby
Marshall Samuel Lockerby in the wagon.   (age ca. 2yrs)

Marshall Samuel Lockerby   (FAMILY NUMBER – 186)
(left – age 14 years / Right – ca. 1950, age ca. 30 years)

Etta Mae (White) Fernley Lockerby and her twin sister Letta McRoy (White) McCoy
Family # 186

(Taken at "Lockerby Town" — back row: Ezekiel Terry Lockerby I, Delphine W. Depew Lockerby, Erwin (in her arms), Mable and Ezekiel Jr. — Front row: Olive, Lena and Herbert. Mart wasn't at home that day.)

Family #95

Family #95 Mable and Olive Lokerby

Margaret Depew wife of Isiah G. Depew

Margaret Depew, wife of Isiah G. Depew, (mother of Delphine who married Ezekiel Lokerby)
Ca. 1900   (She lived to be 106 years of age) – Family #95

William Depew and Maria Melvinnia (Terry) Depew)
Parents of Delphine (Depew) who married Ezekiel Terry Lockerby (family #95)

Ezekiel Terry Lockerby b. 1857 married Delphine Depew (fam # 95)

SOURCE CITATIONS

1. Mary Louise Cleaver, History of the town of Catharine New York (History of the Town of Catharine New York, by Mary Louise Cleaver.), pgs 563-566. .... Beulah Totten Wright, Family Information in 1982 from Beulah Totten Wright. .... Church Register of the Walpack Congregation (Church Register of the Walpack Congregation, Baptisms and Births, 1741-1830 and Marriages from 1741-1769, Heritage Books, Inc, NY, 1913).

2. Mary Louise Cleaver, History of the town of Catharine New York (History of the Town of Catharine New York, by   Mary Louise Cleaver.) .... Beulah Totten Wright, Family Information in 1982 from Beulah Totten Wright.

3. NJ Archives Series- NJ Colonial Documents (N. J. Archive 1st Series V.35. Calendar of Willis 1781-1813).

4. Mary Louise Cleaver, History of the town of Catharine New York (History of the Town of Catharine New York, by Mary Louise Cleaver.) .... Beulah Totten Wright, Family Information in 1982 from Beulah Totten Wright. .... Church Register of the Walpack Congregation (Church Register of the Walpack Congregation, Baptisms and Births, 1741-1830 and Marriages from 1741-1769, Heritage Books, Inc, NY, 1913).

5. Mary Louise Cleaver, History of the town of Catharine New York (History of the Town of Catharine New York, by Mary Louise Cleaver.) .... Beulah Totten Wright, Family Information in 1982 from Beulah Totten Wright. .... Probate Records, Schuyler Co., NY.

6. Church Register of the Walpeck Congregation (Church Register of the Walpeck Congregation, Baptisms and Births, 1741-1830 and Marriages from 1741-1769, Heritage Books, Inc, NY, 1913).

7. Mary Louise Cleaver, History of the town of Catharine New York (History of the Town of Catharine New York, by Mary Louise Cleaver.) .... Beulah Totten Wright, Family Information in 1982 from Beulah Totten Wright. .... Church Register of the Walpeck Congregation (Church Register of the Walpeck Congregation, Baptisms and Births, 1741-1830 and Marriages from 1741-1769, Heritage Books, Inc, NY, 1913). .... 1855 Census, Town of Cayuga, Schuyler Co., NY.

8. Church Register of the Walpeck Congregation (Church Register of the Walpeck Congregation, Baptisms and Births, 1741-1830 and Marriages from 1741-1769, Heritage Books, Inc, NY, 1913). .... 1855 Census, Town of Cayuga, Schuyler Co., NY.

9. Mary Louise Cleaver, History of the town of Catharine New York (History of the Town of Catharine New York, by Mary Louise Cleaver.) .... Beulah Totten Wright, Family Information in 1982 from Beulah Totten Wright. .... 1855 Census, Town of Cayuga, Schuyler Co., NY.

10. Mary Louise Cleaver, History of the town of Catharine New York (History of the Town of Catharine New York, by Mary Louise Cleaver.) .... Beulah Totten Wright, Family Information in 1982 from Beulah Totten Wright. .... NY B&G, Vol. V, 1913 (NYB&G, Volume V, 1913 - Baptism Records of the Dutch Reformed Church of Walpeck, Sussex Co., NJ). .... 1855 Census, Town of Cayuga, Schuyler Co., NY.

11. Mary Louise Cleaver, History of the town of Catharine New York (History of the Town of Catharine New York, by Mary Louise Cleaver.) .... Beulah Totten Wright, Family Information in 1982 from Beulah Totten Wright. .... Family Information from Diane Lockerby (Family information from Diane Lockerby).

12. NY B&G, Vol. V, 1913 (NYB&G, Volume V, 1913 - Baptism Records of the Dutch Reformed Church of Walpeck, Sussex Co., NJ). .... Family Information from Diane Lockerby (Family information from Diane Lockerby).

13. Family Information from Diane Lockerby (Family information from Diane Lockerby).

14. Mary Louise Cleaver, History of the town of Catharine New York (History of the Town of Catharine New York, by Mary Louise Cleaver.)

15. Correspondence from Mary Balow 1985 (Correspondence from Mary Balow 1985). .... Family Records of Linn Gustafson - 1986 (Family Records of Linn Gustafson - 1986).

16. Family Records of Linn Gustafson - 1986 (Family Records of Linn Gustafson - 1986).

17. Correspondence from Mary Balow 1985 (Correspondence from Mary Balow 1985).

18. Mary Louise Cleaver, History of the town of Catharine New York (History of the Town of Catharine New York, by Mary Louise Cleaver.) .... Beulah Totten Wright, Family Information in 1982 from Beulah Totten Wright. .... 1855 Census, Town of Cayuga, Schuyler Co., NY. .... 1865 Census, Town of Cayuga, Schuyler Co., NY. .... 1880 Federal Census of Schuyler County, NY.

19. Mary Louise Cleaver, History of the town of Catharine New York (History of the Town of Catharine New York, by Mary Louise Cleaver.) .... 1855 Census, Town of Cayuga, Schuyler Co., NY. .... 1865 Census, Town of Cayuga, Schuyler Co., NY.

20. Mary Louise Cleaver, History of the town of Catharine New York (History of the Town of Catharine New York, by Mary Louise Cleaver.) .... Beulah Totten Wright, Family Information in 1982 from Beulah Totten Wright. .... 1865 Census, Town of Cayuga, Schuyler Co., NY.

21. Mary Louise Cleaver, History of the town of Catharine New York (History of the Town of Catharine New York, by Mary Louise Cleaver.) .... Beulah Totten Wright, Family Information in 1982 from Beulah Totten Wright. .... 1855 Census, Town of Cayuga, Schuyler Co., NY. .... 1880 Federal Census of Schuyler County, NY.

22. Mary Louise Cleaver, History of the town of Catharine New York (History of the Town of Catharine New York, by Mary Louise Cleaver.) .... Beulah Totten Wright, Family Information in 1982 from Beulah Totten Wright. .... 1855 Census, Town of Cayuga, Schuyler Co., NY. .... 1865 Census, Town of Cayuga, Schuyler Co., NY.

23. Mary Louise Cleaver, History of the town of Catharine New York (History of the Town of Catharine New York, by Mary Louise Cleaver.) .... Beulah Totten Wright, Family Information in 1982 from Beulah Totten Wright. .... 1855 State Census Town of Catharine, NY (1855 State Census Town of Catharine, NY). .... 1850 Federal Census, Chemung Co., NY.

24. 1855 Census, Town of Cayuga, Schuyler Co., NY.

25. Mary Louise Cleaver, History of the town of Catharine New York (History of the Town of Catharine New York, by Mary Louise Cleaver.) .... Beulah Totten Wright, Family Information in 1982 from Beulah Totten Wright. ....

Bible Records of Bennajah and Maryann (Bible Records of Bennajah and Maryann (Terry) Lockerby. Hand written and on file at the DeWitt Historical Society in Tioga County, New York.) .... 1855 State Census Town of Catharine, NY (1855 State Census Town of Catharine, NY). .... 1865 State Census Town of Catherine, NY. .... Death Records, Kent Co., MI. .... 1850 Federal Census, Town of Catherine, Chemung Co., NY.

26. Bible Records of Bennajah and Maryann (Bible Records of Bennajah and Maryann (Terry) Lockerby. Hand written and on file at the DeWitt Historical Society in Tioga County, New York.) .... Death Records, Kent Co., MI. .... 1850 Federal Census, Town of Catherine, Chemung Co., NY.

27. Bible Records of Bennajah and Maryann (Bible Records of Bennajah and Maryann (Terry) Lockerby. Hand written and on file at the DeWitt Historical Society in Tioga County, New York.) .... Death Records, Kent Co., MI.

28. Cemetery Stone - Rockford Cemetery, Kent Co., MI.

29. Mary Louise Cleaver, History of the town of Catharine New York (History of the Town of Catharine New York, by Mary Louise Cleaver.) .... Beulah Totten Wright, Family Information in 1982 from Beulah Totten Wright. .... 1855 State Census Town of Catharine, NY (1855 State Census Town of Catharine, NY).

30. Mary Louise Cleaver, History of the town of Catharine New York (History of the Town of Catharine New York, by Mary Louise Cleaver.) .... Beulah Totten Wright, Family Information in 1982 from Beulah Totten Wright. .... 1880 Federal Census of Schuyler County, NY. .... 1855 Census, Town of Cayuga, Schuyler Co., NY.

31. Civil War Records of Mathew Lounsbury Lockerby (Civil War Records of Mathew Lounsbury Lockerby). .... Family Information from Diane Lockerby (Family information from Diane Lockerby).

32. Correspondence with Diana Lockerby (Correspondence with Diana Lockerby), 9 Jan 1995.

33. Fred Bowman, 10,000 Vital Records of Western New York 1809-1850 (Genealogical Publishing Company 1985).

34. Henry King Olmsted, Olmsted Family in America, Olmsted Family in America, 1912, by A. T. De La Mare Printing and Pub Co., -- Pub 1993 by Heart of the Lakes Pub, Interlaken, NY, p 267.

35. Family data from Mary E. Van Vlack, Recorder of Butler County, Iowa, and desc of Rebecca M. Olmstead, provided by M C --, Family data from Mary E. Van Vlack, Recorder of Butler County, Iowa, and descendant of Rebecca M. Olmstead.

36. Henry King Olmsted, Olmsted Family in America, Olmsted Family in America, 1912, by A. T. De La Mare Printing and Pub Co., -- Pub 1993 by Heart of the Lakes Pub, Interlaken, NY, p267.

37. Henry King Olmsted, Olmsted Family in America, Olmsted Family in America, 1912, by A. T. De La Mare Printing and Pub Co., -- Pub 1993 by Heart of the Lakes Pub, Interlaken, NY, p267. .... Family data from Mary E. Van Vlack, Recorder of Butler County, Iowa, and desc of Rebecca M. Olmstead, provided by M C --, Family data from Mary E. Van Vlack, Recorder of Butler County, Iowa, and descendant of Rebecca M. Olmstead.

38. 1855 Census, Town of Cayuga, Schuyler Co., NY. .... 1865 Census, Town of Cayuga, Schuyler Co., NY.

39. 1865 Census, Town of Cayuga, Schuyler Co., NY.

40. Mary Louise Cleaver, History of the town of Catharine New York (History of the Town of Catharine New York, by Mary Louise Cleaver.) .... 1855 State Census Town of Catharine, NY (1855 State Census Town of Catharine, NY). .... 1850 Federal Census, Chemung Co., NY.

41. 1855 State Census Town of Catharine, NY (1855 State Census Town of Catharine, NY). .... 1850 Federal Census, Chemung Co., NY.

42. 1855 State Census Town of Catharine, NY (1855 State Census Town of Catharine, NY).

43. Mary Louise Cleaver, History of the town of Catharine New York (History of the Town of Catharine New York, by Mary Louise Cleaver.) .... Beulah Totten Wright, Family Information in 1982 from Beulah Totten Wright. .... Bible Records of Bennajah and Maryann (Bible Records of Bennajah and Maryann (Terry) Lockerby. Hand written and on file at the DeWitt Historical Society in Tioga County, New York.) .... 1855 State Census Town of Catharine, NY (1855 State Census Town of Catharine, NY). .... 1865 State Census Town of Catherine, NY. .... 1850 Federal Census, Town of Catherine, Chemung Co., NY.

44. Mary Louise Cleaver, History of the town of Catharine New York (History of the Town of Catharine New York, by Mary Louise Cleaver.) .... Bible Records of Bennajah and Maryann (Bible Records of Bennajah and Maryann (Terry) Lockerby. Hand written and on file at the DeWitt Historical Society in Tioga County, New York.) .... 1855 State Census Town of Catharine, NY (1855 State Census Town of Catharine, NY). .... 1865 State Census Town of Catherine, NY. .... 1850 Federal Census, Town of Catherine, Chemung Co., NY.

45. Bible Records of Bennajah and Maryann (Bible Records of Bennajah and Maryann (Terry) Lockerby. Hand written and on file at the DeWitt Historical Society in Tioga County, New York.) .... 1850 Federal Census, Town of Catherine, Chemung Co., NY.

46. Mary Louise Cleaver, History of the town of Catharine New York (History of the Town of Catharine New York, by Mary Louise Cleaver.) .... Beulah Totten Wright, Family Information in 1982 from Beulah Totten Wright. .... Bible Records of Bennajah and Maryann (Bible Records of Bennajah and Maryann (Terry) Lockerby. Hand written and on file at the DeWitt Historical Society in Tioga County, New York.)

47. Bible Records of Bennajah and Maryann (Bible Records of Bennajah and Maryann (Terry) Lockerby. Hand written and on file at the DeWitt Historical Society in Tioga County, New York.)

48. Mary Louise Cleaver, History of the town of Catharine New York (History of the Town of Catharine New York, by Mary Louise Cleaver.) .... Beulah Totten Wright, Family Information in 1982 from Beulah Totten Wright. .... Bible Records of Bennajah and Maryann (Bible Records of Bennajah and Maryann (Terry) Lockerby. Hand written and on file at the DeWitt Historical Society in Tioga County, New York.) .... 1855 State Census Town of Catharine, NY (1855 State Census Town of Catharine, NY). .... Cemetery Stone - Rockford Cemetery, Kent Co., MI. .... 1850 Federal Census, Town of Catherine, Chemung Co., NY. .... 1880 Federal Census, Rockford, Kent Co., MI.

49. Mary Louise Cleaver, History of the town of Catharine New York (History of the Town of Catharine New York, by Mary Louise Cleaver.) .... Beulah Totten Wright, Family Information in 1982 from Beulah Totten Wright. .... Bible Records of Bennajah and Maryann (Bible Records of Bennajah and Maryann (Terry) Lockerby. Hand written and on file at the DeWitt Historical Society in Tioga County, New York.) .... Cemetery Stone - Rockford Cemetery, Kent Co., MI. .... 1850 Federal Census, Town of Catherine, Chemung Co., NY.

50.   Bible Records of Bennajah and Maryann (Bible Records of Bennajah and Maryann (Terry) Lockerby. Hand written and on file at the DeWitt Historical Society in Tioga County, New York.) .... Cemetery Stone - Rockford Cemetery, Kent Co., MI. .... Plot Map of Rockford Cemetery, Kent Co., MI.

51.   Cemetery Stone - Rockford Cemetery, Kent Co., MI. .... Plot Map of Rockford Cemetery, Kent Co., MI.

52.   Mary Louise Cleaver, History of the town of Catharine New York (History of the Town of Catharine New York, by Mary Louise Cleaver.) .... Beulah Totten Wright, Family Information in 1982 from Beulah Totten Wright. .... Bible Records of Bennajah and Maryann (Bible Records of Bennajah and Maryann (Terry) Lockerby. Hand written and on file at the DeWitt Historical Society in Tioga County, New York.) .... 1855 State Census Town of Catharine, NY (1855 State Census Town of Catharine, NY). .... 1865 State Census Town of Catherine, NY.

53.   1884 State Census Nelson Twp., Kent Co., MI. .... Family Journal of Delphine Depew Lockerby, Delphine Depew Lockerby family journal on file at the DeWitt Historical Society in Ithaca, NY. .... Death Records, Newaygo Co., MI, Death Records, Newaygo Co., MI. .... Beulah Totten Wright, Family Information in 1982 from Beulah Totten Wright. .... Family information Muriel Haggman Whalen, Information from Muriel Haggman Whalen, correspondence of 1982. .... Mary Louise Cleaver, History of the town of Catharine New York (History of the Town of Catharine New York, by Mary Louise Cleaver.) .... Bible Records of Bennajah and Maryann (Bible Records of Bennajah and Maryann (Terry) Lockerby. Hand written and on file at the DeWitt Historical Society in Tioga County, New York.) .... 1865 State Census Town of Catherine, NY.

54.   Family Journal of Delphine Depew Lockerby, Delphine Depew Lockerby family journal on file at the DeWitt Historical Society in Ithaca, NY. .... Death Records, Newaygo Co., MI, Death Records, Newaygo Co., MI. .... Mary Louise Cleaver, History of the town of Catharine New York (History of the Town of Catharine New York, by Mary Louise Cleaver.) .... Beulah Totten Wright, Family Information in 1982 from Beulah Totten Wright. .... Bible Records of Bennajah and Maryann (Bible Records of Bennajah and Maryann (Terry) Lockerby. Hand written and on file at the DeWitt Historical Society in Tioga County, New York.) .... 1865 State Census Town of Catherine, NY.

55.   Family Journal of Delphine Depew Lockerby, Delphine Depew Lockerby family journal on file at the DeWitt Historical Society in Ithaca, NY. .... Family information Muriel Haggman Whalen, Information from Muriel Haggman Whalen, correspondence of 1982. .... Beulah Totten Wright, Family Information in 1982 from Beulah Totten Wright. .... Death Records, Newaygo Co., MI, Death Records, Newaygo Co., MI. .... Bible Records of Bennajah and Maryann (Bible Records of Bennajah and Maryann (Terry) Lockerby. Hand written and on file at the DeWitt Historical Society in Tioga County, New York.)

56.   Family Journal of Delphine Depew Lockerby, Delphine Depew Lockerby family journal on file at the DeWitt Historical Society in Ithaca, NY.

57.   Mary Louise Cleaver, History of the town of Catharine New York (History of the Town of Catharine New York, by Mary Louise Cleaver.) .... Beulah Totten Wright, Family Information in 1982 from Beulah Totten Wright. .... Bible Records of Bennajah and Maryann (Bible Records of Bennajah and Maryann (Terry) Lockerby. Hand written and on file at the DeWitt Historical Society in Tioga County, New York.) .... Cemetery Stone - Rockford Cemetery, Kent Co., MI.

58.   Mary Louise Cleaver, History of the town of Catharine New York (History of the Town of Catharine New York, by Mary Louise Cleaver.) .... Beulah Totten Wright, Family Information in 1982 from Beulah Totten Wright. .... Bible Records of Bennajah and Maryann (Bible Records of Bennajah and Maryann (Terry) Lockerby. Hand written and on file at the DeWitt Historical Society in Tioga County, New York.) .... 1865 State Census Town of Catherine, NY.

59.   Mary Louise Cleaver, History of the town of Catharine New York (History of the Town of Catharine New York, by Mary Louise Cleaver.) .... 1855 State Census Town of Catharine, NY (1855 State Census Town of Catharine, NY). .... 1865 State Census Town of Catherine, NY.

60.   1880 Federal Census of Schuyler County, NY. .... Carol Fagnan, Historian, Town of Catherine, various newspaper articles shared with me in 2011.

61.   1880 Federal Census of Schuyler County, NY. .... Carol Fagnan, Historian, Town of Catherine, Obituary of Willliam E. Lockerby from thre various newspaper articles shared with me in 2011.

62.   Mary Louise Cleaver, History of the town of Catharine New York (History of the Town of Catharine New York, by Mary Louise Cleaver.) .... Beulah Totten Wright, Family Information in 1982 from Beulah Totten Wright. .... 1880 Federal Census of Schuyler County, NY.

63.   Cemetery Stone - Rockford Cemetery, Kent Co., MI. .... 1880 Federal Census, Rockford, Kent Co., MI.

64.   1880 Federal Census, Rockford, Kent Co., MI.

65.   Plot Map of Rockford Cemetery, Kent Co., MI.

66.   1884 State Census Nelson Twp., Kent Co., MI. .... Family Journal of Delphine Depew Lockerby, Delphine Depew Lockerby family journal on file at the DeWitt Historical Society in Ithaca, NY. .... Death Records, Mecosta Co., MI, Death Records, Mecosta Co., MI. .... Funeral Home Notice, Big Rapids, MI (Funeral Home Notice, Big Rapids, Michigan). .... Mary Louise Cleaver, History of the town of Catharine New York (History of the Town of Catharine New York, by Mary Louise Cleaver.) .... Beulah Totten Wright, Family Information in 1982 from Beulah Totten Wright.

67.   Family Journal of Delphine Depew Lockerby, Delphine Depew Lockerby family journal on file at the DeWitt Historical Society in Ithaca, NY. .... Mary Louise Cleaver, History of the town of Catharine New York (History of the Town of Catharine New York, by Mary Louise Cleaver.) .... 1884 State Census Nelson Twp., Kent Co., MI, p.69.

68.   Family Journal of Delphine Depew Lockerby, Delphine Depew Lockerby family journal on file at the DeWitt Historical Society in Ithaca, NY. .... Death Records, Mecosta Co., MI, Death Records, Mecosta Co., MI. .... Funeral Home Notice, Big Rapids, MI (Funeral Home Notice, Big Rapids, Michigan).

69.   Beulah Totten Wright, Family Information in 1982 from Beulah Totten Wright. .... Death Records, Mecosta Co., MI, Death Records, Mecosta Co., MI. .... Funeral Home Notice, Big Rapids, MI (Funeral Home Notice, Big Rapids, Michigan).

70.   Death Records, Mecosta Co., MI, Death Records, Mecosta Co., MI. .... Funeral Home Notice, Big Rapids, MI (Funeral Home Notice, Big Rapids, Michigan).

71. Family Journal of Delphine Depew Lockerby, Delphine Depew Lockerby family journal on file at the DeWitt Historical Society in Ithaca, NY. .... Cemetery Record Rockford Cemetery, Kent Co., MI, Cemetery Record from Rockford Cemetery, Plainfield Township, Kent Co., MI, page 22.

72. Cemetery Record Rockford Cemetery, Kent Co., MI, Cemetery Record from Rockford Cemetery, Plainfield Township, Kent Co., MI, page 22.

73. 1884 State Census Nelson Twp., Kent Co., MI. .... Family Journal of Delphine Depew Lockerby, Delphine Depew Lockerby family journal on file at the DeWitt Historical Society in Ithaca, NY. .... Beulah Totten Wright, Family Information in 1982 from Beulah Totten Wright. .... Marriage Records of Newaygo Co., MI. .... Birth Record (Delayed Reg.), Mecosta, Newyago Co., MI.

74. Family Journal of Delphine Depew Lockerby, Delphine Depew Lockerby family journal on file at the DeWitt Historical Society in Ithaca, NY. .... 1884 State Census Nelson Twp., Kent Co., MI. .... Marriage Records of Newaygo Co., MI. .... Birth Record (Delayed Reg.), Mecosta, Newyago Co., MI.

75. 1884 State Census Nelson Twp., Kent Co., MI. .... Family Journal of Delphine Depew Lockerby, Delphine Depew Lockerby family journal on file at the DeWitt Historical Society in Ithaca, NY. .... Birth Records, (Delayed Reg), Kent Co., MI.

76. Family Journal of Delphine Depew Lockerby, Delphine Depew Lockerby family journal on file at the DeWitt Historical Society in Ithaca, NY. .... 1884 State Census Nelson Twp., Kent Co., MI. .... Birth Records, (Delayed Reg), Kent Co., MI.

77. Family information Muriel Haggman Whalen, Information from Muriel Haggman Whalen, correspondence of 1982. .... Beulah Totten Wright, Family Information in 1982 from Beulah Totten Wright. .... Death Records, Mecosta Co., MI, Death Records, Mecosta Co., MI.

78. Death Records, Mecosta Co., MI, Death Records, Mecosta Co., MI.

79. 1910 Federal Census, Newaygo County, Michigan, 1910 Federal Census, Newaygo Co., MI, Home township, p. 248. .... Family Journal of Delphine Depew Lockerby, Delphine Depew Lockerby family journal on file at the DeWitt Historical Society in Ithaca, NY. .... Marriage Records Mecosta Co., MI, Marrige Records of Big Rapids, Mecosta Co., MI. .... 1920 Federal Census of Pottawattamie Co., IA (1920 Federal Census of Pottawattamie Co., IA). .... Divorce Records, Newaygo Co., MI (Divorce Records, Newaygo Co., MI.) .... World War One Draft Card (World War One Draft Card from Pottawattamie Co., Iowa).

80. Family Journal of Delphine Depew Lockerby, Delphine Depew Lockerby family journal on file at the DeWitt Historical Society in Ithaca, NY. .... World War One Draft Card (World War One Draft Card from Pottawattamie Co., Iowa). .... Funeral Home Notice, Big Rapids, MI (Funeral Home Notice, Big Rapids, Michigan).

81. Family information Muriel Haggman Whalen, Information from Muriel Haggman Whalen, correspondence of 1982. .... Beulah Totten Wright, Family Information in 1982 from Beulah Totten Wright. .... Funeral Home Notice, Big Rapids, MI (Funeral Home Notice, Big Rapids, Michigan). .... Death Records, Osceola County, MI (Death Records, Osceola Co., MI).

82. Cemetery Stone, Whipple Cemetery, Big Rapids, Newaygo Co., MI.

83. Family Journal of Delphine Depew Lockerby, Delphine Depew Lockerby family journal on file at the DeWitt Historical Society in Ithaca, NY. .... 1910 Federal Census, Newaygo County, Michigan, 1910 Federal Census, Newaygo Co., MI.

84. Family information Muriel Haggman Whalen, Information from Muriel Haggman Whalen, correspondence of 1982. .... Beulah Totten Wright, Family Information in 1982 from Beulah Totten Wright.

85. Carol Fagnan, Historian, Town of Catherine, various newspaper articles, including obituaries.

86. Family Journal of Delphine Depew Lockerby, Delphine Depew Lockerby family journal on file at the DeWitt Historical Society in Ithaca, NY. .... Marriage Records of Newaygo Co., MI.

87. Marriage Records of Newaygo Co., MI.

88. Family information Muriel Haggman Whalen, Information from Muriel Haggman Whalen, correspondence of 1982. .... Beulah Totten Wright, Family Information in 1982 from Beulah Totten Wright. .... Marriage Records of Newaygo Co., MI.

89. Marriage Records of Atchison Co., MO, Marriage Records of Pottawattamie County, Iowa, in possession of Marsha (Lockerby) Pilger. .... 1920 Federal Census of Pottawattamie Co., IA (1920 Federal Census of Pottawattamie Co., IA).

90. 1920 Federal Census of Pottawattamie Co., IA (1920 Federal Census of Pottawattamie Co., IA). .... Marriage Records of Atchison Co., MO, Marriage Records of Pottawattamie County, Iowa, in possession of Marsha (Lockerby) Pilger.

91. Death Records, Pottawattamie Co., IA (Death Records, Pottawattamie Co., IA). .... 1920 Federal Census of Pottawattamie Co., IA (1920 Federal Census of Pottawattamie Co., IA).

92. Death Records, Pottawattamie Co., IA (Death Records, Pottawattamie Co., IA).

93. Death Records, Newaygo Co., MI, Death Records, Newaygo Co., MI.

94. Family Journal of Delphine Depew Lockerby, Delphine Depew Lockerby family journal on file at the DeWitt Historical Society in Ithaca, NY. .... Beulah Totten Wright, Family Information in 1982 from Beulah Totten Wright.

95. Marriage Records, Papillion, Sarpy Co., NE (Marriage Records, Papillion, Sarpy Co., NE).

96. Marriage Records of Pott. Co., Iowa, Marriage Records of Pottawattamie County, Iowa, in possession of Marsha (Lockerby) Pilger.

Name Index

Name Index

Name Index

Name Index

Name Index

Ida Adelia, 33, 53
Ida Frances, 43, 63
Jacob, 109, 119
Jacob Smith, 33, 49
James Leaten, 37, 56
Jane, 15, 17, 21, 30
Jay Douglas, 57, 79, 96
Jean Rosella, 76, 94
Jerome Bennajah, 33, 48
Jessie E., 44, 64
Joan, 80, 97
John, 12, 15, 17, 19, 28, 40
John B., 31, 44
John H., 24, 35
Jonathan Michael, 111, 120
Joseph, 16, 19, 26, 28
Joshua Luthy, 109, 119
Joy Michelle, 111, 120
Katherine Barton, 44, 64
Kitty May, 48, 65
Kristan Suzan, 99, 113
Lemuel H., 24, 34
Lena May, 53, 74
Lucille, 80, 97
Lucinda, 24, 35
Lucy V., 37, 57
Luella, 61, 83
Mabel Melvinia, 53, 67
Margaret, 21, 30, 35, 55, 78, 95
Margaret Louise, 57, 79
Marguerito Elizebeth, 62, 83
Mark, 94, 108
Marsha Lynn, 92, 106
Marshall Samuel, 33, 47, 53, 66, 72, 90
Mary, 16, 19, 25, 27, 32, 47, 63, 83
Mary Ellen, 37, 56
Mary Jane "Jennie", 31, 47
Maryjo, 94, 109
Mathew Lounsbury, 25, 36
Maude, 56, 78
Michael Jay, 96, 111
Mitchell Monroe (Dr.), 33, 47
Monte Lee, 92, 105
Moses, 15, 20, 24, 30, 31
Nellie, 44, 64
Nora Delight, 83, 99
Olive Adell, 53, 72
Oscar Dunbooth, 29, 41
Patricia Ann, 106, 118
Polly, 21, 30
Robert, 12, 13, 15, 19, 20, 27, 30
Robert Ellsworth, 96, 110
Rosetta, 24, 33
Sally, 21, 31
Sally M., 32, 47
Sally/Sarah, 24, 35
Samuel, 15, 20, 21, 30, 56, 78
Samuel McCarthy, 37, 57
Sarah, 16, 19, 21, 25, 27, 31

Sarah Ann, 31, 46
Sarah E., 25, 36
Saul Dwight, 99, 113
Seneca Daries, 30, 44
Sharon Ann, 90, 104
Shawn, 96, 110
Sonja Jane, 111, 120
Susan, 33, 49
Susan Elaine, 90, 104
Terry Leroy, 90, 105
Terry LeRoy Jr, 105, 118
Truman B, 49, 65
Unnamed Boy (twins), 76, 94
Vance, 94, 109
Wallace Hiram, 33, 48
Walter H., 24, 32
William, 15, 18, 20, 21, 30, 56, 78
William E., 35, 54
William Edgar, 37, 56
William H., 32, 47
William R., 31, 46
LOCKERBY (TWIN)
  Edith M., 49, 66
  Ethel M., 49, 66
LOUNSBURY
  Leah, 25
  Matthew, 25
LOVETT
  Ann, 49
LUEBKER
  Earl F., 97
LUTHY
  Charlotte, 109
  Ervin Fredrick, 109
LYON
  Herbert, 81
  Jesse Gordon, 81, 98
  Levi, 39
  Maynard, 81, 98

M

M.
  Annie, 80
MALLORY
  Aaron Ebenezer, 39
  Anna, 59
  Charlotte Prince, 39, 59
  Cora Gertrude, 39, 59
  Ella Ruanna, 39, 59
  Judson D., 39, 59
  William, 59, 81
MARER
  Marla Merle, 115
MARKEL
  George, 35
  Mary, 35, 55
  Nicholas, 35, 55
  Rosella, 35, 55
  Siona, 35, 55

MARSH
  Harold A., 102
  Joan Enile, 102
MARTIN
  Cora Elizabeth, 84
  Sherry, 118
MAXIM
  Mary, 92
MAYBEE
  George, 66
MCCURDY
  Desiah T., 37
  Samuel, 37
MCINTOSH
  Gertrude, 105
MCQUEEN
  Lucille, 95
MEHRENS
  William, 83
MEYERS
  Joyce Elaine, 109
MILES
  Samuel, 103
  Sandra, 103
MINER
  Beverly Kay, 89, 104
  Clair, 89
  Craig William, 89, 104
  Gloria, 89, 104
  Jeffrey, 104, 117
  Juanita, 89, 104
  Michelle, 104, 117
  Theresa, 104, 117
MIX
  Delphine, 46
MOE
  Harriett, 65
MOLER
  Sarah, 71
MONKE
  Bruce, 111
  Geoffrey Kyle, 111, 120
  Kelsey Anne (Twin), 112, 120
  Lindsay Mae (Twin), 112, 120
MORLEY
  Blanche, 58, 80
  Edward B., 38, 58
  Eugene, 38, 58
  Hiram, 38
MORRIS
  Janet, 102
  Y. O., 102
MOSHER
  Lydia A., 39
MOSSEL
  George, 101
  John Edward, 101, 115
  Robert George, 101, 115
  Todd Calvin, 101, 115
MUELLER

Name Index

Name Index

Name Index